Submergence of the Self by Shen Chen Hsieh
Mixed media, screen printing, 23 inches by 29.5 inches. 2018.

MOON CITY REVIEW

2026

Moon City Review is a publication of Moon City Press, sponsored by the Department of English at Missouri State University, and is distributed by the University of Arkansas Press through the Chicago Distribution Center. Exchange subscriptions with literary magazines are encouraged.

Submissions are considered at https://mooncitypress.submittable.com/submit. For more information, please consult www.moon-city-press.com.

Cover art by Shen Chen Hsieh.
Cover designed by Shen Chen Hsieh.
Text copyedited by Moon City Press staff.

moon city press
Department of English
Missouri State University

Staff

Table of Contents

Poetry

Flash Fiction

Nonfiction

Fiction

Graphic Narrative

Translation

MOON *CITY* REVIEW
2026

Shivani Gupta

Apocalypse Diary

I used to fall in love
with strangers
and their living
their orange coats
too heavy for september

trembling hands
as we read poems
green mill jazz club
nerves or old age
or the combination

gentle tilt of the cup
barista-in-training created
shapes in my cafe miel
cinnamon dust so suitable
a response to chicago winter

I used to fall in love with red leaves
falling from once green trees
in how they'd imprint
sidewalk a rusty orange
still bright and burning

subway girl's bubblepink headphones
face forward like a cowbelled mammal
in memory we always look

so much younger
than we will ever be

with drivers observing traffic rules
so we could all have safe passage
unaggressive unurgent
face nods & hands waves
we were all trying to get somewhere

& there was still time.

Victoria Martynko

Anger and the Years That Fed It (Sowing Silence)

The mornings are quiet now. We used to watch our outdoor cat
        play with yowling prey,   and miss the bells ringing in mass,
and forget to take out trash until the garbage truck whirred past.
        We still make mistakes, but we used to pay for them:
spats and arguments   into   guilt and reminders
of our original sin.   The mornings are quiet now,
        but we remember the noise.   There was you and me,
crying   at the rabbit guts and fur tufts   on the back patio
as they called us out on our 'theatrics,'   our childish living.
        There was the organ at church   as we learned of shame.
        There was the slam of doors while we prayed. But
the mornings are quiet now.   The cats stay indoors,   safe.

Jeremy Griffin

What Big Teeth You Have

Somewhere in the veil of trees, a woodpecker
bores into a trunk, the drone steady as the peal
of a gong beckoning votaries to prayer. We watch
an osprey haul a branch to its nest atop a warped pylon

jutting from the marsh like the errant fang
of a dead predator left to rot. Here, an eagle skims
the water, ascends with an eel struggling in its talons
before vanishing over the pines. Always, we are waiting

to be devoured. Soon the oyster boats prowling the horizon
will trawl back to shore, misshapen silhouettes against
the varicose twilight. The moon will cast us
in its jaundiced glow, the world coiled

on its haunches, breathing steam. We close
our eyes against what little light lingers beyond
the sky, and we wonder what will awaken
in the dark. We can never be ready enough.

Mario Aliberto III

If It Weren't for Bad Luck

Dinner rush is over, and Charlie says let's catch our break in the alley. Summer night no cooler than grilling steaks on the kitchen line. We hit Charlie's vape pen by the dumpsters as we bitch about the other line cooks, our cars, our girls, smoke billowing out of our mouths like steam off a fajita skillet.

I always spit the same story when I'm stoned. How I was eight years old when a bolt of lightning lit me up on the front lawn. Florida's the lightning capital of the world, don't I know it. Wasn't doing nothing but playing Tonka trucks, digging in the dirt. Pow. Just like that. Wouldn't even known lightning got me if no one had told me. All I remember is waking up in the hospital to a doc telling my old man and Momma the two little toes on my left foot blowed up like popcorn kernels. My Superman belt buckle had melted onto my jeans and a nurse gave it to me as a souvenir. In comic books, a person would have gotten superpowers, but all I got was a permanent limp and people telling me how lucky I was.

Charlie's heard my story a thousand times. He don't think I'm lucky. He's got a bad back from a car wreck that shoulda killed him, and I don't think he's lucky neither. Woulda been luckier for none of that to happen at all. But we get it when folks say we're lucky, what they're really trying to say is things coulda been worse. And they don't mean worse as in dying. Dying ain't hard on no one but the living. That's why we say Momma was lucky to go quick when docs found the cancer in her lungs. Two weeks from diagnosis to grave. Charlie got a grandma with old-timer's going on ten years and don't no one say she's lucky.

As Charlie and I mellow out, we share our dreams of better jobs, better cars, better girls. Talking about girls always ends with me rambling about my old man, and how he ain't been right since Momma's gone. How the doc says he's healthy as a bull, but I keep catching him standing statue-stiff on the front lawn like he done forgot how to move. Charlie says maybe the doc missed something, but I don't think that's it. What Charlie doesn't know is how my old man stands on the spot where lightning got me. Where no grass ever grows. How I gotta remind my old man lightning never strikes the same place twice. How no one's ever that lucky.

Michael Malan

A Different World

This is one of those days when yesterday and tomorrow get mixed up and you don't know what day it is, or really care. Your mother died, you lost your faith, you drink too much. Forget all that. Go into a deep sleep and wake up in another decade in a different world. Start over, get your faith back, find a home where the buffalo roam. Sit on the porch and watch the sun set, catch some trout in a nearby stream. The dream pops like a balloon and you look at the man sitting next to you at the bar. His hands are rough and hairy; you imagine his sharp, retractable claws could rip you to shreds. He is staring at the wall of bottles behind the bar. You see insects in his matted hair, tiny yellow birds flying around his head, a miniature thunderstorm in his glass of gin. You've been searching for an ending to a story you are writing and think this stranger will provide the perfect counterpoint to your fantasy about an adventure that seemed doomed from the start. You imagine he is driving along the Oregon coast in a dune buggy, listening to the Beach Boys sing "Sloop John B." The ocean is gray and flocks of seagulls are soaring like clouds through the sky. He finishes his drink and leaves the bar without saying anything. A few minutes later, another man, just as silent and surly, opens the door marked EXIT and brings the night in with him.

Josh Russell

The Garden of Earthly Delights

Your wife of nearly thirty years looks lovingly at you while you sit side-by-side on the couch, watching a K-drama on Netflix, then reaches out as if to stroke your cheek, and instead yanks from your nose a hair she's noticed because it, like your beard and what's left of the hair atop your head, is now gray, almost white. When you yelp, she smiles, apologizes. Since you've got her attention, you decide to try out the profundity that's occurred to you: "*Where's Waldo?* is our *The Garden of Earthly Delights*." She keeps grinning. "Hieronymus Bosch," you clarify. "Okay," is all she says, which pisses you off. You'd hoped to talk about clutter in art, weird multiple focal points, the ambiguity of image. You'd hoped to propose to her that *Where's Waldo?* and the central panel of Bosch's triptych are both depictions of freedom, not damnation, but also to allow the counterargument both depict hellscapes. Instead, just "Okay" and she heads to bed. You switch over to a dull World Series game, turn it off after an inning. In the bedroom the curtains glow, lit by the full moon.

Rebecca Bernard

The hummingbirds have left.

It's taken me a week to notice their absence. I look up how long sugar lasts. Afraid of what's left in the feeder, its state when they return. I wonder why they didn't tell me they were leaving but they don't have voices, at least not human ones.

I could research their migrational pattern, but wouldn't it be more fulfilling to let them return when I least expect it? When I most need a tiny vision, a belief in circles and shapes. A low, dull affirmation from the universe.

The unexpected return. Unexpected because most of the time it never happens. The un-returned more like it.

My high school boyfriend's an example. When's he coming back? He isn't.

There'd be no reason for him to other than realizing he still loves me, can't live without me. But he's filled these decades with other bodies, weekend trips to the mountains, abortions, board games, hugs. What do I know about it?

I knew him once, but that doesn't mean always.

My husband wouldn't like it either, of course. But I can still dream. Everyone I ever loved returning to me. My insatiable heart satiated. Wet and red and gorgeous with fulfillment.

I see it all happening. Faces slack with age, wrinkles mirroring the geography of lives lived simultaneous and apart.

Come in, come in, I say. *I've made cake!* White icing at the tips of my fingers.

We have nothing to say to each other together, so my lovers take turns flitting through the rooms. I squeeze a one-night-stand's rough fingers in the pantry, whisper raunchy jokes in the linen closet with my crush from philosophy of science class. The boy from summer camp revisits my lips in the sunroom. My high school sweetheart makes eyes at me in the sea foam bathroom, our bodies perched side by side on the old porcelain.

How long for an intimate to become a stranger. The other way around? *Not everything's a boomerang*, my husband says.

I must learn to appreciate departures.

One year the feeder's abuzz. The next who can say it won't be silent? And what do I do with the lack?

I mix one part sugar to four parts water; I go about my life.

In the evenings, my husband and I stream nature shows on the television. A grouping of hummingbirds is called a charm, but I've only seen them one at a time.

Unless it was always the same bird, here for a few seconds, back again an hour later? I can't be sure.

When they migrate, they do it alone.

As darkness falls, I set the table for dinner. The air inside sweetly silent, the house warm as sheets from a recently departed bed. My husband hums to himself as he peels ginger.

Outside, the star glow's masked by clouds. I wouldn't know if they'd returned, and maybe that's best.

From the kitchen, the stovetop crackles. Brown sugar caramelizing in the pan. Water set to boil.

You coming? my husband calls to me.

No sweetness ever meant to last.

Ray Kruger

Pipe Cleaner Bouquet

Sometimes when I'm with you, I wonder if I'm actually a shitty person.

And it's not your fault, but sometimes you'll be talking and you'll say a certain word, and a memory resurfaces like the painful snap of a rubber band against my wrist, and I can't help but flinch from the pain of it. You'll keep on talking, not paying me any extra attention, and I'll get swallowed up by that memory as I watch it unfold in this new and terrifying light, all to reveal how shitty of a person I pretend otherwise not to be.

One of those memories unfolds now.

You say, "This one is different, I really like her. I think I'm going to ask her to be my girlfriend next weekend, so that way we'll be official before Valentine's Day. I even made her a flower bouquet out of pipe cleaners; it turned out so cute. Do you want to see a picture?"

The memory snaps into focus faster than I can help it, and it takes everything in me not to hiss aloud in front of you. I see a pipe cleaner bouquet inside my head, not the one you made, but one from someone else. And then I see her too, eyes as big as yours but without the same shine to them. It must have been Valentine's Day then too, because she hands me a pink gift bag and inside is this strange jumble of color that I struggle to decipher right away. I pull it out, this assembly of red, blue, green, and purple pipe cleaners twisting in every direction, and she tells me she spent a week making it. I turn it about in my hands, trying to keep the confusion from contorting my face into an expression that would make me look ungrateful. I ask what it is and she tells me it's a flower bouquet. She asks if I like it, her eyes so wide with anticipation they're nearly as big as yours. I say I do, thank you. And that's that.

Later, when I got home that night, I put the mass of fuzzy colorful pipe cleaners on my nightstand. Because they don't need a vase or sunlight and it's a gift, so I should keep it somewhere I'll at least see it every day. I'm not ungrateful. It's just that the colors are so bright they hurt, and the touch of them makes my sensory issues go haywire, and some of the pipe cleaners are glittery with bits of metallic foil, so overall it looks a bit like an elementary school art project. But because I at least appreciate the gesture, I let them sit on my nightstand undisturbed. And as time goes by, and the bouquet gets swallowed up by poetry books, and junk mail, and tubes of hand cream, and licked-clean candy wrappers—it doesn't even matter anymore. Because in August, she breaks up with me in the passenger seat of my car as we sit in the parking lot of an ice cream place, leaving me with handwritten notes with little hearts drawn next to the words explaining how she's not happy with our relationship anymore. She hadn't been for a long time but didn't know how to tell me. We were never good at talking.

And in September, I gather up all the pieces of her that still linger in my room and throw them into a trash bag, because everyone is telling me this is how you move on from a long-term relationship—you throw it all out like she did to you. So I don't think, as the pictures get torn off the walls, as the letters are crumpled between my hands, as the matching necklace I used to wear every day is thrown away, and then all that's left is this ugly-ass pipe cleaner bouquet. This is the one thing I don't have a problem discarding, and for a moment I allow myself to feel a little glad rather than sad. I save the guilt for later, and that's that. Until now.

Now it is January, and I'm well past self pity and I'm cured enough from my breakup hangover to realize why she was so unhappy with me. And why her eyes always reminded me of yours. And the sting of it all is painful enough for me, that I can only imagine how it felt back then for her. So yeah, maybe I'm a shitty person.

Because I never liked that pipe cleaner bouquet she gave me.

But, maybe I would have kept it if it was from you.

nat raum

journal (take #5)

after O Brother, Where Art Thou

dear diary, when the weather is like this—artscape hot, the kind of heat you can see reflecting off the asphalt—i wish i was a siren in a river in rural mississippi, dressed in ditsypink floral dress and wringing laundry as i serenade unsuspecting wanderers. dear diary, i swear i won't try to transfigure anyone when the boys in the Model A scream *pull over* and discover me and sisters, translucent cloth clinging to curves while we inch closer, closer. while we swing jugs of shine from doll's fingers and tip them over into men's mouths. dear diary, what we'd do would be dirty but what we won't do is love a man up and turn him into a damn toad. we'd circle like he was an open drain and each of us a current, poised to inundate. and don't judge, dearest diary—we'd turn him in for the cash, too.

Connor Beeman

fawn bodies

I keep having this dream

where we're fawns and your father

is a better man.

instead of his knife and your best

attempts at gutting, I've seen our bodies,

fragile and intentioned, imagined

us with slender and shaking legs.

what would we trade

for small cloven hooves?

sharing chapter books in the deer stand,

the green plastic shell of your Gameboy,

berries, lumpy crabapples, our new fawn mouths

stained with fruit.

how long has it been since you've dreamed?

I miss imagining

you without violence—

your back like mine, soft and lean,

dusted with lush white spots.

August Reid

One Summer

slick and shiny like a fountain penny,
you burst from the pool water and hold
my bare shoulders, years and years of
skin to touch, touch because you can here,
now with summer shading us, with hesitance
stripped bare like every other pink-soaked
body and swirling shame. we press into
a bathroom stall, dripping water and want,
your mouth makes me ache for cherry slushie,
communion wafers, and your ruby red chapstick
melted in the back of my mom's malibu.
your body is a thunderstorm under my palms.
i only want to hold it for now, please. i don't know how
to capture something so persistent, so anxious.
my hair sticks to your neck like beach sand
and a soft rumbling swims from your throat, a growl
or a whimper, praise or humiliation. light sneaks
in from the window above, drenching us in gold.

while you suck bruises, bite into my flesh,
it's hard not to think of god.

Patricia Q. Bidar

Velvet

Beside the door, Derrick's bag is packed. His leather hat and multi-pocket shorts. His SPF50.

Passport.

Tanya has music on. Joe Ely. He was no quitter. A million years ago, Tanya's dad jammed with him in Lubbock. Derrick wasn't interested until she told him Ely toured with the Clash in Houston, San Antonio, Laredo, Lubbock, and Juarez. That he sang in Spanish on "Should I Stay or Should I Go." When Mick Jones barked, "Split!" he was talking to Ely.

Derrick calls them bite trips. And it's not only passion; he's making money. Has sponsors. Last year, Derrick asked and received permission from Tanya's father to shoot on the family property. Derrick said that Tanya would work as an assistant. She cleared some brush, wiped dust from clothing, and checked Derrick's face for dirt. But she can't be heard in the YouTube video of the velvet ant. That honor went to the unflappable camera operator, Jesus.

Harvester ants! (Sixty stings!)

Fire ants! (Derrick shoved his hands into their nest!)

Velvet ants! (Really a solitary wasp! Tanya all over!)

It occurs to Tanya now, as she is going down on him, that Derrick is distracted by thoughts of rolling around on the ground in Costa Rica, a tiny dinosaur stinger jammed in his flesh, soft-eyed Jesus bent over him and murmuring, "Are you OK, man?"

Now, breath coming fast, Derrick mutters, it's hard to feel anything unless he is being stung. He adds that the bullet ant strikes fear into the hearts of men. He is so close, he says.

Tomorrow, Derrick and Jesus will find the bullet ant nest. Together they will get one bullet ant into the glass container. Derrick will extend a protective arm and tell Jesus, "Back up back up back up." He'll implore Jesus, "Your legs, dude! Check your legs!"

The Clash were serious. One can imagine Joe Strummer offering his arm to be pierced by an insectoid dagger. But Tanya bets it is Joe Ely who has actually done it.

When Derrick leaves, Tanya will shake out the bleached sheets. She will check under the bed and in all her shoes. That squeaking sound she made will hang in the air. Both genders of velvet ant make the sound. But only females can deliver a wound.

"Go on; split!" Tanya cries. And more quietly, "I quit!" Then she puts on more Joe Ely, something hard and driving, loud enough to pierce.

Laura Leigh Morris

Eve Eats the Apple

Here's what no one tells you about why I ate that apple.

Adam could be an ass, always pointing to the scar on his side, saying I wouldn't be here without him. Then, he'd wave at rocks and scratch at bugs in his hair, say, "We're in paradise," ask, "What more could you want?" And I was left wondering why he *didn't* want more, but try telling him that, and he'd shake his head, say I didn't get it. Like I was the one with the problem, while Adam sat there muttering about how I was never satisfied, how Eden should be enough, how I couldn't even find bliss in a place that *literally* meant bliss.

Still, he was a means to an end. You women know—sometimes you do what you have to.

Oh, you might say I could still have had my boys without eating that apple. And maybe you're right. Except you're not the one who had to live with him saying, "Doesn't the word bird just make you think of flying?" or, "There's something about that neck where the name giraffe just fits, you know? The long double-f does all the work." All damned day. Like he would never brag, but he wouldn't not either.

Besides, there's something about the agony of childbirth. You get closer to death than you ever have before, the whole world dark and full of pain. Nothing but pain. And in the end, you're left aching and deflated and exhausted, but you also have a baby in your arms. And it's screaming and demanding from its very first breath, and you know who can give it what it needs? You. You're the only one who can feed it.

So Adam stood there while Cain suckled my breast, and for the first time in forever, he didn't say one damned word about that rib. And I'll tell you what, I'd have eaten that apple sooner if I'd known it would finally shut him up.

Gary Fincke

The Vanishing of Nuns

after Gary Fincke

After his student's accidental death, the aging professor calligraphies her workshop poem about the possibilities of love, reforming her imagery for desire with intricate loops and decisive slants. Her setting is the garden of St. Paul tended by two ancient nuns who, each day, catalog how the light is altered by the arrangements of decorative trees. Aside from May and June, those nuns, she wrote, prune the rose bushes monthly to allow room to kneel for the raised right hand of a smiling Mary.

Pausing, the professor calculates it has been years since he has noticed a nun. Because they have abandoned their habits, he decides, and remembers how they rode the streetcar in pairs; how they gathered at the museum where, as a boy, he was transfixed by dinosaur bones, mummies, and animals stuffed and mounted.

He has always loved the desire to preserve. He once loved the way Lenin's body was displayed, how it testified that death flatters just as well as a costly, tailored suit. Years ago, he learned that when the Germans, during World War II, neared St. Petersburg, Lenin's body was moved to Siberia, where almost anything, from prisoner to icon, could be hidden. Longing for usefulness, the soldiers who guarded Lenin's body, it's been reported, drank themselves daily into sorrowful songs while Lenin lay silent.

His student's sixteen lines were a gospel of surfaces, touch after touch where nerves nearly breach the skin. They detailed blossoms that flourished like sacrifice; they added topiary that shadowed erosions from frequent storms, the nuns often singing. The professor recalled *Soeur Sourire,* the Singing Nun, her song about Dominique relentless on the radio, her Ed Sullivan minutes, how he followed her brief career, discovering she had left the order for a woman, nothing certain by then but the pull of desire.

Years ago, in Florence, surrounded by faith, he had been startled by loud, recorded "Shhhs," a single "Silencio" from above meant to minimize a thousand tourists. Cameras were shuttered by decree; everyone listened through rented ear buds to the near-whisper of the guide, and some paid for candles to light and wish upon. He had shuffled close to a sarcophagus roped off like a crime scene. This saint, the guide murmured, was so selfless her body was shared by the cathedrals in competing cities.

The priest who blessed his wedding fled the church for a woman who had spent seven years as a nun. By then, when nuns in the mall laughed loudly, he dreamed them touching each other or men they once had disciplined in schoolrooms, hissing the "Shhh" of holy admonishment while their habits rustled.

Later, Sister Smile killed herself, nuns beginning to become improbable as faith. Now, a collection of habits is on display at his city's museum where he sees teachers gathering their restless students to hear a young, uniformed guide explain what those dark, dowdy outfits signified. Her skirt stops short enough to turn his head toward her mystery, and he meditates on which vows she would be willing to break, her history yammering somewhere else.

His student, at last, had shifted to the white statue of the garden saint, his blessed hand smooth from centuries of kisses, her poem ending in an astonishment of prayer.

Jenny Stalter

Lawn Chair Baptism

She's sitting naked in a lawn chair on her back lawn during a thunderstorm. She hasn't bathed in three months, or is it four? The thing is, she's just so tired. Can't imagine climbing into the tub where they cleaned together. Where she fell asleep, arms falling gently to her side. Accidentally letting go. She grips a bar of soap, some fancy organic shea butter soap that smells of almonds and reminds her of pistachio pudding because you put almond essence in pistachio pudding. The packaging says it's for men and women, like soap can have a gender. The packaging says it's an exfoliating bar. And that's the only important thing about the soap. The exfoliation. It's summer, and the day's heat hangs around even though it's the dead of night. The rain is cool, and she scrubs herself with the bar, working it into a thick lather. The thunder bangs and the downpour rinses everything into the grass. Anything that could still cling, a skin cell that might have touched his milky skin, any milk that might have dried on her breasts, baby drool remaining in her hair because he liked to put her hair in his tiny mouth and suckle. The lightning tears through her ablutions, and for seconds at a time, the sudsy remains are strobing there in the grass, the rain stippling her skin that is letting go.

Jenny Stalter

Lovers

Today, I cried because an internet stranger's cat died. Your belligerence still rocking me weeks later. Then I watched a reel of flowers made of rice paper—so delicate—but they only bloomed in smoking-hot oil. You knew a level of intimacy was unlocked, my specific tendernesses that allowed you to hurt me. The way you watched porn when we fucked, forcing me to compare myself to the young women. Their taught bodies versus my middle-aged thighs and breasts. Doggy-style always made me think of the fight when you shouted that you wished I died and not the dog. My only reply to you was the scream I let out as I heaved the wine bottle that smashed behind your head. Not dissimilar to the scream climax on my knees. My pain was another window you climbed through. The way you crawled through the kitchen window when I locked you out drunk. The way you milked my love until I was tapped. Today I cried about the flowers and the cat but not about leaving you.

Tonight, I'm on a date with Simone de Beauvoir. I tell her my pain was a window you used to slink through and she sucks on her cigarette and blows out a big whirling cloud. It looks like a ghost because I feel like a ghost. Like an illusory thing that comes after the real thing. I died in the war. Which war? The War of Living Things. No. Wait. The War of Wounded Women? She says it doesn't have to be that way. Her face smells like rose oil. She removes our pussycat bow blouses. She brings saucers and we drink milk like kittens. We are ageless. We are gentle. We remove our silk bras and show each other our breasts. We do not compare them. We only love them.

My younger self is around here somewhere. I wish I could tell her about you and windows and little deaths. Let her know she is rice paper.

Naphisa Senanarong

In the Future

In their eggs, the hatchlings made wet little chirps, like baby birds choking on their own saliva. Quickly, I grew to love them. It might be hard to imagine, from the outside looking in, how one could fall in love in such industrial conditions. In the wild, the crocs' mothers would climb back into the nest and the vibrations of their bodies would trigger the hatching. At the farm, we kept them in incubation tents. Rows after rows of steel wire rose up to shelter the eggs, delicately perched. We inspected them for bands of fertility. These stretched like birthmarks over the translucent shells. The infertiles were allowed an extra month of hope.

In our white lab coats and hair nets, Rai and I walked the rows, our ears preened for gurgles. I was fifteen; Rai, sixteen. We gathered trays that showed signs of breakage and brought them to a white-tiled room where we peeled away the shells and nestled the newborns in our palms. In these moments of weakness, relatively brief in the scheme of their long lives, they craned their necks up and slow-blinked at us. Cats, kissing with their eyes. Before Rai showed up at the farm two months ago, I had been the only foster parent to the hatchlings after Mom left the farm for Bangkok. Like the other boys, I wanted to be a trainer, to wear red and learn to walk among crocodiles. To be so still I could offer a limb or two without provoking them.

"Pretty boy," Ake, the man who'd hired me and Mom, said. "You'll stick a head into a croc's mouth when your balls have dropped."

Emerging from the heady heat and mucus smells of the tent, midsummer nights in Samut Prakan can feel light on the skin. A breeze can bring you to your knees. I loved the look on Rai's face when she tore off her hairnet. Her mouth mellowed out in an exhale, somewhere between exhaustion and pleasure.

We spent sunrises knee-deep in green water, wading into the enclosure with buckets of tiny fish and rat parts ground into sausages. Mom was the one who showed me how to handle the young crocs. Soft, naked underbelly weighed against her palm and forearm, tiny tail tucked against her body, into the crevice between her breast and armpit.

"They're flexible," she'd said. "You have to point them away from you when you let them back into the water." We'd practice letting go of them together, making sure to release the neck and the tail simultaneously, and watch them slither back into the water without a backward glance. They rarely bit us. I showed Rai this maneuver when we checked the babies' skin for signs of infections, blemishes. She learned quickly. We developed favorites and named them. Ai Jud for the one whose pattern was so evenly knitted he looked polka-dotted.

I tried to break her gently into the world of reptiles. I showed her how to make the feed. She did not flinch at the smell or the slimy texture thickening in our hands. When she bent a knee and plunged her gloved hands into the water, I couldn't keep my eyes off of her. She had a long, lean torso in proportion to stout, muscled legs and looked like what I imagine Mom must've around the time she had me: stubborn and brash and beautiful, if you looked at her closely in private. Her black hair shone with a sheen of mulberry dye that made me think of twilights in the paddy fields. It was on one of these mornings, me echoing my mother's words to Rai, positioning a young croc in her arms, a scaly young thing of our own, that she told me she was pregnant.

Sometime in the month, Mom called to tell me she had found a nannying job with a new family, having left the previous one because the Burmese maid who'd been with the family before her framed my mother for theft. She'd used the kitchen knife to shave off her toe nails, scattering the clippings like bird feed all over my mother's bedding. The little girl my mother was raising now took piano lessons in the big hulk of a mall they'd just slapped onto the banks of the Chao Phraya River. It had an indoor floating market and trees growing upside down from the ceiling instead of the crystal chandeliers we saw on daytime soap. The ceiling was curved, which, Mom admitted, made her sleepy for the rest of her day. That or the air conditioner. While the girl took her lessons, Mom sat in a cafe overlooking the river that wound its way out of the capital, down to the gulf. From that great bay window, she thought of me at the mouth of the river.

Over lunch, I showed Rai the picture of the café Mom had texted me. Gleaming white tabletops surrounded the centerpiece sculpture: half of a woman's torso, bound in flowers. In the brim of the photo, you could make out the top of the little girl's head, pigtails plaited tight to her scalp.

Rai said, "I'll be a host in a place like this." She spoke about our lives like this, with the certainty of fortune-tellers. "And you'll work with your mom's new family. Once you can drive. In the future."

We ate our lunch in the souvenir shop, away from the smells, although each time we left the air-conditioned haven, we had to retrain our noses—recalibrate to the norm of rat parts and animal shit. Once the nausea and heat of pregnancy got the best of Rai, we hid when we could. I stole a bandana from a rack in the back of the store and fashioned a filtration mask for her.

It was a slow day. We picked out useless things from the racks and play-pretended: shopped for our lives in Bangkok. I made a crib mobile out of souvenir keychains. She modeled handbags, hip cocked dourly to one side. The bags—stripped from real croc skin, copiously lacquered—looked stiff and imitative. Slung from the crook of her bony arm, she made the gaudy seem somehow intentional. In the souvenir shop mirror, we stood together.

She said I needed a new name. Anuwat is not the name of a receptionist, an office clerk, a cocktail waiter. It is not a Bangkok name. I agreed. I should be Sony or Winner. The baby will be Andy, Nino. She pressed her forehead into mine and said, "You have the face for a better name."

Sometimes, the children of tourists would peer over our shoulders, feign interest in the contents of our Styrofoam boxes. Lately, the tourists had all been from Mainland China. They arrived in vans and crowded the souvenir shop, poring over the same handbags and belts made from crocodile skins, dyed tangerine orange or electric blue to disguise the blemishes that came from infection, fight wounds. Westerners shied away after allegations of animal abuse or else came in with an air of bashfulness.

When the kids paid us interest, Rai would drape a toy crocodile over her head and crouch, growling behind the aisles of cheap knock-off sunglasses and mugs advertising *Samutprakan Crocodile Farm.* They loved her and so did their parents. Toddlers were hoisted onto her lap, as she puppeteered the stuffed animal for the kids, chattering away in stilted English. With her sparkly drugstore makeup, the blue mismatched for such small warm eyes, Rai made for an excellent local anecdote. She smiled wide for photos with the kids. I loved her prominent canines, the way they balanced out the softness of her eyes.

Later in the afternoon, for extended time with the hose and clean, cool water, we filled a bucket with earthworms and squeezed the dirt out of them like bits of crusty toothpaste. Clean earthworms were easier for the fragile digestive system of young crocs. Afterward, we hosed the enclosure and each other down, dirt, earthworm guts, running slick down our elbows.

I tried, then, to picture the two of us out there, in the city. Me and Rai in the type of restaurant my mother fell in love with. The malls and hotels and cinemas my mother loved. A gray mass of overpasses and skytrains hunkered over millions of lives.

Boom tried to get me to confess to seeing her naked. He wanted the details. He insisted that girls like Rai, *dek jai thaek,* liked to be jerked around. Leave them to dangle a while. It gets them horny, he said, it gets them restless.

"I banged this girl who worked in a salon once. Trust me." Fingers slicked with gel, Boom smoothed my hair back towards the crown of my head. I let him talk at me the way I let him work products into my hair, shaping the long, overgrown strands into the ridge of spikes sported by him and the other crocodile trainers. Unlike the rest of the older boys at the farm, who treated me with a mix of coddling and taunts, Boom considered me one of his own. He'd started at the farm at around my age, all on his own.

In the amphitheater, Boom was always smoldering, flexing his wiry biceps, puckering wet joker kisses. Mom used to say that she couldn't picture him anywhere else, doing anything else, other than sticking his big head into a crocodile's mouth, teasing the pretty Chinese girls in the first row with a toothy grin, staggering towards them as if he'd been bitten, before producing a crushed flower from the pocket of his red-and-gold uniform.

Back when my mother worked at the farm with us, she used to shave both our heads clean with a buzzer.

She said: "The trick for keeping your head out of trouble is keeping it clean and down." Boom would say his trick for keeping his head out of trouble was knowing when to pull out, watching for the tiniest twitch of a jaw, the inward roll of an eyeball into sockets and filmy lids. It's the same with girls, he said: Pull out before shit sours.

"Close your eyes and swallow eight seconds of this." Boom pulled out a bottle of cloudy liquid the color of light rust. At about four seconds, I started to sputter. "Pinch your nose," he said. "You'll thank me."

If I told Boom the truth about Rai and me, about our plan to raise the baby, he would tell me to get the fuck out. He would echo Mom when I saved up my minutes and called to tell her, not about the pregnancy, but about Rai, her very existence. Mom told me that one could tell if a girl had had sex by the width of her hips. A gold anklet or a piercing anywhere but on the earlobes, she said, these are signs of *dek jai thaek*—children with shattered hearts. She said she didn't want me to get hurt or to have someone else's past foisted onto me. I thought it was hypocritical of her to judge but kept this to myself.

Rai borrowed Ake's motorbike for the evening. She had a coarse, charming laugh that she used on most people. It usually got her what she wanted. On the bike, wind hit our faces on the open road framed by rice paddies, shrimp farms, and mangroves on one side and the drift of smoke from factories on the other bank of the river. As I circled my arms around her waist, I thought about how roughly a month and a half from now, she would likely begin to show. The salty wind and the heavy aftertaste of rice whiskey produced a pleasant red swirl in my mind.

When we reached our destination, Rai dropped Ake's bike on the empty road. On one side of the road was the dark, dense curl of mangroves, all wrangled together in a thicket of brine and mosquitos. On the other side: a gas station.

Rai asked me if I'd ever swum before. I told her no.

"It doesn't matter." She pulled her hair into a bun at the nape of her neck. "It's only a matter of letting go and holding on."

With our hands linked, we pushed our scrawny bodies beneath the underbrush, slapping mosquitos dead on our legs and, laughing at each other, tripping over the roots of trees. When we reached the enclosure that opened up in the middle of the thickets, my heart swooped with the drop. There, hidden somewhere I would've never found on my own, was a blue hole. Around the rocky frames of the enclosure, the water was a crisp, magical blue, but towards the center, light lost its way and gave out to murky green. Rai released my hand. I watched the mud swallow her footprints as she advanced towards the opening. It was not a deep fall, and the rocky walls would provide enough traction for our hands and feet to grip, for our bodies to pull their way up. I don't remember if I told myself this at that moment. I remember watching her lower herself down the side of that swimming hole, sharp elbows and quick hands working so efficiently. I wanted her to look back up at me. When she was a safe distance from the water's shimmery surface, her body pushed off the side and, briefly, disappeared beneath the surface. I knew following was stupid, but I emptied my pockets, my phone, neatly onto the bank of the water and made the descent.

In the center, she resurfaced, witch hair plastered both sides of a large, grinning face. I could see her T-shirt, her flat chest, the murky ripples her arms made to keep her afloat. I couldn't see her feet.

"Push," she called.

I said, "How deep is the center?"

"Push."

I lowered one foot into the water, as if I were testing the temperature for someone else's bath.

She ducked her head beneath the surface, flipped her body around with mesmerizing litheness, and resurfaced closer to me, only to disappear again. Each time her face broke the surface, her coarse laughter rang up and up the hole, towards the sky, as if she were expelling a part of herself. The water brought out a levity in her that I had seen the first time I watched her face as she plunged gloved hands into the hatchlings' enclosure. I surveyed the walls of the hole for protrusions, a large rock or a tree branch that I could use to pull myself back out later. I was a good climber, but more importantly, I didn't want to be seen as a coward. I reached a hand towards her outstretched one.

"Let go," she said and I did.

In the water, I clung to Rai for dear life, knowing that I shouldn't, unable to let go. She kicked her feet for the two of us, gulping water through what looked like laughter but could have been protests, pleas. Her broad face bobbed up and down in the water, her eyes filling up with something wet. I waited for her to slip beneath the surface, then I let go.

When I went under, beneath our feet, I saw a tunnel of water leading somewhere I couldn't begin to imagine, harder to picture than the concrete-and-steel network of malls and hotels and parking lots that we'd spent our lives planning for. She pulled me out by the neck of my T-shirt.

On the rocky shoulders of the hole, we reconvened, sputtering. Night had swallowed our little enclosure. I looked at her through bleary eyes and felt, for a second, like my insides were swollen with water, air, and what could only be love. I hacked it all up. We coughed together, and I must've thought we were laying ourselves bare for one another, there in that blue hole. I rolled over to her, clothes darkening in the wet mud, propped myself onto my elbows, and leaned over her. Her sleepy, smiling face.

Then I remembered. "The baby."

I thought of my body grasping, holding Rai's down, beneath the water as I struggled to stay afloat. Bile and something acidic, the rice whiskey, burbled up my throat. I thought of her eagerness, the abandon. My fists clenched in the mud.

"Why did you," I said. She kept still and cold.

I said, "How could you?"

My fingers reached the roots of something, the filmy carapaces of little shrimps, carried here during the rains and floods from one of the nearby shrimp farms. I thought of runaway crocodiles, rogue creatures that escaped from the farm once or twice every few years during the floods. How forecasts of big storms made people around here nervous. I thought of the two of us, surrounded by them now, in the dark. In the wild, this was the type of place they would nest. Foggily, I scanned the dark for a flash of red, the guanine crystals in their eyes that become refractive at night. Only the night stared back. I balled the mud in my fist and examined her face for some kind of response. "Did you do it on purpose?"

I raised a fist dripping with mud, hovered it over her face. I wanted her eyes to dart, some kind of admission to flit across her face.

"The baby," I said. The baby tumbling like rocks in a crocodile's stomach. The baby losing oxygen, sinking, while my body held hers down, tumbled with hers in an endless whorl.

I brought the hand down, slammed the mud over her mouth. I painted the dirt from her chin to her eyes, like a blind. I didn't want her to see me. She opened her eyes under the mud mask. I dug up more mud and raised my hand again. She expelled a short sound, not quite a laugh. She caught my wrist.

"The baby is fine." Rolling away from me, she spat out the mud. She wiped the sleeve of her shirt across her face. When her face emerged, half clean, I felt ashamed.

I tried to apologize, but she stopped me, tugging my elbows gently out from underneath so that my body flattened onto hers. We wrestled on the muddy banks until she was on top of me. We shed our wet clothes. The night sky swaddled us in its wet hold. She smeared the cold dirt on my chest. Of my first time, it's this image I recall best: the muscles along her shoulder rolling left, right, and left again under skin.

Afterward, we lay next to each other, and she began talking aimlessly. She talked of life in Trang, of sitting with her back against the wind on the nose of a long-tail boat headed out to sea. She lived with an uncle who was a scuba instructor. In emerald water that draped out like moving glass, they'd tether themselves to tanks of oxygen that allowed them to both sink and float simultaneously. It was like being in an upside-down world. She talked of the perils of cave diving, how you could lose track of which direction led you to the surface and which one led you farther down. I think in her own way, she must have been warning me. People have different methods of coming clean. My mouth was too slow and sleepy at the time, but if I could, I would have told her that I knew, I knew, and it didn't matter.

Before my mother made the decision to take me from the man who would've been my dad, he used to braid her hair. Even though she could smell the lies on his breath, knew that he ran loose with promises, silky, high, and unfounded, she kept her head in his lap when he came back for her, parted his fingers in her hair. I don't know if any of those memories were mine or solely hers, passed on to me. I braided Rai's hair for her away from her face when she threw up.

To hide her pregnancy from Ake and the others at the farm, I worked for two. I told Ake she was sick but I was handling it. The other boys cooed, "Pretty boy, how's your wife?" when I passed by them on the walkway overlooking the pit, where they readied their hands and their heads for another daredevil performance.

I called Mom under the pretense of nostalgia. I wanted her hardship stories about being a pregnant teenager without her realizing what I was really up to. I asked her if she could help us find a cheap apartment in Bangkok. "I don't know, Anuwat," she said. Across the static of a long-distance call, she sounded distracted: "I'll ask around."

I couldn't have been more ready. In the new-hatchlings' enclosure, they could sense my impatience. They yapped when I fed them, tore apart the rat sausages I tossed to them, and made a mess of the minced meat in the pool that I then had to clean. "Don't be like that," I said. "You know I loved you guys first." Ai Jud burrowed his small body in mud, like he was returning his body to the mound, to the nest his mother made. I didn't have the heart to tell him that his mother gave birth to him in a cubicle, a shaft built and labeled and attached to the fencing of the communal breeding pool.

Rai's nausea subsided. We celebrated the return of her nose unoffended by the smell of blood and rot by helping Boom bind flayed, raw chicken onto long fishing poles to be extended over the enclosure. The tourists loved baiting the crocs to jump.

Rai folded the wings of a chicken over its breast neatly, like an undertaker preparing a body for burial. Boom bound the wings together in prayer and handed me the headless body. I picked up the chicken and thumbed the fat of its neck like an earlobe before piercing a hook through it, tying a rope around the whole thing and securing it to a fishing pole. We were an assembly line, and in our farm uniforms, the tourists took as many photos of us as they did of the crocodiles. We were on one of the walkways that framed the communal enclosure.

"That's a juicy one, ladies and gentlemen," Boom kept on saying when a crocodile morphed from stone to living being, jaws closing in fluid motion over a chicken. "And there's another contender," he narrated as the animals fought each other over a discarded breast.

I was propping up some finished poles against the balustrade. Boom was flirting jokingly with a group of university students. The girls were giggling, giddy with his attention more than the actual prospect of him, but Boom knew this. Rai was talking to a neatly dressed woman around Mom's age. A thin cardigan in the heat, a handbag. I tried to catch Rai's eye so that I could point out an adorable toddler in a crocodile hat being wheeled away in a baby stroller. A large family of tourists intercepted me. I equipped them with crocodile bait.

"Pop," I said, imitating a crocodile lunging for the poultry. The kids laughed. Out of the corner of my eye, I tried to see if it made Rai smile, too. The children were tugging on my arms, demanding more crocodile, more lunges. "Pop!" they echoed, pretending to bite. I crouched, gearing myself up for the pounce. "Yai!" they demanded, calling out the name of our main attraction, the alleged largest crocodile born and bred in captivity. Like the other crocodiles we kept at the farm, he was a Siamese-Saltwater hybrid which made him humongous and aggressive. The saltwater genes, woven in by captive breeding, overwrote the generally non-aggressive, timid nature of the endangered Siamese freshwater crocodiles. I turned in Rai's direction just as the woman in the cardigan handed the handbag over to Rai.

The woman in the cardigan took off her shoes, left them neatly by the balustrade as if she were entering a home. She stepped around Rai, who still had the woman's bag slung obediently from the crook of her arm. Her slim frame slid between the gaps in the steel bars that were only chest high and stood for a second, graceful, on the ledge. Then, calmly, as if answering the door for a guest or perhaps some call from within, she stepped off the ledge and down into the pit.

A week after the woman ended her life in the pit, Rai told me what she wanted to do. We never talked about the contents of the handbag, the suicide note, which were quickly covered by the press, as they would be just as quickly forgotten. It was not a unique story if you stripped away the gore. Not here, in a country that had known steep hopes and steeper declines. After the crowd dissipated, the body parts scavenged for and removed, the blood drained from the cement pool, we hid in the souvenir shop and watched a Chinese tourist don a jacket made out of crocodile, dyed electric blue. A body constrained in borrowed skin.

The next day, I borrowed Boom's motorbike and we rode across the province line in search of the clinic she'd already found on her phone. They gave Rai pills to take in the privacy of her home. That night, we rode back to the farm, past mangrove trees that grew with the sort of abandon that felt like violation, scraggly limbs twisted into the crooks and hollows of one another's bodies. In a storm, the telephone lines would embrace them and lose themselves in the tangle. The sky swelled with impending rain. I prayed for a flood that would break open our hatchlings' enclosure and give them what I couldn't.

In the small bathroom in my dormitory, I held Rai's hand as she swallowed the pills. We'd pressed two chairs against the doors to keep the other employees out. Although we were both used to the smell of blood, it smelled different in our own bathroom. Curled together on the floor, Rai prayed for forgiveness. When the pain got to be too much, I gave her the Percocet, like the doctor recommended. As she hurled into the toilet, I began braiding her hair.

In bed, we turned to face each other, and I remembered the first day we met. It was towards the last leg of the breeding season. In her low-rise jeans and sparkly tank top, Rai was brought straight to the crocs' communal pool by the boys. They watched her with gluey eyes as she leaned against the railing overlooking the concrete hole where 250 crocodiles clustered at their sexual peak.

The first time I'd heard their mating call, I was six years old. That first day at the farm, Ake took us on a tour of the place. He brought us to the communal breeding pool. I held my mother's hand and made myself look down. From moss-green water that smelled like waste rose the low guttural sound, a prehistoric exhalation. I felt my legs give. I thought only of the fall, the railing disappearing beneath my fingers, the green that I would meet below. My mother knelt and wrapped one arm around me, pointing with the other. "Look at them dancing."

I'd pointed this out to Rai on her first day. Barely visible in the grimy water, the male crocodiles' bodies thrummed. The low vibrations of their bodies rippled the surface, creating baby fountains across the otherwise-still pool. I thought about how long the dance has been around, how little evolution occurred in a species.

"What's the first thing we do when we get to Bangkok?"

"We'll stay with my mom. She'll take us to a restaurant made out of marble."

"I'll find work there."

"I'll make us a home."

"And where would we live?"

"In an apartment that opens up to the sky trains."

She smiled.

"Your mom will like me," she prophesied under heavy-lidded eyes. The blue of her makeup smeared into the hollow beneath her eyes. I thumbed a streak of sparkle down her face, all the way down to her chin. She turned her back to me and nestled into the nook of my body. "We'll go," she said. "In the future."

"We'll go," I echoed and watched for the rise and fall of her breaths, elongated, grown steady, as she surrendered to sleep.

"I promise," I said and twisted an elastic band from my wrist onto the tail of her braid, completing it.

Rachael Hershon

After Your Father Dies

His friends try to fuck your mom.
They gather solemnly in your driveway
        for the ceremony of giving away possessions.

The night before, your mother boxes watches
he never wore—big, gaudy things with purple
        and yellow faces. One for each of his closest friends—

Matt, Kevin, and Danny—all standing dumbly, eyeing
your mother's breasts as she works her way down the line,
        dropping watches into cupped palms, cracked and swollen

with labor. Almost in unison, they slip their hands
through silver bands, clip them on, rotate wrists, glass glinting
        in the sun, as if trying on your father's life. Jewels of sweat

forming on foreheads at the thought of future adult
stepchildren. For several months, each appears
        unannounced, eager to offer their trades to your mother—

a widow's tears, the most powerful of aphrodisiacs.
Matt vaults himself onto the roof in search of loose
        shingles, lingers in the kitchen over a cup of coffee,

leaning in closely, toolbelt sagging. Kevin
checks the pines for root rot, invasive species, work boots
        leaving heavy indentations in the dirt. He calls your mom

late at night to confess that when she and your dad first started
dating, he had the hots for her too. Danny offers to buy
          your dad's truck for parts at his junkyard, inventorying the car's

inner workings. Cowboy mustache and nose hairs trimmed
for the occasion, he asks to take your mom for a drink.
          She calls you, stunned, remembering the day these friends

slung dirt into his grave, shovels in hand, joints grinding
under dress shirts, leaving the cemetery crew with little work.
          The rabbi's remarks circling her as he watched them:

Never seen anything like this before. Must have been
so loved. Such devoted friends.

Rachael Hershon

A Member of the Hevra Kadisha

I am the last human
touch. Not his kids,
not his wife. I massage
holy waters into ulcerated
feet. Cleanse the curtain
of flesh that drapes above
genitals. Wrap the body
in linen. Press Jerusalem's
dirt onto feet, heart, eyes.
Pray for his soul's resurrection
when the Messiah comes.
It's comforting to know
they're in such caring hands,
the rabbi says. But I have
grown to hate my dead.
How they expect too much
of me. How one mistake
takes away a man's entry
into The Coming World.
How Malakh Ha-Mavet
has a constant eye on me.
He follows me on the drive
home, craving car crashes.
Cranes his neck while I dice
potatoes, eager for the blade
to split veins. Salivates as I eat
dinner, hoping to chew the sludge

stuck in my throat. Cradles me
when I fall asleep, tempted
to slow my heart to a stop.
In a repeated dream, I wake
with phantom pressure
between my temples, earth lodged
deep in my skull. I dig and dig
for a shaft of light only to be met
with the scrape of bone.

Mary Kovaleski Byrnes

Elegy in Fractals (Chaos Theory)

And where my organ of veneration should be—
wormwood and gall. Grudge sliver.
— "After the Angelectomy," Alice Fulton

When Tammy dies, someone says, *It's God's will.*
He wanted her for himself, to make her an angel
and I want to cut a bitch. I hold her one-year-old
on my hip, her four-year-old takes my hand.
Her daughters remember her out loud.
This will only last a year, until their brains grow
wider, burying their mother again, memories like planes
into the Bermuda triangle, like swimmers out too
far, past the rope, beyond the break. Someone

smarter wouldn't be so pissed about the angel
comment. They'd tell you about chaos theory—
randomness, no matter how cruel, isn't random,
but set off by something we just can't see. In
other words, I'm in the fractal, somewhere,
a woman holding on to the hands of many children
standing on a planet that's floating in constellations
of stars shaped like a snowflake, or a fern leaf,
something perfectly balanced, symmetrical.
But they derived *fractal* from *broken* in Latin, *angel*
from *messenger* in Greek. Tell me again about

angels, how they comfort the grieving. How if
you're really listening, you might hear one speak.

Mary Kovaleski Byrnes

Intelligent Work

By sixteen, I'd mastered a language
allotting for silence. For repetition

in symmetry with the recent and distant
past. Held my mother's flute to my own new mouth

pasted strawberry lip smackers and another
aperture of time, patience

and what they called *intelligent work* rising
from those antique pads under white brass

even then I found the song
perhaps too predictable, featherweight

yet essential, she taught me
performance, how to concentrate

so much perseverance toward the shape
of the lips, the mouth—

what music can come of this?

I carried her flute across the state
of Pennsylvania. On its case

mascots to a history of violence and pillage,
a crusader and a raider—I watched myself

in the rearview, over her shoulder,
as we drove toward mountains,

toward ruin and coal rivers she knew as home,
their archaic mouths once embouchure

for an entire blooming valley, the whole
of me cut off in that mirror except my lips.

Emily Rinkema

This Is How They Learn

The tornado is just a metaphor when the Adults lock the sliding door to the kitchen and pull the curtains closed, leaving the Kids in the yard. The Kids are between the ages of nine and twelve and it will be a few years before the first one runs away, the first one starts cutting, the first one breaks the church window with a baseball bat. But you can feel it in the air, the coming storm, thick and still, clouds darkening over the church, which is weeks from quietly closing because of photos they will find in a box in the minister's office, the minister who is one of the eight Adults currently drinking Cosmopolitans in the now-locked kitchen of one of his parishioners at just after two p.m. on a Saturday in June as a tornado slowly moves towards them.

The tornado isn't really moving slowly, probably about thirty miles per hour, which is impossibly fast if you're trying to outrun it, but almost three times as slow as the speed at which one of the Adults, the one currently asking the minister, his best friend since childhood, if he can hang onto a box for him for a bit, will drive into the quarry. And the minister, who is on his second Cosmopolitan, says of course, just bring it by my office, and he doesn't even ask what it is, what's inside the box, because they've been friends for so long that it doesn't matter. Later, he'll have so many questions, but they will get lost under the metaphorical debris of should haves and what ifs and the real debris from the storm.

As the tornado gets closer, the Kids are in the yard playing a game they call War, which involves two teams trying to stay out of sight of each other by running around the house. The porches are Safe Zones. They all have slightly different understandings of the rules, and they fiercely defend their own understandings, which leads to accusations, which escalates to screaming, which is maybe why the game is called

War and definitely why the Adults turn their music up louder. One of the Kids quits, goes to sit on the swing set, looks up from her sneakers and notices that the sky is dark, really dark, like weirdly dark, but the rest of the Kids are still warring, so she doesn't say anything, a skill she has lots of practice at, keeping secrets from her friends, from her mother, from her minister. She won't have to keep the secrets for much longer, but she doesn't know that, and even if she did, she's too young to find that comforting.

The tornado is only a few miles away now and the air is heavy and the trees in the yard are swaying and the Adults are also swaying and one of them thinks maybe they should check on the Kids because aren't they oddly quiet all of a sudden? Or maybe it's just that the music has gotten louder, and another one of the Adults thinks he hears the wind, but then thinks that he has to figure out a time to get the box that's currently hidden in the garage to the church office, so stops thinking about the wind. And another one of the Adults wishes it were always this simple, always as easy as drinks in the afternoon and Kids old enough to take care of themselves, and still another Adult wonders why her husband was whispering with the minister in the corner, why he's so distracted, and she pours another drink and decides to ignore it, ignore him, because maybe if he sees her dancing, spinning, he'll remember that they used to have fun together, that's it's not all accusations and screaming.

Now the Kids see the tornado, a real tornado, which is almost here, and they stop yelling about War and start yelling about the funnel that is incredible, right out of a cartoon, the way it moves, its perpendicularity and its power, and the wind is so strong that the swings are swinging on their own, empty now, and one of the Kids runs to the sliding door of the kitchen and bangs on it and tries to open it, but remember, it's locked, like the box in the garage, and the rest of the Kids run around the house and try the other doors, but they are all locked, and isn't there a key under a pot? There's no key, and the Adults hear the banging on the door, but they're laughing and dancing and drinking and one of them says they should let the Kids figure out their own problems, and another says she would love having the kind of problems the Kids have, and another says that this is how they learn to grow up, to be functioning adults.

Scott Garson

This Is Where I Live

She told me I was beautiful, so I followed her to the city. Her name was Rae. I wasn't doing anything major with my life.

She had a ground-floor place. But zero furniture. Just a mattress, which was our bed.

Some nights I presented my chest, my barbed throat, like I was a six-part gift.

The building was old. The windows were deep and barred. Mornings we would step outside with coffee and perch in the sill, right close to the street. Passers-by would glance at us, wondering if we were looking for cash.

Rae got mad with some frequency.

She went walking, and I was alone.

This is where I live, I sometimes thought. Like I had nodded off—just then opened my eyes.

I got a job making sandwiches. Rae didn't need a job; she had money. One day she came back with a car.

What's that for? I asked.

Driving? she said. She pantomimed gripping the wheel.

I didn't point out that it would be hard to find parking, or that our requisite shopping was easily done on foot. I didn't point this out because Rae was fuming. That was clear.

I said earlier that the double mattress was all we had in the apartment. That's not quite true. After Rae took off in the car and abandoned me, I did a bored search, discovering within a hall closet a sizeable rug, rolled up and tied. I crooked it for extraction, muscled it out, then did the unfurling.

And wow. This beautiful Persian rug. Maroons, impossible blues. It was magnificent. That was the word I used out loud in the barred apartment.

Maybe a couple of days after that, somebody knocked at the door.

I wanted to think it was Rae, come back to repent. But it was another person entirely. *Maddie Anderson*, she said.

Turns out? It was her Persian rug!

Oh, I said. Right. It's beautiful.

We went inside to gaze upon it.

Do you need any help like moving it? I asked.

Maddie Anderson didn't say anything. Something was telling me I should shift gears, so I asked if she wanted some coffee.

She sort of frowned. Maddie Anderson pursed her lips. I thought that she thought that my offer was maybe off-key, or somehow off-color.

Also, I thought my analysis was probably totally wrong.

Yes, she said drily.

Yes? I said.

Yes, I'd like some coffee.

Long story short, Maddie Anderson moved in. That same night.

She joined me on the floor on the mattress. (I'd thought to put on fresh sheets.)

Maddie Anderson was a person of interesting foibles, like everyone is once you know them. She often worked her nose muscles to pinch or sharpen the tip. She did this always at certain times: when she wanted you to know that she had some thought. But didn't want you to know what it was.

I tried to read the room with Maddie Anderson. This was not as easy as you might think.

In bed she turned away from me but liked for me to pull close. This, I believe, was a help to her as she coped with her journey to sleep.

Often, in the depths of the night, when we were mostly unconscious, we would tussle. This was a consequence of Maddie Anderson's terrible eczema. Asleep, she'd be trying to itch herself raw. Asleep, I'd be trying to stop her.

Maddie Anderson belonged to some community groups. Because I never accompanied her (because I might have complicated her image—or so I deduced), I never managed to memorize which community groups these were.

But she was gone a lot. Just as Rae had been. Also like Rae, she came home once with something unexpected: a bona fide handgun.

Is that a gun? I asked.

I thought that Maddie Anderson might respond by working her nose. But she said, It's not a pizza.

I nodded, for this was true.

Her fears had to do with living in the city on the ground floor, even though the windows facing the street were fitted with bars, as I've said. If I went to bed before she did, Maddie Anderson would sit with the gun at the tiny table she had brought in. She'd sit with the gun on the table next to an ounce or two of cranberry juice, contained in a Daffy Duck jam jar.

That handgun was left on the table at all times, for ease of access.

Even when she was gone, even when I was pacing the room by stepping on each cerulean shape within the Persian rug, the gun would be sitting there. Like Maddie Anderson herself on occasion, it would seem to have something to say.

Eventually, I got a text from a friend, asking if I would accompany him to Los Angeles in a pickup truck, so he could reclaim the possessions he'd lost in a breakup. That's a whole other story, of course. This one ended with me moving out, though I don't recollect my doing so (saying bye to Maddie Anderson, for instance).

Instead, I remember sitting at Maddie Anderson's table, next to the gun, which I might have concealed in a drawer if this could have been done without use of my hand. I remember sitting there, thinking the oddest thoughts. Thinking how someone might wake in my mind, some other person entirely. Someone might come, like mentally teleport, and blink, and be using my eyes. And what would they see, this brand new resident? What impressions might they form of the scene, this place where they lived?

Pamela Painter

Revenge

Seconds before the accident, I felt it coming, is what I tell the policeman who, his siren blaring, showed up with two ambulances and three police cars minutes after the accident. I admit I knew it was going to happen. My car was going to swerve into theirs, run them off this mountain road, their Chevy now upside down and bent over the railing, its doors leaking booze, while broken teenagers are being pried free and lifted into ambulances. Minutes ago, their car was paused next to me at the light, kids swigging half empty bottles of vodka or gin. They were revving their engine, giving me the finger—daring someone old enough to be their grandmother—into a senseless race. It was the sort of situation I suspect I've been looking for ever since my son's death a year ago. Exactly a year ago when another car packed with senseless kids celebrating something stupid with half-empty bottles of vodka or gin swerved into my son's car filled with his family coming home from a day at the shore where he was teaching his daughters to swim. I tell the policemen I didn't know I wanted revenge, not in so many words till the car with drunk teenagers pulled up beside me at the red light, and suddenly I saw red, not literally, but well—Yes, officer, yes you can take me in.

Caroline Beuley

It's a Monster, Baby

It is winter, and the snow is falling in gusting hushes, and I am going to the greenhouse. The nubby, pilled fingers of my gloves click and close a knife so that it snicks and shuts in tune with my footsteps. Night is slipping down the skyscrapers, and the city is never safe, but especially not after dark.

Every day they find more bodies, wet intestines shining like jewels in the bright light of morning. *A serial killer*, ABC 7 says. But that doesn't account for the quantity. A roving hoard of serial killers? The greenhouse glows green in the distance like a shot of absinthe. Snick. Click. Snick. Click.

This is the greenhouse where the girls go, the one they all told me about, way down at the tip of the island, by the jetty, where the concrete washes into the water. There's nowhere else to go for what we need.

When I reach the greenhouse, a padlock dangles from the door on a thick necklace of chains. But I have the key. A girl, who got it from a girl, who got it from another girl, gave it to me.

Inside, the greenhouse is a riot of plant life, wet and close. I am reminded of pressing my face to the dirt as a girl. I am still a girl, but not in the same way as I was when I pressed my face into the soil and my fingers searched for earthworms.

Shadows bubble and burst in the steamy half-light. I start at each shape, searching for the woman we all know but do not name—for her safety, and ours. She emerges from beneath a hanging monstera, watering can in one hand, pruning shears in the other.

She asks what she can help me with, and I say the code word: *Seeds.* She points her shears down a long row of carnivorous plants. Leafy jaws open and close like baby mouths as we pass. At the end of the row, there is a shed. Inside, it smells like back home. Fertilizer, grass clippings, and a freshness I had to leave behind when I moved to the city to find work.

The woman procures a seed packet from the back of the shed, presses it into my palm. *Take it with water,* she says. *Alone.*

Will it hurt, I ask.

She nods. *But by morning it will never hurt you again.*

The other girls say she does not accept payment, and this also turns out to be true.

Thank you, I say.

She waves me away. *I was a mother once, and now I'm a gardener. This is what I do.*

I wonder if she will say anything else, if *I* should say anything else. But she only turns to an exuberant bush of basil and begins plucking the buds from the junctures between the leaves. My mother used to do this to the pot on our porch. *If you let them flower, the leaves will turn bitter*, she told me.

When I turn on the lights back in my studio, the white bottom of a dresser drawer gleams in the fluorescents like an erased whiteboard. I close it with my hip. He left it open, I think, to make a point, to remind me of the empty spaces he will leave behind in my life.

I fill a glass of water from the tap, place the seed packet beside it. He has taken his toothbrush from the cup by the sink. I am not a monster. I do miss him. But I have heard stories from the girls of other girls who confided in boys. Boys who changed their minds, developed a conscience after the fact. Girls who were subsequently arrested (or otherwise imprisoned).

Alone, the woman said. There is no other way to do this safely.

I open the seed packet. Inside is a clear capsule. When I turn it in my fingers, dried plant matter tumbles like snow in a globe. I swallow it with water.

Curled on the couch, I contemplate my apartment. It is the biggest I can afford and yet still much too small. In the fridge are two packs of Reese's cups and a half-dozen Diet Cokes. In the bathroom, pink mold collects in the cracks between tiles. Old toothpaste spit clouds the silver sink spout.

The pain starts an hour later. Jerky, wrenching waves of it. I cover my mouth to muffle moans. A glutinous wet pulses into my pants. I scrabble off my sweats, rolling onto the floor to save the couch. Something splats between my legs. It is long and tentacular. It wriggles. I close my eyes, and my scream becomes a snarl as my muscles contract and push.

When I open my eyes, the thing is on the floor in front of me, heaving in tune with my breaths, its tentacles flexing and stretching like newborn fingers. It lets out a low mewling. The circular mouth in the center of its slick, bulbous body yawns open, revealing concentric rows of razor-sharp teeth.

The girls told me about the greenhouse, and the key, and the code word, and the payment. They did not tell me about this part. I don't blame them. I won't tell anyone.

The thing gnashes its teeth and oozes at me. But I am not afraid. I have already given my portion of pain to the creature. It seems to understand this, and drags itself over to my window, tentacles slapping and sucking across the floor. With a quick jab, it shatters the glass, hoists itself up, and drops from the sill.

I stumble over to the window, watch as it shudders across the dark street. I worry it will hurt someone. I know, and the girl before me knows, and the girl before her knows, and all the girls before them know, no one is safe from something like this. I grab a piece of cardboard and tape it over the shattered window.

Ryan Pierce

Rag and Bone Man

for Rafaat Alareer

The baby sleeps through the night now, but I do not.

I surface, instead, after a gorgeous three hours bought with Black Label and diphenhydramine citrate and stumble onstage into the dream I've somehow made my life. My wife breathes from her cocoon of blankets beside me, the softest snore. The dog adjusts himself to warm my shifting feet. An early spring breeze moves cotton curtains like a jellyfish's bellows, sweeping in abundance, drawing out self-doubt, sweeping in renewal, expelling black, shattered asteroids of regret.

Which is to say: Insomnia is easier than it used to be.

It hasn't rained in weeks, but I've come awake to a concerto of droplets on the skylights, their polyrhythm anchored by a deep and distant groan from the barges on the river. I often hear the sounds of unfathomable tonnage settling in a hold, or a grain elevator yielding open its rusted bay, or the complaints of whatever ailing remnant of the industrial age is staggering to its knees on someone else's graveyard shift.

Above, under, and between all that is the racket of rubber wheels on the driveway, plastic flapping, sardine cans clattering on cement. It is not trash night and hasn't been for what feels like months. The moon illuminates what the busted streetlight no longer does: The Rag and Bone Man has chosen our house this dark morning.

I catch him with his finger poised at the bell. Wake my baby and I'll smash your skull, I will. He licks his thumb instead, extends a hand that I somehow can't not shake, although what's this? It's not a hand he's offering but the torn-up rootball of an olive tree. Crumbs of dry earth shower my bare feet.

"You must be mistaken," I begin. My voice sounds meek and wavering, damp laundry on a line.

He clicks and whistles, and a gust of rankness knocks me back, which I worry will read as an invitation to enter my house, but the Rag and Bone Man does not. He rifles through his rucksack to find a shibaried plastic bag, unbinds its twine, and presents a stuffed, plush gazelle. I know it's a gazelle, because I saw them in the wild, once, on a miserable safari.

"Okay," I say. I begin to explain that I need to fetch my wallet before we haggle on a price, but as I turn away, the Rag and Bone Man turns, too, shuffling into the night with his wretched contraptions, leaving me to stroke the toy antelope on my unlit front stoop in the night like a madman.

"Daddy got you a toy!" My wife sounds surprised and maybe even pleased. She is always the first and sometimes the only one to think of the baby's needs, to order the next size of onesie or something called Developmental Caterpillar.

The baby coos and mashes the stuffed creature against the shelf that used to hold our record collection. Something is awry, though, and I coerce the gazelle away to find hairy, maroon larvae wriggling from the seam where its legs meet. I can barely hold on long enough to get it outside to the garbage. The baby screams, apoplectic at my theft.

Three nights later, my neighbor leaves his window open and falls asleep with the TV on. I can't understand the words, but I sense the strained enthusiasm of a game show host long beyond a dignified retirement. The wind shifts direction, slapping the neighbor's flag against our house across the alley where we store the trash bins. The neighbor is a cave person who justifies his apocalyptic politic with customized lies from AI chatbots. He likes to bait me, lacing casual racism into banal observations: "I guess it's raining too hard for the mail today; I hear those people are superstitious about rain." He wants me to bristle at who he means when he says "those people," but I remind him that it's Sunday and we have never gotten mail on Sundays.

The wind lifts again, and a shuffle-scrape rides the draft. I meet the Rag and Bone Man at the curb. The clarity of predawn makes his ensemble all the more troubling: the cardboard visor and crowded teeth. Definitions blur between hood and chin, between eyes and their inferred meaning. I summon some gumption.

"Can't you come at a more reasonable hour?"

The Rag and Bone Man smiles at my simple-mindedness. We'd set the dogs on him, of course, if he chanced the light of day. Too slowly, too gradually, he spreads a threadworn blanket on the apron of the driveway, and too tenderly he moves aside my many unread newspapers in their plastic husks to present me with his pitiful wares. A burnt pot with a pewter spoon fused to its bottom. A cheap faux-oak frame with a family picture, its subjects sun-bleached to abstraction. A model airplane—or starship, perhaps, some futuristic toy conjoined to a remote control with gaffer's tape. That's what I opt for tonight, as it seems most appropriate for a baby and unlikely to host a parasite.

This time, I've come prepared, with five dollars in the elastic of my pajama bottoms, but the Rag and Bone Man isn't interested. He reaches into my mailbox and presents me with its contents: an update on our investments, a tax thing, and the catalog they've sent us every month for years because we bought nice sheets after our wedding. I fumble in my waistband as he regroups and clambers away, but the cash is missing, or so I think, before I find it folded on the kitchen counter.

The toy is well designed. With a nine-volt and a bit of fiddling, I can fly it from the mudroom to the nursery. The baby chirps and claps her hands. My wife arches a brow but seems happy for the distraction. Like a languid black wasp with a single red eye, it thumps dumbly against the window. When my wife throws open the door to let some air in, the spacecraft zooms off, ignoring my frantic handling of the joystick. It is its own master now, and my wife says it's lost forever and good riddance, but I feel it hasn't gone far.

There is a certain high whine, for instance, any time I watch TV, the subliminal hum of a lost octave that seems to distract both me and the news anchor. Her words are misarranged; they clatter like hollow plastic, devoid of meaning. Six dead in a shooting at a big box retailer, the gunman bought his weapons in the store and unboxed them to commence killing—but then here are some teens taking neighborhood cleanup into their own hands, laconic youths dragging garbage bags, stabbing at litter with slender pikes. I like the funny and familiar insurance commercial that plays at every break.

I dream of the black craft lurking in the birches past our fence or just at my periphery, keeping its unblinking digital eye on me when I scuttle from the house to the car to drive to work and from the car back into the house again.

I find the Rag and Bone Man in the greenbelt that separates our development from an identical-except-less-affluent one. He is occupied, I see, with bundling rolls of gray, stained gauze into paper lunch bags, adding dried flowers and a pinch of grain. He sings softly to himself—or rather to his packages, which he tucks together with great deliberation, patting them as if to give them comfort.

"I could help you," I offer, opening my hands to show both my capacity for labor and will for peace. The Rag and Bone Man ignores me.

"I have money. And I know some people. Influential ones?"

The song he's singing sounds familiar, but I can't place it. He is embellishing his project by tearing small pages from a travel bible and pasting them to the Kraft paper with a honey-flecked spoon. It is the last hour of night, and the sprinkler heads lunge like snakes from their burrows to shower the perfect turf with clean, clear water, soaking my ankles and my calfskin slippers, soaking the Rag and Bone Man or his apparition, his pathetic gifts and jalopy bazaar cart, the mar of his unwelcome existence at the addled boundaries of my mind.

From the dry creek bed, crickets join the Rag and Bone Man's song. From behind the scrim of branches of the dying ash trees, a red eye watches in silence.

Dennis Hinrichsen

Scandanavian dance party with Max von Sydow and a dead mouse

performance of the soul with none
of its

stink :: that's what I want ::
not

dead mouse
stench

because I left one

in a trap
for six days :: I forgot :: they

raid our larder ::
I had to take it :: its ethereal

tremor snapped :: poor
thing ::

last musk of soul ::

there is no
minor

seventh in language
to convey

my feelings :: I'm not a killer
though I kill ::

so I considered its eyes ::
those portals

perfectly
rounded obsidian pearls :: jet

to shallow depths ::
then bagged

the body :: upstairs

The Seventh Seal :: that
witch-

on-a-cross scene ::
von Sydow

blasting tears down gaunt
and granite

cheeks :: but he had nothing
on me ::

I had a dead mouse in a bag
and so

I turned away :: *dramatically* ::

as the woman does to her fate
in the film

because she knows there is
no God :: just

fire :: endless fire ::

even the mouse and I agree
on that ::

as for von Sydow ::
he just rides

away :: the woman? ::
they cut her down :: she's

been
hanging there for hours ::

it might've been Take #17 ::
the set is

closed :: she is already
out of her

sackcloth
in the Scandinavian night

saying
(as the mouse might say ::

or even me) to anyone ::

please :: stay ::
hold me in your arms a minute longer

Blue Fay

The Brick

Around the time you disappeared, someone threw a brick through the windshield of my car. I was staying in the San Francisco, parking around the Castro without a permit. One morning, I woke up and found blood splattered along the fenders. I drove through the carwash and the next day it rained ash. I had a recurring dream about driving the brick down to Orange County, to the parking lot where you were stabbed to death. Night after night, I climbed into the passenger seat and threw the brick back at the windshield of the afterlife. You unzipped your own body bag. You were knifed back to life.

Grant Clauser

46,000-Year-Old-Roundworm Gives Birth in German Lab

The world tells us it's the little things in life
that matter, how a stranger paying
for the lab assistant's coffee
on a cold Cologne morning after the MRI
shifts something in both of them
the way the hour after good news
feels like a break in the weather,
and on her drive to work she hits
every green light on Zülpicher Strasse,
finds her favorite parking spot in front
of the university lab is empty, and she drops
the four euros she saved from the coffee
into the hands of a homeless man sitting
in his usual spot by the building's revolving doors.
The grain of his face reminds her of her late father,
and now she strolls in three minutes early,
and that's when her colleague shares the news—
It worked, a life suspended in Siberian permafrost
since before there were words to describe it.
Just a mere thing, stuck to the glass plate
of a microscope in a world turned inside out
a thousand times, and despite all the forgotten
history, freeze and thaw, an insignificant
nematode rescued from the maws of time
makes every banal day in her short life
break into their component parts, becoming
small beautiful things, just for today.

Dan Pinkerton

Time Machine

Two guys showed up with the time machine strapped in the back of their pickup. "Want to try it out?" asked one of the men, who said his name was Gary. He introduced his partner as Doug.

"Sure," I said. "Where do I sign?" I was dreaming of Giza, Versailles, ancient Peru ....

"No signature needed. But you can only go forward two hours."

I thought about this for a minute. "But why me? Isn't this a game-changer? I mean, time travel! Couldn't you sell the machine to the government for millions of dollars?"

"We could, but we're patriots," Gary explained while leaning against the fender of the pickup. He spit into the grass. His pants were grease-stained, I noticed. There was dirt under his nails, probably from tinkering with the machine. I didn't quite understand the patriot comment, which must've shown on my face.

"We're populists," Gary continued. "We want everyone to have a go at it, not just the elite."

"Are you scientists?"

"Basically," Gary said. "We don't want to see the machine locked up somewhere, out of reach. We've been up and down your street, asking everyone."

"And the neighbors tried it?"

"Without exception. It changed their lives to see the future."

"Even the Dunagans?" I asked. The Dunagans were skeptical of everything.

"Yep, the Dunagans loved it. We gave them a family discount."

"That's odd," I said. "The Dunagans don't have children."

"Well," Gary said, spitting on the ground. "You know, two can make a family just as well."

"Okay," I said, convinced. "I'll try it. I mean, if the Dunagans loved it …."

"It's a one-hundred-dollar donation to science," said Gary. "You know, to further the work the lab is doing."

I frowned. "I don't have a hundred dollars."

"Well, how much do you have?"

I scrounged in my billfold. "Maybe eighteen, nineteen bucks."

"That'll work," said Gary.

The pair started loosening the straps securing the machine to the truck's bed. They peeled back the canvas. It was impressive, lots of stainless steel, much like the apparatus in a microbrewery or fancy coffee house. They wrestled the time machine to the driveway. After I counted out the remaining bills from my wallet into Doug's dirty palm, I climbed into the machine and thought I could even smell the residue of brewed beer. Maybe I just had beer on the brain.

Gary handed me a strange pill.

"What's this?" I asked, voice echoing in the steel chamber.

"It'll help with the nausea. It's not like you're just taking a ride around the block. This is time travel we're talking about."

I dry-swallowed the pill, the machine started up, there was much loud banging and whistling, as of pistons and steam, and I lost consciousness. When I came to, I peered out. The men were sitting in folding lawn chairs, listening to a football game on a small radio at their feet. They were eating Cheetos, the big ones, the Puffs, which I remember reading somewhere were invented by mistake, a lab accident. Maybe that's what this time machine was, with its two-hour limit, a lab accident, the Cheetos Puffs of time travel.

"How was it?" Doug asked.

I looked around. Everything was different now, more vivid, the hues of grass and sky. The hairs on my arms stood up. I glanced at my wristwatch. Two hours had elapsed. "Wow!" I said. "The future!"

Gary raised his hands, palms upturned. "You're looking at it."

"It works!" I said, crawling out of the machine. "It really works!"

"Was there ever any doubt?" said Doug.

Both had risen now, folding up their chairs, tossing them in the back of the pickup, wrestling the time machine into the bed.

"Need some help?" I asked, noticing that in the future I was more willing to lend a hand, even if it meant a sore back the next day. I liked my future self, glad for this glimpse of things to come.

"I think we've got it," Gary said, doffing his cap, a very old-world gesture.

Some things, I guess, never change.

Mitch James

Anatomy 5000: Advanced Human Dissection

I was the first to cut into you, then Niko, then Aniya, and I was the first to take from you, your triquetrum, pisiform, then lunate, washed clean, like curds in my hand. Then there was the day of clinical augury, where I sifted through your liver and gallbladder, stomach and spleen, and emerged into a new world, where it was no longer possible for anything to belong.

Caden couldn't understand how, after seven years, organs proved it impossible for us to ever truly be together, but if he could see inside you too, how it all fits like one big hug, everything clutching at each other, he'd understand closeness, the beauty of proximity. I have made you hollow, then full again. I have wept.

We're birthed. Taken from. That's our introduction to the world. Separation. Is there a greater violence? But inside we're whole from the start.

Did you know when we form, everything within our mothers, what had a home all those years, must migrate, drop or spread, curl under, cradle or climb? Then, when we're gone, it comes together again.

They must cut into you too. You are the hardest thing to share. After each class, we slide less and less of you back into cold storage. Last night, Niko said we've left you looking like something found in the savannah. But I saw you first. It was I who sturdied *Gray's* atop your belly, guiding that first incision. I was the first to feel you full. No matter how ravaged you are now, how empty, I have felt you full.

Alan Michael Parker

Edison Liu Needs to Disappear

Like on a freighter, dude	It wasn't stolen stolen	Suzan used to	The Benjamins in Cal's foot locker	Like Ohio
Pappa's pocket watch	APB	Dude knew who had the car	BASE jumping looks the rizz	Suzan's real clear on lying
"In recovery, the patient can drop below baseline, and have no upward recourse." -Dr. D.D. Hodges	Smugglers go back, right?	**Won't vs. Can't**	On a mountain, or like in one of those caves, for real	335-hp V-6
105 mph, lights off	Who told Suzan	The two adrenal glands rest just above the two kidneys	Mom	Like Harry Potter
Suzan's going to kill him	Cal has a plan	No passport	He was only trying to	Release of norepinephrine in the amygdala

Michelle Ross

Because the Bike, Because the Coffee

I dreamt that I left a bike-share bike unattended while I ran into a coffee shop to use the bathroom. Not wanting to be irresponsible and place the bike at any more risk than necessary, I hurried in and out of there without buying a coffee, which I felt guilty about. In many ways, I am rebellious by nature, but not in this way, not when it comes to courtesy. So using the establishment's bathroom without purchasing anything bothered me, but I did it anyway—because the bike.

When I returned, however, the bike was gone. No sign of it, though I searched all around the building and up and down the surrounding streets. I opened the bike-share app, which I had downloaded just before renting the bike because I am nothing if not organized. I intended to report the bike stolen, but the FAQs offered nothing about what to do in the case of a lost or stolen bike. So I called the company. The young man who answered seemed not to understand my situation. He said, "You pay until you return the bike." I said, "Surely, I can simply pay for the cost of the bike and be done with it. If I lose a library book, there's an option to replace it with a new copy. I'm not doomed to pay book fines for said book until I die." But there was no reasoning with the guy. He merely offered up that my rental rate, 17 cents a minute, would remain locked in at the price upon the time of rental; I would not be subjected to inevitable rate increases over time. He said this as if it would be a comfort to me.

If the matter could have been resolved by stealing someone else's bike-share bike and returning it as my own, I confess I would have seriously considered it, though that too would have made me feel guilty. But, of course, the bikes have unique IDs and so returning someone else's bike would have done me no good. So I kept searching for the bike. Every time I spotted someone on a bike-share bike, which, oddly, I thought, happened only three times in all my searching, I hounded them into letting me check the ID against what showed in my app. The first time was easy. I spotted the bike as the rider was waiting at a red light. The woman, who was wearing a sequined dress, by the way—sparkling silver like the scales of a fish—watched me warily as I got out of my car and ran over to her. But she didn't object to my looking, and I was quick so that by the time the light turned green, I was out of her way. Two I had to chase down on foot. I never would have caught him if he hadn't turned to look at me over his shoulder and so ridden the bike into a parked car. After checking the bike's ID, I offered to help him to his feet, but he said that if I wasn't gone by the time he stood, he'd punch me, "lady or not." I spotted three as I was exiting the wine store with a bottle of white, which at this point, owing over a thousand dollars to the bike-share company, I could not afford. I didn't even have to run to catch up to her. She was right there in front of the store, in the process of mounting the bike. But when I told her my situation and that all I wanted to do was check the ID on the bike, she refused me. I had to jump in front of her and block her from leaving. A tussle ensued.

I checked the bikes at all the bike-share stations in town, too, in case the bike had been returned and perhaps there was a glitch in the meter or the company was trying to scam me. But none of these bikes was the one I'd rented, either.

Eventually, I did find the bike. It was, in fact, where I had left it when I'd gone into that coffee shop. Leaning against the red brick just as before. It was as if I had been in the coffee shop all that time; or, I thought, maybe an alternate me was still in the coffee shop right this minute. In any case, I got on the bike, and I quickly rode it away, before someone else—another me or not—came looking for it. Only, here's the thing: now I couldn't find a bike-share station with an empty slot to which to return the bike. I searched and searched, riding that bike all over the goddamned place, but every bike-share station I found was fully occupied. I called about this, too, but again, there was no reasoning with the person on the phone. The woman on the line said, "You have to return the bike to an open slot." She told me that if I downloaded the company's app, I would be able to click on the various bike-share stations to identify one with an empty slot. I informed her that I had the app and that I had already searched every station in town, and there wasn't even one empty slot. She said again, "You have to return the bike to an open slot."

It was in the midst of my hiding out near one of those bike-share stations, waiting for someone to rent one of the bikes and so leave an empty slot, that I woke in a sweat. I realized that I was feeling sorry for myself. It had all been so unfair. As often happens when I catch myself feeling sorry for myself, self-pity quickly transformed into self-castigation and shame. I considered how the whole thing was probably all my fault for not having ordered that coffee.

Scott Repass

The Tick-Tock Traps of the Time Commander

We wheeled, Aurora in her wheelchair and me wheeling the wheelchair, out to the patio. It was to be the last time Aurora would go outside, the last time she would breathe an atmosphere that wasn't piped and filtered and processed. "The patio" was what the staff called it, although to anyone with even the flimsiest grasp of reality, it was just an eight-by-eight concrete pad, twenty-five feet from the back entrance along a cracked path, a road too long for Aurora to travel alone.

"No more cigarettes," Dr. Pulaski had said. "None." But vice and virtue are meaningless when you are near death. I took out Aurora's tubes and hung them around her neck, like a lanyard. The nurses there adored me, the steadfast spouse, and doted on Aurora, the pleasant patient. One amiable RN, armed with a conspirator's wink, had shown me how to de-tube her so she could smoke. I lit a cigarette and put it between Aurora's cracked lips. She jerked her head at the oxygen tank strapped to her chair.

"Just smoking isn't dangerous enough for a notorious adrenaline junkie like me," she said. "I need the added rush of smoking near explosive gasses." Her voice was a saxophone with a cracked reed.

Car engines idled. The bench was built entirely of concrete and radiated heat. Aurora closed her eyes and turned her face to the sun. She was thirty-nine when I first brought her in. At this point, eyes closed, cigarette clutched in her crusty hand, she might have been seventy-nine. I lit a cigarette and closed my eyes, too, but I didn't turn my face to the sun.

"You should go home," the nurse said to me while reinserting Aurora's tubes. "Get some rest."

She was right. At night, I sat in the stiff armchair by the window, my feet propped on my duffle like a traveler stranded by delays. I watched basic cable. Shatner and Picard and Dr. Who. Shows where the rules of our world don't apply. Hygienic spaceships and helpful computers. Neat uniforms, neat resolutions. In my episode, I am an immortal being the Team encounters on a distant planet, a planet the ship's computer tells them is hospitable to life yet completely lifeless. I have lived and will live forever, I tell their captain, so their computer's concept of life doesn't apply. To me, life and death and time are all empty words.

"I travel through time as I please," I tell them. "Only the past is infinite to me. The future, as a concept, does not exist if you can travel whenever you want."

"Does anybody read magazines anywhere besides hospitals?" Aurora huffed, slinging a slick journal onto the floor. She had had lots of visitors at first, and the room was peppered with the things people think perk up a hospital stay—flowers, balloons, magazines. They were just brash, glossy specks in the cold claustrophobia of the sterile space.

A cat clock hung on the wall, a gift from one of Aurora's grad students. Stolen, really, from the wall of the grad-student lounge. A bright-eyed black cat in a bowtie. Its tail twitched each second, click click.

The room was glacial, and the thermostat was somewhere else, somewhere not there, controlled by someone with an agenda that did not include Aurora's comfort. Every day, I asked, and every day, Aurora shivered. The nurse brought her a gray blanket that felt like fiberglass. Every day, I asked. I pleaded politely; I complained not-so-politely.

"I'll see what I can do," the nurse said every day.

I will lie in the summer heat, shirtless and tanned under a beach umbrella. A cold beer and coconut sunscreen. Aurora will be swimming in a blue bathing suit in the pale blue waves, further and further into deeper and darker water, a speck, almost nothing. That evening, at a special restaurant for a special night, the kitchen staff will write "Happy Anniversary!" in chocolate on our dessert plate, and Aurora and I will eat the happy wishes with whipped cream.

I am shirtless and tanned when the Team finds me. I have lived a thousand of their lifetimes, I tell them. I am cordial and generous, but the audience knows something is not right. My hair is yellow platinum, my toga gold lamé.

Aurora couldn't concentrate enough to read anymore. She was never really much of a reader. In what we assumed was the evening, we watched movies on my laptop. Aurora only wanted to watch things she'd seen before. Butch and Sundance jumping off the cliff. DeNiro the bounty hunter chasing Grodin the bounty. When she'd fall asleep, I would pause the movie and turn back to basic cable.

I tell the Team a story about a soothsayer on my planet. A sexy Shakespearean witch in well-placed rags who also grants wishes. I go to her when I am young and in love and deliriously happy and beg her to make me immortal.

Holding her hand to my heart, she says, "You alone shall live forever."

Soothsayers are notorious equivocators.

Hospital rooms are eddies in the time flow. Sometimes, the time there goes faster than time in the outside world, sometimes slower. But never at the same speed. We bickered in the mornings about who slept worse, an argument I always let Aurora win, because of all the tubes. I knew the truth, because I watched her sleep.

Once a day, maybe, the doctor would come to Aurora's room. His gray tie was always straight, his long white coat crisp and unblemished by his work. Dr. Pulaski had dark skin but eyebrows that were so sun-bleached they were almost invisible. Every day, he wanted to chit-chat first, chattering being an integral part of his bedside routine.

"What's new?" he'd say. Nothing. How could it be.

He'd tell us the results of the latest tests, the lab work, the blood work, the scans, the prods and pokes. The numbers didn't move. They didn't get worse, but they didn't get better.

"We'll just have to wait and see," Dr. Pulaski said.

Blithe and Aurora will walk on the seawall, holding hands, her little steps doubling Aurora's slow, strong gait. They will point at gulls and whisper about bicycles and share jokes and it will be wonderful to watch. This day with her will be more Aurora's day than mine, and it will be hard to explain why that brings me such joy.

We will walk to get ice cream. Blithe will wear a pink sundress that is already too short on her, and Aurora will wear loose shorts and a blue t-shirt. What I will wear is irrelevant. The sun will glow its late-afternoon glow, and they will be happy and I will be happy and I won't be able to look away.

The machines beeped and wheezed. If there was a pattern to their noises, I never perceived it. I'd try to tap out the rhythm, try to find some meaning to the clicks and beeps and slow hisses. My brain tried to lay some framework over it all but, in reality, things beeped and things wheezed and I never figured out why.

Aurora was on a respirator at night.

"It looks like a mad scientist's lab."

"Fitting," said Aurora the scientist.

Aurora watched Tom Hanks talk to a volleyball, watched scientist Will Smith talk to mannequins. I flicked through my phone, answering fewer and fewer messages. Emails from yesterday. Wheeze. Beep.

Shelby, one of Aurora's campus comrades, came to visit. She snuck in a bottle of whiskey, if you could call it sneaking. Nobody cared anymore if Aurora had whiskey.

"A bottle of Old Granddad for the old grandma," Shelby said, pouring shots for me and Aurora and her into the plastic cups the nurses used to bring pills. Shelby pulled a chair close to Aurora's bed.

"Sunny, sonny," Aurora said when she asked the question everyone asks the woman in the hospital bed. Shelby leaned close and threw her black hair back and shared the latest campus gossip. The room filled with her perfume, sweet artificial flowers that briefly overpowered the lingering isopropyl and urine.

"I'll see you tomorrow," Shelby said, as if we had any concept of when tomorrow was.

Aurora will teach Blithe to ride a bicycle. Around they will go, around and around in the gray orbit of our cul-de-sac. Squeals and screams and hoots. I will sit in the shade of the front porch and watch. I will carry lemonade, and the glasses will be wonderfully wet and cool.

The effort of the visit and the whiskey sent Aurora into a nap as soon as Shelby left the room. The TV was on with the sound off.

The truth can't stay hidden, of course. The Team ascertains that when I travel through time, to any moment other than the one I share with them, I cannot touch it. I cannot interact. I am just an observer.

"He can be an audience to any moment in the eternity of the universe," says the commonsensical Team member. "But he is not in that moment. He is a specter, a ghost. Almost nothing." Only here, in this exact moment, on this empty planet where, in some other time, I was stranded by a witch and a wish, can I speak to others and be heard by them. In all the universe and in all of eternity, the Team has stumbled onto, into, the one moment when I live.

"The odds against such an encounter are staggering."

The hospice team was burdened with telling me the truth, as they must always be. The truths they told were truths I already knew. Aurora's breathing was thin and dry. She couldn't keep her eyes open. She couldn't talk.

"Ice," was her last, cold word to me.

She couldn't watch Bruce Willis struggle through the air ducts, couldn't watch Snake pull apart the cassette tape. I let the movies play, over and over, my laptop lying on the beige food tray that wasn't needed for food.

"When are they moving her?" I asked the beige woman from the hospice team. Beige skin and beige scrubs and beige shoes.

"Let me see," she said, pulling out her laptop.

Blythe will move. One hot August, she will load up the cheap-but-reliable car Aurora and I will give her for graduation. She will bounce on her toes in her pink sandals while gray Aurora and maudlin me hold hands and watch, giving advice we know she will ignore or never remember. From that moment on, my concept of Blithe's life will end in a question mark. She will move away, and her life will no longer be a satellite to mine. My life will be a satellite to hers.

Aurora was moved to another room and another bed. I was moved to a different uncomfortable chair but the same basic cable.

Although my episode is titled "The Tick-Tock Traps of the Time Commander," it is obvious by the end that I am not in command of the time I flit through. I am alone from day to day, epoch to epoch, watching always, waiting always.

We didn't move all the gifts to the new room. We didn't move the balloons or the flowers or the plush toys. We didn't move the cat clock.

Shelby brought another bottle of whiskey. Angel's Envy. This room had real glassware, as drinking there was common. We poured each other shots, and we poured Aurora a shot and set it next to her on the bedside table. There was almost nothing left of Aurora.

She was evaporating. She was brittle and thin under the thick white comforters, their comforts wasted on a body wasting away.

"I'm here for you," Shelby said. And then she was gone, too, of course, and I was alone with the TV and the remnants of my wife.

Through a contrivance of pseudoscience and commercial breaks, it is discovered that the arrival of the Team on my planet, at this exact spot, at this exact moment, has given me a chance. A chance to become corporeal, to rejoin the flow of time. There is, of course, a catch. The only way for me to shuffle off this immortal coil is for a Team member to replace me. For me to regain my life, one of them must sacrifice theirs.

"She's getting very close," the hospice nurse told me, meaning that she was getting further and further away. "If you want to be here at the end, you should stay the night tonight," she said, meaning that if I didn't want to be there, at her very last moment, I should leave. I closed my eyes, and she reached up and turned off the TV. "Not all spouses stay," she said.

In the end, I am magnanimous. I stay. "In this way," I tell the captain, "I can see my wife, my children, eternally. In this way, I can be with them." The Team leaves me, alone forever, on a planet that is hospitable to life but lifeless.

"His is a road," the captain says as his ship burns through the cold claustrophobia of sterile space, "far too long to travel alone." Vice and virtue are meaningless here. I can't see her. It is quiet and the piped-in air is cold. Somewhere not here, the cat's tail flicks.

Chelsea Guo

American Girl Starter Pack

One sock on the sill, Adidas white.
One foot teasing a neon Croc—
one My Little Pony charm gone summer-warm.

One August of pollution folding
the Xi'an skyline into orange silk, roofs
veiled pink, balconies wired into birdcages.

One untouched bowl of sunken wontons
submerged in broth tarnished as old gold—
faintly sour, like characters left out too long.

One glass of soy milk gone grainy
with sugar packets. (Three, always.) Sometimes
the granules refuse to acclimate. Why

does America sweeten the unfamiliar
until I can't even remember bitterness at all?
One white triangular hat for one man

steaming up a buffet kitchen as he folds
dumplings on the hotel's twenty-eighth floor.
One dad, too transfixed with textured tofu

to notice his daughter watching his hometown
through the glass window, just rice
folded in with pork, childhood reviving his tongue.

American Girl Starter Pack

One green basketball court, students
scattered, dark blue crumbs
with shiny black hair, shadows stitched

to a netless hoop. Girls lean against fences, watch
boys scrape across the paint, shoes
squeaking lightning from the rubber.

One sweatshop, characters neatly blocked into its side.

One hometown, Dad's idea
of a layover—every fourth summer, his daughter
turning salmon pink from the pollution.

One set of five neat soldiers, marching
their hearts into perfect rectangles.

Ronda Piszk Broatch

A Horse Weighs, on Average, Eleven Hundred Pounds

Rather than trot circles in the closed arena, sometimes Horse wants to gallop. Horse is the age of Jesus, say, and his back is stiff. The arena is long and narrow, the sawdust is thinning a bit in the corners, and Horse doesn't corner well anymore. When you fall together, Horse doesn't land on you entirely. You get up, dust in your eyes, and stumble your way toward the gate. Horse follows.

You haven't ridden in more than thirty-some years. You haven't fallen from the saddle, your foot caught in the stirrup, no moment of temporary blindness. On The Gong Show, a guy rolls out on stage on a saddled sawhorse, sings *It's so lonesome in the saddle since my horse died*, finishing two seconds too short to get gonged. You haven't had a horse since Horse died.

Horse dies, kicking up his heels in the pasture at the age of Jesus when betrayed by Judas. Horse, on a cold, frosty morning, had no illusions of death, of going down on the sun-slick slope like a sack of bones. Horse never wonders how the earth feels, shouldering the shuddering impact, lighter because you're not there.

Ronda Piszk Broatch

Horse, When I Tell You

God doesn't bother me as much as words
sewn and modified to grow more thistle
than the fact.

We're alive and walking together,
you, eating grass, and me, pulling burrs
from your tail. Somehow,

we've dropped from the stars, arisen from muck,
crowned and spiked microbes,
grown synapses,

given a way to stave off entropy for lengthening
gallops of time. Horse, when you ask
why I haven't been to church,

I say I've been tracing electrons and photons
across rows of sunlit seats, a kind of oblation,
a sort of feedbag

of faith my mind isn't composed to readily accept.
Horse, the problems come in the form
of messages, every report of war,

and since when did six-year-old children begin
taking handguns to school, never mind shooting
their teacher in the abdomen? And it seems

the resurrection seeds we've been left with morph
in the telling, multiplying and dividing.
If God is the shadow that brushes against me

in the meadow of dead horses, whiskered lips
against my palm, the apple in my hand says,
Let's reclaim the sweetness of the mystery.

Alexandra van de Kamp

Best Western Sonnet

How many episodes of *Forensic Files* can my husband and I absorb
at this beach hotel with swampy air-conditioning? The answer:
a pelican throat-load of them. It's all the bad decisions people make—
the world a gumball machine of jealousy, panic; the sad stagger

of loss marching into other lives due to one person's fake
identity or shaky accounting. One lesson: You never know
who will rear-end you. Another: The body is a disposable thing.
It's 77° dewpoint, and there's a diaphanous, uneasy map aglow

beneath our daily routines connecting us to god-knows-what: The single
mother who leaves her abusive husband and four days later is knifed to death
by the male neighbor who helped her move her mushroom-colored
couch. How many *Coffee-mate®* commercials can we diligently watch—

the Willy Wonka river of creamer poured by a lipsticked woman
into a squat white gleaming mug?

Will Musgrove

Tourist Trap

From behind the counter, I watched a customer pick up a ceramic bison from the shelf and check the price printed on the sticker under its hoof. His eyes bulged like in a Tex Avery cartoon. He set the bison down and wandered down the aisle, glancing over his shoulder once as if saying goodbye to a dear friend. So I rounded the counter to meet him next to the prairie dog plushies.

"Ten minutes, out by the dumpster," I said, pretending to organize a shelf of commemorative shot glasses. "Bring twenty bucks, and I'll bring the bison."

"The what?"

"The buffalo."

The customer nodded and disappeared behind a rack of rodeo postcards. A lot of people confuse bison with buffalo. Long ago, they'd started calling the animal by the wrong name, what they believed it was, and it stuck.

I told a coworker I was taking a smoke break. In the back of the shop, I unwrapped another ceramic bison. It felt light in my hand, not worth what we charge, and I fought the urge to smash it.

Everything inside Not So Badlands is expensive except for me. The gift shop pays me twelve bucks an hour to hawk souvenirs to tourists, tourists who'll later arrange them on their bookcases to remember the time they played cowboy. I often fantasize about sneaking into their suitcases to hitch a ride to whatever city they came from. I fantasize about watching them leave to make-believe somewhere else.

Sometimes I even tell myself, "Nothing's keeping you here, just go," and I'm booking an imaginary Greyhound to some metropolis. Then what? I can be anyone and do anything in this faraway place in my head. Before I can decide, though, the electric bill shows up in the mail, or my landlord calls about the rent being late, and I'm no longer a person lost in this pretend place but a cowboy hat or a decorative dreamcatcher. I'm an easily spotted souvenir, a different kind of tourist, one who clocks in to observe life at a distance.

I exited through the employee entrance and placed the bison on an upside-down milk crate so it could see its flesh-and-blood relatives grazing on the hills across the road. I lit a cigarette right as the customer showed up with a twenty hidden in his palm. After slipping me the money and stuffing the bison in a plastic Walmart sack, he turned toward the hills and exhaled.

"Thanks for doing this," he said, hand over heart as if reciting the Pledge of Allegiance. "I sure do envy you, getting to see this view every day."

He saw beauty when I saw just rocks and grass. Since I couldn't eat it or pay my rent with it, the view had faded like an old photograph. But when I looked at the customer, at his I Heart SD T-shirt and fanny pack, I saw a different setting, saw skyscrapers and variety, saw a life not bound by nature. We each focused only on what we lacked.

The customer shook my hand and left. Staring at the hills, I took a drag. I tried to force myself to see what the customer saw, wanting this view to be enough, but all I could muster was a lot of vast emptiness. Sure, I oohed and aahed at the world around me as a kid, but the awe had depreciated like a new car driven off the lot as I struggled to get by.

I flicked my cigarette butt toward the hills, imagining it riding the wind to the dry grass. I imagined the bison fleeing as flames engulfed everything, including me. I imagined the ceramic bison escaping in the plastic sack, imagined it running away in the night to chew a new life of exciting cud. Instead, the butt landed a few inches from the dumpster, its orange tip fizzling, and I walked back inside to finish my shift.

After work, I drove past the turn to my apartment. I do this whenever it's been a long day. I need to keep moving, even if I'm going nowhere. The low-fuel warning flashed on my dash, so I chucked a U-ie. A bison now stood in the road, blocking my path. Sitting there in my idling car, I stared at the animal. "Buffalo, buffalo, buffalo," I repeated. "Buffalo, buffalo, buffalo."

Luanne Castle

Last Happiness

We lay there, the sand molded around us, our coconut oil scent intensified by our body heat, sunlight glinting off his honey hair so that it seemed haloed, the sound of the waves rocking us toward a glazed awakeness that resembled sleep since we didn't want to let this time go, wanted to bask in our slippery flesh, errant sand grains the only other between us, our love so sure and ready for the future, his job driving the van to pay our tuition and mine at the library to cover our rent, work was something outside our time together which was our genuine life, and maybe he had the same thought at the same moment as we often did and propped himself on his elbow and brought the hash pipe to his mouth to light, the scent of the smoke brought me back to the first time we had sex in a clearing in the dank woods, parkas on but no pants, and I began to laugh and mentioned it to him, and soon we were hysterical in the private little setback in the dune, my bikini top thrown I didn't know where, and the gulls soared overhead and one perched on the towering peak to monitor our antics and I thought of our little Molly Wawa at home, her barking, happy to see us so late every night and a fleeting moment of regret rustled through me like a silk flag and I briefly wondered if we should go back to our place, but that passed very quickly when he gently cupped my breast, then pulled me toward him and as he did so I noticed the boys down on the beach where we could see them, but not them us and they surrounded a gull but not the one above us, now cawing and cawing and cawing, but one with a bent wing, and I nudged him to see, and the boys who were nearly full-grown and thickset, kicked sand over the bird who could not fly away nor walk past their circle like an iron ring around him, and I wrapped the sandy towel around myself and stood up to run down, tugging on his hand to follow, but he pulled me to the ground and whispered, *shut up*, his hand now over my defiant mouth, as the cut glass laughs of the boys carried up to us, so far away from that helpless bird, far as if we were on the dunes of Mars.

Laurie Blauner

Natural Disasters

On the television the sign that said *If You Lived Here You'd Already Be Home* was burning, succumbing to fractal, auroral flames that could be seen from a distance. No one wanted to see the fire up close, with its roaring, crackling devastation, with its intense heat and smoke. There were elegiac floods, whirlwind tornadoes, hurricanes, and destructive earthquakes with different and yet similar narratives. Moments created stories, the before, during, and after.

I enjoyed my quiet life in my small, inherited house with my cat, plants, and fish on the edge of a forest I knew well enough. But every place was dangerous, especially when I paused between the highlighted minutes of meeting you. At that time the forest was covered in sparse grass. Trees were still romancing the birds that laced their branches while sky thought about various ways to rearrange everything. I glimpsed you hunting for mushrooms in your moss-green clothes far enough away. I had not seen you there before. I slid behind a tree. I had been walking, so I began hurrying in the other direction. When I looked back sunlight had entered the space between us in a haphazard way. I was silently talking to myself about the problems in this crazy world when you started speaking to me. You must have come up behind me. I was startled.

Look here, you said, pointing at something white on a decaying tree trunk. *Oyster mushrooms feed on dead trees*. You plucked the cluster and stuffed it in your bag. *I didn't mean to scare you*.

As if you were invisible. *I see you*, I declared. Sometimes I lost time. It went too fast or too slow.

Did you want to be alone? you politely asked, your fingers twitching in your pants pocket. A dog barked somewhere. You stared at me, your beard swaying slightly in a breeze that felt hardly there.

I wondered if I should run. Anything could happen and nothing stays still for long. Some things are targets but others aren't and things usually go one way or another. I missed my bedroom at home, my cat and fish. I should have been more careful.

I dreamt there were already red flowers blooming deep in this forest last night. I tried to say this cheerfully. But you gripped my arm. I kissed your hand, then you pulled it away. There was nowhere close to go, but I ran, anyway. Evening was arriving as I tried to leap over rocks, bushes, and grass as quickly as I could without falling. You were right behind me when you fell onto me. I kicked you and scratched you hard but you were stronger.

Now you're my forest wife, you declared, accompanying me home and moving immediately into my house. You didn't own any possessions.

I didn't know how to get rid of you even though I plotted. But even when you were briefly away you were still with me. I tried to lock you out. You slept outside once but then you broke a window to enter. Outside or inside, it didn't seem to matter. But I knew that nothing stayed still and there would be a time. One day when I came home the cat was gone. *I'm going out to look for the cat.*

You rubbed your beard. *Fine*, you claimed, *but be back before dinner.*

I entered that primordial forest where trees appeared to quiver as I passed them. Grass looked trampled and bush branches seemed broken by something very large. Sky yawned and clouds emerged. I angrily hoped the terrible forest and thoughtless clouds would fall into the sky's gaping mouth. I was living an unintended life.

I called my cat, but she didn't come. I reached the place where I had met you. I didn't want you, but you watched my every movement. I removed matches from my pants pocket. I set one tree on fire. I watched the flames catch onto everything surrounding it. The same way you caught me. I liked the fire's intensity, not quite like the wildfires on television, but better in some ways. I saw a small animal hurry across a far road. I ran, called my cat, and scooped her into my arms. The heat was already at my back and wherever you had touched me I could feel my body burning.

Lana Spendl

Found Piano

after Julie Schenkelberg

The artist with blonde hair tours abandoned factories in the Midwest, scavenging for broken furniture, textiles, metal beams, and shards of glass. She binds her sculptures together with cement. To audiences she explains that abandoned factories are our version of ancient cities or temples to the gods. People, in thought, tilt their heads.

Her latest installation stands in the center of a great hall, almost reaching to the skylight. On the floor, at one end, stands a broken piano. On top of it sit piles of folded rags, and under the keyboard, where one would otherwise press the pedals, stands a piece of iron fencing. Behind the piano rise fruit crates and suitcases and a dresser with a tilted drawer. Behind that, debris—chunks of chairs and plaster—extends over the gleaming floor like the tail of a wedding dress.

On opening night, after the artist has delivered her talk in red lipstick and a black suit and the hall has emptied out, silence and darkness reign. Moonlight filters through the skylight, tumbling over the edges of the installation. Like a landfill heap in the great hall of kings.

And through a wall, a ghost drifts in.

He is a slim ghost, sickly. Thirty-two. He wears dark trousers, a white shirt, suspenders, and a bowtie. From his undereye circles you can tell he hasn't slept in a century. Life (or death) can be so hard.

The ghost comes from Maryland and is looking for a place to land. Back home, before the accident, he'd play in basements that spun with tunes and colors and dancing, and women in drop-waisted dresses approached him at the piano and perched nearby. In between sets, he'd twist on the bench and chat. There was Louise with her black bob. And Livia with those almond eyes.

In darkness now, he tucks his hands into his trouser pockets and examines the white colonnade against one wall. His upper back is curved, humble, as if he's afraid to step to his full height. His eyes land on the peak of the heap, near the skylight. Then, like the moonlight, they tumble down and fall on the piano.

His spine straightens as if a cord has pulled his head toward the ceiling. It is the same instrument he'd play all those nights. On impulse, he pulls his hands out of his pockets and turns this way and that, wanting to tell someone, anyone, *That instrument is mine.* What a concept. *Mine.*

On his way to this Midwestern town—drifting through streets and intersections and town squares and parks—he had forgotten all about *mine.* The possession of this great instrument brings up others' admiring eyes. Those nights he'd keep his gaze on the music sheet, focused, as if interested only in pressing the next set of keys with the right pressure at the right time. As if shaping sounds like a sculptor. But inside, his whole being ballooned with the importance of their admiring gaze. Afterwards, he'd wander night streets and replay how he had been watched by this one or that one, or how that comment drifted over about the smoothness of his sound. He wanted to play bigger places. He wanted to be a star.

But then the accident.

Now, with slow step, he approaches his piano. Like a relic on an altar. When he steps to it, he is struck by how ordinary the familiar music rest looks. There is something touching, even heartbreaking, about the fact that this instrument that cradled him through so many nights has remained nearly intact. He hovers a hand over the keys, almost feeling their bones. He is not sure if to laugh or cry. He wants to see it whole, he decides.

And then he does what ghosts sometimes do. He solidifies.

This process takes a lot out of common ghosts. The only ghosts who can do it with mid-level effort are former athletes. And so, he focuses his single-pointed mind on the effort—shaking all over, sensing his muscles near fail—and when he feels his chest and arms and face congealing, he swings a forearm against the rags piled on top of the piano.

But the rags, like a brick wall, hit back. He grabs at his pained forearm with a hand, holds it to his chest like an injured child. He remembers, back in life, what it was like to slam into furniture or metal poles.

He grows confused, uncertain, and he wanders to the piano's side. It might be easier to knock away the crates. He focuses on the wavelets of solidification left inside his body, which are now subsiding into calm, and attempts to shake them again into great big currents like a storm. And he shoulder- and face-slams into the crates and falls on his side with a moan.

First, he feels numbness, then a burning pain. He sees stars. And all his energy is depleted. He lies there, a quivering mess.

What has happened to his piano? Or is it him? Have his abilities diminished over time? Does that even happen to ghosts? He was always a loner, so he has no one to ask. Shame fills him, and he wonders if his cheek will turn black and blue from impact. Do ghosts get bruises? Do they get scars?

Mae Juniper Stokes

The Spinster House

I

There were three of us at first, in the house that was the cobbler's until he left to join a city guild, and we discovered that three spinsters' earnings could lease a cottage with a garden dark and toothsome. There was no richer dirt in all of Edgewode. Royse said this was because the brook chattered through the garden like a child. Amice said it was because the cobbler had paid a fine to let his cow defecate on the garden at night. Ibb brought chickens, and they left enough excrement to make up for the cattle, or so it seemed to us.

We loved the chickens, gave them names, knew their personalities and the complicated social and political forces that moved their society. Only Ibb had the stomach to wring their necks for feast days. She assured us her methods were quick, that before she did it, she smoothed their feathers and kissed the tops of their heads. When a wolf ate half the flock and left the others to suffer the devastation of this great social upheaval, we wielded knives, tracked the wolf to its cave, and took our revenge. It was a she-wolf, nipples swollen, and when we saw the pup, we wept.

II

We noticed right away that the house was bigger inside than the outside rightly allowed. We each kept this to ourselves. We lived there a year before Royse drank enough mead to mention it out loud. We laughed with relief. Some tension that had been strung between us broke. There were five of us by then. We fit comfortably around the hearth, with its great iron pot slung above it like a spider fat with eggs. The smoke stained the center of the ceiling black and thickened the air to the texture of dreams.

Amice knew the herbs to make a fire burn brighter than is natural, so we'd stand or crouch around it with our spindles and distaffs and finger the wool into fine, even thread. The work hypnotized us, and to exaggerate that quality, to revel in it, we sang. Darkness cupped the house in its hand. The fire danced and spit. We threw our harmonies against the walls, against each other, and conjured string from clots of wool.

III

We were not afraid of the house. An ancient oak held its cape over the roof. Acorns knocked cheerfully, rolled, and landed at the threshold. When Meggy moved in, she brought two elder saplings and planted them on either side of the entrance. The next year, Dye arrived, and she steeped the elder berries in crab apple vinegar and honey from a hive she stole from the woods. When the whole village grew ill after Christmas service, every one of us in the spinster house took the oxymel and survived. That year, there were nine of us, most still young enough for marriage. Five village maidens died of that Christmas plague, and the villagers begged us to end our strange woolly hermitage and court the lonely village men. But none of us desired marriage. That was, in fact, why most of us lived in the spinster house.

The lord instigated a new fine for unmarried women. The fine was just higher than the amount a spinster could pull from her distaff. Meggy and Ibb and Royse left at once for the city and came back bearing two gleaming, intricate spinning wheels. Such a dazzling invention seemed strange at first, next to ordinary Edgewode women. But soon, we saw each other in this technology: beautiful, complicated, and capable of spinning more than should be possible.

IV

We knew the wolf was the pup we had orphaned because she bore the same dark markings around each eye. She laid Dye's favorite chicken on the porch like a cat will a mouse, then watched us from behind our wagon, panting. The chicken's neck ended in a blunt, bloody unfurling. It brought to mind a bouquet.

We gave our chickens away to the village cunningwoman, who we knew had uncanny ways of keeping her flock safe. Then we began to leave the wolf our scraps. We crowded the window to watch her pounce, crack bones, clean herself, and nap. We could smell her, like the first scent of winter on a late autumn day: iron, musk, and ice. It would be another year before we let her inside to sleep by the hearth, and then only Royse dared stroke her warm, coarse coat.

V

Twelve is the most we gained from Edgewode. After that, spinsters took pilgrimage from villages all over to stay with us a while and then, if they liked us, never leave. There were hay beds in the east room and the west room and up in both lofts. We kept the spinning wheels on either side of the hearth. They were never unoccupied, and the rhythmic whir comforted us. The fire cast spiky wheeled shadows at night, black spikes the wolf paced through. We had many mouths to feed but also many hands and a garden of riotous abundance we could hardly contain. Always the scent of garlic, apple, parsley, and cheese.

Many of us thought we were the first to take another spinster as our lover. It was an open secret and then not a secret at all. Eventually, this way of loving grew mundane, so much so that when we attended markets or the midsummer celebrations, we had to reacclimate. We'd born witness to a delicious truth: There was no unnatural sex. We found the only way to bear the world outside the spinster house was with a detached amusement. But it was hard to move through the village without bewilderment and fury. Still, the sweetness and heat of these encounters invigorated the whole household. Later, we'd agree that this first break from the narratives we'd inherited is what primed us for the discoveries to come.

VI

We grew careless. When Margaret and Amice were caught howling their pleasure together in the May Day dew, it was only the threat of our wolf that kept them from the ducking chair. The fine they were charged was no burden, but out of caution, we purchased three more spinning wheels. By then, we were a household of 25, and the villagers viewed us with outright hostility. They were terrified we'd send the wolf to eat their children. In truth, the wolf was a wild thing and would eat or not eat who she pleased. She laid headless rabbits at our door. We turned these into fine stews and threw her back the bones.

We had children ourselves by then. Brought with the spinster widows or collected, filthy and ragged, from the streets of the city. We, too, were afraid of the wolf, but knew she was essential to the preservation of our way of life. We kept a shepherding watch over our children at play and prepared ourselves to kill the wolf if necessary. The wolf was occasionally a snarling thing but more often docile, if distant, in our presence. Some of us believed her practically tame, an enormous, looming, moony, and elegant dog who would never hurt us. They were viewed by most of us as sweet but dangerously naive.

VII

Our first spinning wheels mounted the spindle horizontally and were turned by hand. One year, we bought a great wheel but found the resulting string flimsy. We were accustomed to spinning the musky, oily wool of sheep, but after we acquired two flax wheels, we learned to beat fiber from flax and weave tender, clean-smelling linen. Rowena and Blake designed and built a treadle so that the fibers could be spun by foot, freeing the hands. Several of us burned by then with an obsession with spinning technologies. We whittled and smithed several inventions. Most failed, but those that did not improved the enjoyment, efficiency, and scope of our craft.

This tradition of curiosity extended to our loomwork. Flyta brought with her an ancient inheritance: a warp-weighted loom with fanciful pottery shards dangling from the weaving like moths made of clay. And, of course, we had our floor loom. We progressed from the tabby weave to twill and discovered a range of seventy-two dyes. The spinster house was by then far larger than the lord's manor when viewed from the inside. We acquired two more floor looms and spent winter days gathered round to watch the work of our most accomplished weavers, encouraging their spirits with song. Our harmonies, too, reached woven, colorful complexities of dissonance and resolution. As we sang, our children danced and bickered and rolled upon the floor.

VIII

The children, of course, had their own complicated relationships with the wolf, one of ferocious familiarity, of longing, fear, and romance. When she grew feeble and patchy and then died of age, our youth who had known her most of their lives padded away in the night and killed a mother wolf, as we had done. They brought back her seven pups. This echo of our early violence disturbed us greatly, so much so that a few of us took our children and left the spinster house forever. The rest of us knew what the children knew: The villagers hated us and we needed to keep around a wild protector.

Our youth could not tame the pups but managed to create a tentative, risky familial state. That is, until one of the adolescent pups bit off Dena's left hand—brave, ferocious Dena who had led the charge into the woods to gather the pups herself. We put our feet down then. No more wolves. Helpless in their half-wildness, they could not be led back to the woods and expected to stay. There was only one way forward. We assured our children the wolves' deaths would be quick, that first we'd stroke their fur and kiss the tops of their heads.

Our youth revolted. They stood between us and the wolves and threatened to run away from us to start their own wolfish community. Dena herself, they said, had been eaten by the wolf she loved the most, and when they brought us to her, recovering in the eastern loft, feverish against infection, wrist packed with yarrow, she raised herself, wincing, on her right elbow and told us that if we killed the wolves, we would never see her or the other youth ever again.

There were forty-eight of us by then, and the youth in question were as old as many of us had been at the founding of the spinster house. Rather than tempting exile, we initiated them into our collective understanding of self but insisted they take responsibility for their beasts, protect the children against them, as we had done. They—we—rose magnificently and with great courage to this challenge, and we went a long time before another incident.

IX

Our experience of gender had long since changed. It began with the way the multiple genders of the children interrupted our understanding of ourselves as a group of women. But soon, some of those who had been in our original group took on male names and wore male clothing or clothing ambiguous, experimental, or plain. We had no end of fabrics to play with. When we learned that our beloved Heather had been first christened with a boy's name, that settled it. We were spinsters, wolf-people, of liberated and self-defined gendering, the outside world be damned. We made no formal announcement to the outside world, but those like us must have smelled some familiar magic, because new pilgrims amassed and our numbers surpassed a hundred. The spinster house stretched to hold us, the hearth burned with happy vigor, and the elder trees grew to unnatural size. Their berries knocked like red bells, full of blood.

X

We began to notice that the fiber arts—the spinning, the weaving, the piecing together—spoke in conversation with other elements of the earth and heavens. We noticed, for instance, that stars wove across the sky in consistent and intersecting patterns, creating a glittery fabric. We set up a third loft—newly appeared—for the purpose of investigating these observations. On clear nights, we removed the waxy wool tarp from a gap we'd cut in the ceiling and tracked what we saw with ink on precious sheepskin parchment. Udele had run away from a monastery and brought with her three illuminated manuscripts, a box of parchment, and the ability to read and write. Eadwig brought with him a royal education in mathematics and alchemy. All this, too, we devoured.

We were especially interested in the peculiar mathematics of the spinster house. The implied dimensions from an outside view never changed. It was an ordinary cottage, big enough for a single household of perhaps six—plus a goat to crowd in at wintertime. Inside, it was larger than the castles some of us were born inside. We were filled with a persistent intuition that this inconsistency in the world's usual nature had something to do, metaphorically, with the lengthening and solidifying of wool and the crossing of strings.

XI

It was around the time Ibb died of age that the villagers began to hunt our wolves. The first was Deorwine's favorite wolf, a handsome and docile slate-colored being who often lay with his head in her lap while she roasted fish in a fire beside our brook. They left his head at our gate and burned his body in the commons.

Some of us called for the formation of own spinster knighthood to threaten the village back with military might. Others among us feared the consequences of this escalation as well as the brutal effects of war on us and our children. Some pointed out the unpredictability of wild things, that even we valued a healthy fear of our own wolves.

Perhaps better communication was required between us and the village. Dena, Blake, and Royse volunteered to act as ambassadors.

We discovered our reputations had morphed into grotesque and mythological proportions. The villagers were terrified of us. Their children were raised on stories of our monstrosity. The lord had offered a free season's lease in return for every wolf killed.

Our ambassadors brought with them offerings of our finest clothing. We hung a tapestry we'd labored over for an entire year in the village church. For some, this only doubled their suspicions, but for others, it formed a wary but hopeful feeling of neighborliness. This kept us, for some time, from an outright hunt of our particular wolves, but the lord refused to rescind the award offered for the hunting of wolves at large. Wolves, he said, were a widespread menace, and the order for their extermination could be found throughout the land, sourcing, in fact, from the king. It wasn't, in other words, personal. We suspected this last part to be untrue.

XII

As the years progressed, we began to discover the true limits of what could be done with weft and warp. It was midwinter, the oak tree scraping its icicles along the rooftop, when we first managed a Weaving.

Charity sat at the star-loft loom and Heather at the flax wheel below. They spun and wove their calculations, witnessed a great flash of light, and in an instance found themselves in the room of a dozen strangers. The air hummed with strange heat and humidity. These strangers seemed startled, if expectant, but for one woman at a loom of unfamiliar and genius design, whose own dark eyes dazzled with triumph and delight. Before there was time to attempt conversation, Charity and Heather found themselves back in our spinster house.

It was a very long time before we managed another Weaving, and this time it was instigated by two women whose names we learned to be Karânî and Sa`îdah, who each operated a spinning wheel they called a charkha. They appeared in our star loft on a warm clear night, crisp with the light of the moon. We all sensed the impermanence of their and our spaces existing together at once and worked through the night to learn enough of each other's languages to begin a collaboration of our studies. Indeed, by morning, they were gone, but they left us with the precious and invigorating realization that ours was not the only spinster house who'd advanced its practice into the threading together of space itself.

As we continued these studies, we found that it was not possible to Weave to anywhere we desired. Weaving could only be achieved through the collaboration of two spinster houses aligned in their desires for contact. These moments were rare, but through them we met Quyllur, Nina, and Urpi of Tawantinsuyu with their intricate backstrap looms. We worked with these women to discover that fibers could be used not only to traverse space, but time. We began with short time disparities, Weaving to Hsu Wen-Mei with her marvelous silk-reeling machine. Then we advanced to thousand-year spans, meeting a household in Çatalhöyük weaving hemp, and Egyptians along the Nile River weaving flax.

Future travel was more difficult to achieve, but we managed a few hours with Anni, Gunta, Friedl, and Otti of the Bauhaus school in Germany. We sat in their slender metal chairs, the noisy sunlight pouring through their studio windows. They confirmed what we'd begun to fear: The great violence of future fiber trades and the eventual industrialization of the practice made Weavings to humanity's future nearly impossible. They set their woven artwork aside then and opened a large book decorated with what looked to be colorful moons. This was where they hoped to go next—into the sky and towards the stars, which, we learned, were suns, every one of them, each mothering their own clutch of worlds.

XIII

I, Dena, make an end to this record. We are myself, my lovers Oriel and Felberta, the children in our care, and the nine wolves who walk beside us. My own interests have always lain with the wolves. I have no patience for the fiber arts.

It is dangerous here. The village no longer tolerates our presence. The spinster house is gone, and we plan to retreat to the woods. Oriel grieves mightily. I fear she will never recover from her feeling of abandonment, but I am glad to be left behind. I feel that some of us ought to stay here, in our own corner of space and time, to defy the limitations of this moment's imagination. There ought to be some Eden here, for those discovering within themselves the vast possibilities of love and sex and self. Just this morning, Hortense, grandchild of the lord, crashed through the bracken, the hornbeam, oak, and nettle, to find us and beg we take her in.

I cannot say the exact destination of the spinster house and its 296 occupants, but I know that the day before the house disappeared, they spoke of an extremely distant future and alien spinsters who live far beyond the visible stars. This is beyond my own comprehension. But I hold the memory of the spinster community who raised me with infinite tenderness and will defend this record of their doings with my life.

Lynn Domina

Anthropological Description of the Human Species

They enjoy certain phrases, *freak accident, fluke, one of a kind, one in a million, fat chance.*
    They convert sequence into narrative. Their favorite conjunction is *because.*

They prefer symmetry—two eyes, ears, five fingers on the left hand, five on the right. Yet (then)
    they invent Cyclops, Cerberus.

They distinguish between weed and crop, predator and prey, pet and livestock, though particulars
    shift across generations and continents.

They believe certain acts should be committed without concern for profit, hence *mercenary, gold*
    digger, simony.

They devote themselves to adornment—silk, satin, handlebar moustaches, muttonchops, gold or
    gold-plated or gold-colored bangles, cameo brooches, French braids, boas, tattoos of hearts, eagles, quotations from Thoreau.

They trust violent solutions, hence *war—on poverty, on drugs, on cancer.*

They imagine other worlds, afterlives. They choose sequel over conclusion. They insist most
    emphatically on those things they can never know.

Kurt Olsson

In Answer to a Self-Assessment

I like people.
I like people who like me.
I like to be with people.
I like to be with people, particularly if they like me.
I like to be with people who like to be with people, and even with those who don't.

People, I hope, like me.
People who like people I hope like me, even if I sometimes like to be with people who don't like people.
I hope you, the person—or more likely people—who designed this test, like me.
I imagine you all in office chairs tilting back, sipping cappuccino, wearing sweatshirts with smiley emojis.

True, I do sometimes like to be alone, but when I'm alone I assure you
I'm thinking wouldn't it be great to be with people,
at least some people, some of the time.

For example, I like to sleep alone, which is, I hope, okay with all you people,
because I can't imagine sharing a bed with a lot of people,
even people who like people,
or people like you or people I like—

there'd never be enough blankets and surely someone would have eaten rice and beans for dinner
or forgotten to trim their toenails.

They say in the old days people often had to sleep with other people,
even people they'd never met and weren't sure they liked or should like.
Abraham Lincoln slept with people, though I'm not sure he always liked people,
but given the circumstances, I think we can forgive him.

I like Abraham Lincoln, and I'd like to think he would have liked me, in those periods when he was liking.

How am I doing?
Because in your writing all these questions about whether I like people
and like to be with people, which I do,
I assume you want me to like people, which I do.

Let me make one thing clear:
I'm all about people, and liking people, and liking people who like people who like them and like to be liked.

But if it appears I'm doing too much liking, I will admit (confidentially, between us)
I sometimes don't like people, because, and I think you'll agree with me, there are some people one shouldn't like.
Even if they like people.
Even if they like wearing sweatshirts with smiley emojis.

Trinity Richardson

Requiem for My Childhood Dog

I.
We put down my childhood dog
on a Tuesday.

It was a clean break—
clean as in broke clean in half—
leg dangling obscenely,
perverse in its disconnect,

He yelped when touched,
brother was the last one to hold him—
I did not want to hurt him, could not fathom it.

But I was there—oh god, I was there—as he slipped
into peaceful oblivion.

II.
When I was young, I was transfixed
by the idea of slow-dancing.

I envied the proximity of it—
hand on hip, hand on shoulder,
even cheek to shoulder, god forbid.

No leaving room for Jesus,
just fear of discovery,
of stove-hot face and unsanctioned body.

III.
In my childhood home, dogs were not allowed
on couches or in the kitchen.

Denied the comfort of cushions,
they begged, then learned better,
settled for cold floor.

IV.
I hope death does not begrudge me
a slow dance, one final nap on the couch,
is not scared to hold me close.

In the end, there is just this:
were you held gently? Did you hold gently?

Justine Sweeney

What Happens When Your Dog Dies

A week after my dog died, Kenny from two streets over and two grades above, came to the front door. He muttered a few words, then edged past me, wandered on into the living room like we were friends or something.

"Got any more of those?" he said, eyeing the strawberry Pop-Tart I'd been eating cross-legged on the floor. In those days I sat right up close to the television set, kept the volume low.

When I returned from the kitchen, he had pulled all the board games out from a bookshelf in the corner.

"Why do you have Mousetrap?" he said, shaking his head, "It's a kid's game, isn't it?"

I shrugged. Pieces missing, anyway.

"Wana play Risk?"

"Boring," I lied. It was the best game. My family had spent so many evenings on the battlefield, everyone yelling, laughing, begging for pee-breaks. My dog would rest his head on the table and whine once it started to go on for too many hours. I just didn't have the energy that particular day to lead troops, fortify my borders or fight for new territories.

Kenny surveyed the pile of colored boxes, cardboard splitting at the corners. He looked like he was going to stick around until I played something with him.

"My aunt bought me a Super Nintendo yesterday," I said.

"No! Where do you get an aunt like that?"

I pulled the sealed box out from behind the sofa. I'd slipped it in there, hadn't wanted to bother dad with the setup.

And so, we connected up the console, slotted the Mario cartridge into place, played after school most days for the rest of that year. I didn't care so much about the princess, but man did I love banging my head off those mystery blocks, knocking their coins out, one electronic bleep at a time. Sometimes I forgot about the dog as we rocked around on the floor, thumbs pumping the controllers. Don't fall off screen, don't run out of time, don't touch lava. But even if we lost all our lives, we could always start again from the most recent save point.

As the weeks went on, Kenny helped himself to the snacks, made microwave popcorn and dug through cabinets to find the big bowls. He learned when to say *hello* to mum and dad, when to creep around invisible, knew to close the door if they started arguing.

One day my mother walked in, face puffy, "You boys wanna go for ice cream?"

We hopped into the car, I let Kenny get into the front seat and he talked the whole time. *How are you doing Mrs. B? You got to look after yourself Mrs. B, my mom, she doesn't look after herself. You're a good driver Mrs. B. I'm gonna learn in a few months, soon as I turn sixteen.*

One day when I was loading up the video game—we'd moved on to Donkey Kong by then—Kenny picked up a framed photograph from the fireplace, stared hard at it for a while. "You know, one time when Billy Murph was beating up on me—last summer before I started high school—your dog came out of nowhere, jumped into the middle of it."

"He did?"

Kenny put the picture down carefully, stuffed his hands into his short's pockets, eyes drifting to some place up the wall where his memories were popping. "Yeah, your dog laid into Murph that day, chased him off. It was nice, you know? He didn't have to help me like that."

"Right."

"If there's ever anyone giving you trouble in middle school, you just let me know, OK?"

"Sure," I said.

He was a good dog.

Other people were sorry about my dog, too. Mrs. Anderson the neighbor would call me up onto her porch, ask about school, my parents, make me take a handful of Hershey's miniatures. I didn't like them, but I knew she liked to give them to me, so I kept them for Kenny. Coach Madison picked me for the class team a few times when there were better pitchers on the bench.

It's like that when your dog dies.

"Sorry about your brother," Kenny had said at the door that first day, because I never had a dog. It's just easier to talk about dogs than it is to talk about brothers.

Andrea Marcusa

Cold Comfort

My seventeen-year-old rescue, Ernest, a chihuahua mix with a bulldog's scowl, died at home in his sleep, twenty-six days, four hours, and eleven minutes ago. In New York City, you can't bury pets in parks or tree beds. I couldn't bear taking Ernest to my unfriendly vet for disposal. And I'm not the cremation type. So I tucked him into my freezer until I figured out what to do. Even a dead, frozen Ernest was better than no Ernest. But I still missed his warm tongue on my face each morning, or how he greeted me at the front door when I returned—even after only a half hour—like a sailor who'd been lost at sea.

Last Saturday, hoping to distract myself from my howl of canine grief, I rode the subway downtown to Union Square in the sweltering heat to the farmers market. Everyone had dogs. I heard "Good boy," jangling collars, and then caught the face of a dachshund giving me that open, soulful gaze you can't turn away from. I was undone all over again. I found refuge at a compost demonstration table where an enthusiastic devotee drew me in. There, I witnessed firsthand the virtues of composting. The specialist, her name was Sahara, called the desiccated scraps of food "black gold" and compared it to a blank slate, raw matter awaiting transformation. Despite my eagerness to embrace her mission, when she opened the black cover of the giant recycling barrel, all I saw were zealous bugs hovering around a bin brimming with wilted carrot tops, black banana peels, gray-furred potatoes, and a corpulent rat skittering under the table where the devout compost evangelist stood.

But Sahara's expression shifted when I mentioned Ernest, and became almost teary-eyed as if she, too, had once lost something beloved. I told her about how, as a puppy, I could fit him in my purse.

When I visited my mother, not a fan of canines, while we drank tea and nibbled cookies at her kitchen table, Ernest awoke from his nap, popped his head out of my purse and released a tiny puppy yap. So startled, my mother's heart lurched into an arrhythmia, which, thankfully, Mom subdued with a cocktail of pills. Sahara and I laughed about Ernest's surprise introduction, and how my mother ended up saying he was the only dog she'd ever liked. "I wish I'd known him," said Sahara. After our chat, I noticed that for the next few days, it didn't hurt as much to walk to the store and greet the local dogs.

When grief descended again with a thud, I thought connecting with my neighbors might help, so I attended our building's tenant association annual meeting for the first time in years. I sat among forty or so tenants and listened as the self-satisfied association president cited two things I've been unable to let go of: Our building superintendent is a reliable, efficient, and helpful source of support; now that the city was imposing a composting law on all its residents, we should store our food scraps in our freezers until their Friday pickup. The tenants, who I expected to guffaw, eyeroll, perhaps murmur under their breaths, "You've got to be kidding," sat placidly, nodding along, as if clueless about what it would be like to squeeze a week's worth of wet garbage between the tubs of Maple Bacon and Lavender Anchovy ice creams. And in my freezer, Ernest's frozen corpse. Still there. Where I can open the door and peek at him and say goodnight.

While I listened to the president drone on, I struggled to name one "helpful" thing our super had done this year. All that came to mind was the time he managed a work crew in the apartment above me—a crew that left open a valve and swamped my bedroom and living room with three inches of water, as if a hurricane had blown in a window.

In closing, the tenant association president thanked us all for the collegial and courteous community we represented.

I looked around. Had anyone listened? Several pecked at their phones. One picked at a growth on his thumb. The man on five kept nodding out and jerking himself awake. This was my community, and I felt no warmth whatsoever, not a smile, or friendly nod, or even a hasty hello when I first sat down, despite my elevator greetings and pithy comments about the weather in the lobby. I felt alien. Even my mail often arrived for the other Emily in 11E, not me in 4A.

In that lobby where we sat, a low murmur of approval emerged along with head nods. A seemingly clueless, baffling consensus rose among them.

Then I thought of Sahara, how despite my cynicism toward rotting scraps and my distaste for the entire process, she had patiently walked me through her spiel and showed real concern when I told her about Ernest, saying, "Oh, that's terrible. I bet you really miss him." I looked back at my neighbors. Did I want to reach out and connect with anyone?

No. There was nothing there.

Sahara, for all her zeal for the rotting, had made me feel like me and Ernest mattered.

When the tenant meeting ended, I picked up a handful of the green compost recycling bags that the city had provided and rode up to my apartment. I opened the freezer, slid Ernest into a bag, and sealed it. As I hurried to the subway, I hoped Sahara hadn't closed her booth for the day.

I didn't say goodbye. I didn't even know if composting a dead pet in New York City was legal. I didn't care.

I just tucked the bag under my arm and left before I could change my mind.

D.E. Hardy

It's Never Too Late to Have a Happy Childhood

My dad likes to tell his caregivers stories about his childhood dog, Lassie, a border collie with an uncanny ability to help others: how Lassie walked my dad to school and picked him up at the end of the day, stick in her mouth, ready to play fetch all the way home; how everybody at school respected Lassie, my dad was a short guy, skinny, which might have proved a problem for other boys, but everyone knew Lassie had my dad's back, one wrong move and Lassie was there—the school yard, behind the soda shop, in the alley by the five and dime—ready to knock any bullies with a nose punch to the crotch; how Lassie was a gift from his real dad who he couldn't see anymore on account of his drinking and the fact that his mom was remarried now and didn't want the neighbors to talk—this was 1950, remember—his mother kept his dad's letters from him, stopped visits, but Lassie got through, showed up on his doorstep every morning until the neighbors started asking his mom why she never let her dog in, forcing her to do exactly that lest she have to explain about her ex; how even when his mom and stepdad had a baby who was so cute that people couldn't shut up about it, Lassie still loved him best; how once Lassie pointed my dad to an abandoned well on old man Johnson's farm where a neighbor kid, Timmy, had fallen, Lassie barked and barked as my dad ran to find help, the local paper taking a picture of him and his hero dog, first page news; how the squib beneath the photo listed his stepfather's surname, not his real dad's; how this pleased his mother, relieved her; how the name switch felt like a betrayal; how Lassie kissed away my dad's tears as he felt the shame of it, just like his real dad would do if he could, Lassie, always there, so close, all the time, forever and ever and ever.

Sarah Lynn Hurd

Strawberry Girls

Mara woke me on Saturday morning and said we should get tattoos. I rubbed my eyes, sleep-swollen, and covered a stale-gin yawn with my hand. She knelt on the floor beside my bed, chin resting on folded arms, gazing at me like a hungry cat.

"Okay," I said. "Sure."

Mara was staying with me for a week. I'd texted her twenty-four hours earlier—I'd finally broken up with what's-his-name. She drove ten hours from Baltimore, arriving just in time to take me out for too many long islands. *Fuck that guy*, she'd said.

I grew jealous at the bar. Mara was effortless—oxblood lipstick, wine-flushed cheeks, one of those French bobs no one can pull off. How did she do that? Did she seriously just order a negroni at a Midwest dive bar? She'd always been so fucking cool, even in high school. Maybe I was bruised from the breakup, maybe I was drunk, but I cried on the walk home, whined about my split ends and late-twenties, acne-prone skin. Like a bad romcom, it started raining. She looped her arm through mine.

Let's run, so we ran.

I didn't have any tattoos—always worried my favorite things would fade like dreams upon waking, or the lovers I'd held hands with throughout my twenties. Mara was a canvas for little bits of art—some surreal, some ironic, some sweet—all beauty: the most delicate crystal glass on her forearm, a crescent moon with the face of a goddess, three curved-stemmed tulips peeking from behind her ear, an ace of hearts. If you asked her about one, she'd say something like, *oh, this? I found it in a notebook of my grandmother's drawings.*

"What should we get?" I asked while we picked at scrambled eggs, hoping to transcend our hangovers. I'd deferred to Mara as long as I'd known her. Even as eight-year-olds, I'd eat the leftovers from her plate: burnt fries, discarded tomatoes, too-soft strawberries that had gone deep red, puckered around their leafy tops.

"We'll get whatever you want, my love."

"You have better ideas," I told her.

"Not true," she said. "You're the coolest person I know."

I buried my face in the crook of my arm. I hated when she slathered on compliments like too much butter.

In college, we invented our own little world. Sharing a room had been a childhood dream—we stacked the beds, hung string lights, and hid Boone's Farm Strawberry Hill in our bottom desk drawers. She helped me pass biology and meet the first guy to ever see me naked. I edited her term papers and followed her from club to club as we sampled backpacking, ballroom dancing, and frat parties. I promised I'd never let her stay out alone again after some guy on the soccer team fingered her when she blacked out. She promised she'd share every meal with me when I stopped eating and lost twenty pounds in one month.

After graduation, Mara got a job in Chicago—it came with a salary, a big-city neighborhood, and a thirty-five-year-old boyfriend. I moved back home and worked at a local café, picking up a bartender fuck buddy and a binge-drinking habit. Now, at almost thirty, I was still running after her like in high school track, lap after lap on the hard concrete.

"You pick one for me," she said, "and I'll pick one for you."

"What if you hate it?"

"I won't."

She held my hand at the tattoo parlor, biting her lip whenever I squeezed too tight. I closed my eyes, remembering how she'd nearly broken my fingers when we got our ears pierced in sixth grade. She'd said she wasn't afraid, *but do you want to go first?* I didn't want to, but I did it for her.

"How's it look?" I asked, trying to contort my arm to catch sight of the new permanent accessory above my elbow.

"Perfect," Mara said. "The sweetest fruit for the sweetest girl." The artist held up a mirror and I examined the small strawberry outline—this one would stay forever ripe. Mara raised her forearm into the reflection, the bisection to my intact berry replicated there. "I can't believe we chose nearly the same thing."

I could. I'd spent my entire life trying to mimic her: her clothes, her snort-laugh, the way she covered her mouth while chewing, her dance moves, her magazine subscriptions, all of it. I wondered, after all these years, if the only thing I'd never been able to replicate was her unconditional affection for me.

I traced the raw-red outline of the strawberry now inked into my skin. She'd chosen bold, confident lines with high contrast for mine. I'd picked tender, delicate linework and a soft interior for hers. I wondered what that meant.

James Keith Smith

Heavy Lifting

"As a kid, I wasn't interested in practicing scales," says my best friend Mike, as we burgle a third floor walk-up off Seventh. "After I picked up the clarinet, I learned guitar—that's when I realized I had a voice." He removes a television from the wall mount, puts the long screws in his pocket. Mike says he's going to try out for America's Got Talent. He's fifty-eight, stands at six foot four, and weighs two-eighty: the Susan Boyle of Buffalo.

Three nights a week, Mike hosts karaoke at the Oak Tavern. I'm a regular—it's where we met. Mike's a fantastic host, quick to coax a newcomer out of their shell, always ready with a compliment. Between sets, he plays his own songs. Sweet, plaintive originals. Real "tears in your beer"-type of stuff.

"Why don't you and Terri come tomorrow night?" he asks.

I tell him Terri and I aren't on speaking terms, she's finally moved out.

"So you broke up for good this time?"

"Well, this might do it," I say, because we're in Terri's apartment, and it's her things we're stealing. Only Mike doesn't know that.

We make a trip out to the van, my beat up Dodge double parked in the alley. Mike's huffing and puffing up the stairway. I'm worried about him, his heart. He's already had a triple bypass. He drinks too much—we all do—and forgets his pills.

Back in Terri's apartment, there's a set of speakers, an espresso maker. I take the New York Jets refrigerator magnet, the little stuffed dog I won for her at the State Fair, her hiking boots.

I wrote Terri a song once. I didn't have the nerve to say "I'm sorry," but I thought a nice melody might do some of the heavy lifting. I invited her down to the Oak, told her I had a surprise. Mike called me up to the stage. I took my Gibson acoustic from the case and began to play.

"Don't quit your day job," someone shouted from the back.

Mike has one end of the sofa, I've got the other. We're both tired, sweating. I'm beginning to rethink my life. Maybe I should've learned a trade, given up the bad stuff, stay single for a while this last time.

We stop at the top of the stairwell. There's a vein sticking out of Mike's forehead. He knows, somehow. He's caught on, and now he wants me to explain, to tell him we're not doing what he thinks we're doing. She's his friend, too, after all.

But before I can explain, before I can say, I know, I know, he grabs his chest, and it's not good—that frightened look, the sudden catch of breath—it's not good at all.

Eric Rasmussen

The Buchanan Street Standoff

It first occurs to us as we stand in Manuel and Rachel's driveway after Lance Gregory Nevin's death: If you don't count tax fraud (and believe me, none of us do), that boy was the first real criminal to ever set foot in our neighborhood. We're almost certain. Whenever someone new moves onto Buchanan Street—or even just visits—we do our homework. Social media, court records, you name it. Lots of us have kids.

Priya passes around a plate of key-lime bars; Evan swats at the stink bugs hovering above our heads. Across the street, firefighters spray the smoking remains of Lance Gregory Nevin's car. "Isn't it funny how people refer to serial killers by all three of their names?" says Marissa.

"It's to protect the other Lance Nevins." Vernon pops the cap off another beer bottle. "Can you imagine sharing your identity with a famous psychopath?"

"Better than having a common name," says Onkwani (whose last name is Kipkemei).

"How would you know?" asks Sarah (whose last name is Johnson).

Six months earlier, all we had known about Lance Gregory Nevin was that he was a high-school dropout who worked as Assistant Manager at the Dairy Queen where Vernon's daughter Amberleigh had gotten a job. She's charming and attractive (track-and-field star, nursing-home volunteer, future pediatrician), so it's not surprising Lance Gregory Nevin asked her out. She agreed; he was a handsome guy, despite putting zero effort into his appearance. His idea of a "date" was a late-night drive to a secluded spot in the woods, so Amberleigh declined any additional romantic encounters, but he was already obsessed with her. She told him to back off, and that brings us to the moment in question: Lance Gregory Nevin, with a butcher knife and a Beretta M9 resting on the passenger seat, drove down Nixon Street, turned onto Buchanan, and became the first actual villain to enter our neighborhood.

If you've never had the chance to visit our neck of the woods, you really should. It's only twenty minutes outside the city. The houses are a little on the big side, but they're not obnoxious. Let's just say no Buchanan Street property has ever stayed on the real-estate market more than a few hours. A day, tops.

Anyway, that night had been unseasonably humid, which might be why the situation escalated so quickly. Lance Gregory Nevin parked his rusty Corolla under the basketball hoop and called Amberleigh. "I love you," he said. "I never want to be apart from you."

"You're a freak." Amberleigh peeked through her bedroom-window blinds. "Get the hell out of my driveway."

"Come out now or I'll kill your family," he said.

"Are you trying to be funny?" she asked. "The cops are on their way. Enjoy prison, you sociopath."

Lucky for Amberleigh, a police officer happened to be patrolling two blocks over. By the time Lance Gregory Nevin unbuckled his seatbelt and double-checked that he had enough bullets for her parents and two younger sisters, a cruiser with siren wailing squealed into the driveway. The cop saw Lance Gregory Nevin's gun, so she hunched behind her open driver's door and called for backup. "Drop your weapon and no one gets hurt," she shouted.

This was when the neighbors started to notice. Robbie was washing dishes when the red-and-blue lights reflected off his new Williams Sonoma flatware. Marissa heard the sirens as she planted her heirloom-tomato seedlings in the corner of her garden. Sasha was doing yoga in her front room when Lance Gregory Nevin's response to the officer's directive echoed through her open windows. "I don't want any trouble," he cried. "I just need someone to love me."

It broke Sasha's heart a little. Who hasn't felt the dull ache of loneliness sharpen into agony in the presence of someone we desire?

As the neighbors emerged from their houses and congregated in Manuel and Rachel's driveway, another cruiser arrived, then another. "Everyone get back," said the sergeant who leapt from the third police car.

We all moved one driveway over, to Beth and Sarah's, kitty-corner from Vernon and Bahiriya's. "Is this far enough?" shouted Priya.

"No," responded the sergeant. "He's an armed fugitive."

"I'm not moving," said Kurt, quiet enough so the officer couldn't hear. "It's a free country."

Gretchen stepped forward. "If we're going to be out here for a while, I'll get everyone some drinks."

She returned a few minutes later with a cooler of beers and spiked seltzers. As Onkwani set up lawn chairs, the cops negotiated with Lance Gregory Nevin.

"Throw away your weapon and we'll make sure you get what you want."

"You'll give me Amberleigh?"

"Exit the car and we'll see what we can do."

Lance Gregory Nevin could tell they were bluffing. He stayed put.

By 9:00 p.m., there were a dozen vehicles in the street, blocking Vernon's driveway. We watched, listened, and whispered to each other in between blasts of the bullhorn. At 11:00 p.m., some of us headed home. "If I'm late again tomorrow, the boss'll be mad," said Manuel. He downed the rest of his beer. "Oh wait, I am the boss." The cops put the bullhorn away around midnight, transforming the standoff into a bizarre silent film.

"Will they let us back into our own house?" asked Vernon.

"The kids are still in there," said Bahiriya. "We'll sneak through the back door."

The clouds parted and the moon shone. Just after 2:00 a.m., Alice and Evan, the neighborhood's night owls, collapsed their chairs and headed inside.

The next morning, everyone poured coffee and approached their front windows to find the same scene as before: Lance Gregory Nevin in the driver's seat of his car, parked in Vernon and Bahiriya's driveway, surrounded by cops. Surely, the officers were different from the night before; shifts end, people need to go home. But if the department had substituted different personnel, none of the Buchanan Street folks could tell. Around 8:00 a.m., the lead negotiator picked up the bullhorn again, as if quiet hours had just ended.

"They'll have this taken care of by tonight, right?" Beth asked Marissa when they passed each other on the sidewalk, walking their dogs.

"I'm positive," replied Marissa. "They must have protocols for this exact situation."

The neighborhood kids went to school; a full month remained before summer would relieve them of their academic responsibilities. Their parents went to work or dove into their domestic routines. Nine or so hours later, everyone returned home to find the situation unchanged. Marissa, who was "between jobs" after her frozen-yogurt franchise went belly up, texted the entire neighborhood.

I listened in all day. Come over this evening and I'll explain everything—I've got ice cream sandwiches!

(They were frozen yogurt sandwiches, technically, because her freezer was still full of the leftovers).

While we stood in a circle and licked the yogurt dripping down our hands, Marissa shared everything she had gathered from the police scanner and from eavesdropping on the cops and their negotiations with the perpetrator:

1. The police had searched the empty lot behind Lance Gregory Nevin's parents' house and discovered, in his childhood tree fort, a bizarre menagerie of mutilated raccoons displayed like pieces of art.
2. They talked to his high-school teachers, who described him as a "quiet boy who was desperate for attention" before they shuddered and added that he was a "deeply troubled individual" with "crazy eyes."
3. A car similar to his had been observed in the area of several murders of homeless people in Chicago. The victims' bodies had been displayed in a fashion eerily similar to the raccoons. ("That means he killed those unhoused people, right?" asked Sarah. "Of course," said Lars. "It's a classic escalation pattern. Textbook.")
4. The police were prepared to wait him out; he'd have to emerge for food or water eventually.
5. Lance Gregory Nevin had enough pilfered Dairy Queen food in the back seat to last him "months, if necessary." ("What about our Memorial Day block party?" asked Robbie. Yue Pheng responded, "We can set up farther down the street.")

The following day, we brought our breakfasts to Beth and Sarah's driveway. It was only 7:00 a.m., but already the temperature had climbed into the mid-80's. "That boy must be suffocating," said Gretchen. "Do you think he has air conditioning?"

The police sergeant crossed the street to join our half circle. Rachel offered him coffee. He declined then smoothed his mustache with his fingers. "Apologies that this is still dragging on," he said. "You folks probably want to get back to your regular lives."

"If it wasn't this, it'd be something else," said Vernon.

"Unfortunately, it doesn't look like he's leaving anytime soon," said the sergeant.

"Can you call in a sniper?" asked Kurt.

"Don't I wish," replied the sergeant. "We only use non-violent tactics now. Since this kid doesn't pose much of a threat, we're actually going to dial it back. Plus, he'll give up soon. He must be roasting alive in there."

Gretchen raised her hand. "Isn't that cruel-and-unusual punishment?"

The sergeant chuckled. "His choice, not ours." He rocked back and forth on his heels. "You folks have nice days now."

A little while later, most of the neighbors left to get ready for work, but Marissa stayed. So did Priya, Alice, Gretchen, and Robbie, who all worked from home. "You think the boss would let me take a sick day?" Manuel asked. "Oh yeah. That's me."

By lunchtime, only half of the cops remained, and the ones who had stuck around ordered sandwiches. After the delivery guy left, they gathered around the trunk of one of their police cruisers. While they unwrapped their subs and offered each other onion and tomato slices, Gretchen crossed Buchanan farther up the street, by Evan and Robbie's place, then crept back towards the standoff. She crouched to pick her way through the lilac bushes that lined Vernon and Bahiriya's driveway under the basketball hoop then tapped on Lance Gregory Nevin's passenger window. He sat up slowly, and she gestured for him to roll down the glass. While the officers squirted their lunches with foil packets of mayo, Gretchen handed Lance Gregory Nevin a bottle of ice water. He pressed it to his forehead, its condensation dripping down his face. "Thank you," he mouthed to Gretchen. "You're welcome," she mouthed back.

For three weeks, we snuck Lance Gregory Nevin all sorts of snacks and cold drinks. Onkwani suggested the kid might appreciate a change of clothes. Evan and Robbie offered the portable toilet they no longer used, ever since they stopped camping. Marissa bought him two cell-phone chargers so she could replenish one while he drained the other. We always waited until the police officers were distracted to deliver our packages, but they had to know. All the sneaking through the lilac bushes had carved out a little tunnel. Also, Lance Gregory Nevin would set his dirty dishes on the concrete underneath his driver's-side door, and he obviously hadn't brought along a full set of Wedgwood tableware to kidnap the girl he worked with. We kept up the charade until the first Sunday in June. That was the day Manuel dragged his grill over to Beth and Sarah's driveway to make hot dogs, and we could see drool glistening on Lance Gregory Nevin's lips.

"This is ridiculous," said Lars as he grabbed a hot dog off the platter. "Everyone deserves a hot dog." He marched across the street; the officers who had been leaning against their cars stood up.

"Go about your business," said Lars. He maintained his speed until he reached Lance Gregory Nevin's window. The serial killer held out his hand, took the hot dog, and offered a thumbs up, which Lars returned.

"You can't do that," said the closest police officer.

"I just did," said Lars as he re-crossed the street. "And I didn't break any laws."

The cops looked at each other and shrugged. "Got any more hot dogs?" asked the youngest patrolman, in back.

Lars waved for them to come along. "Of course we have more hot dogs. As many as you can eat."

Our neighborhood is a safe place, full of camaraderie, support, and laughter, but it does have an unfortunate flaw: We tend to get so competitive. It doesn't matter what it is—Christmas decorations, snow forts, our lawns. Last year, it was the battle of the hot tubs. Yue Pheng and Marissa had one installed, then Evan and Robbie copied them but with a pergola. Each new backyard spa one-upped the previous until Priya and Kurt won with a full patio, twelve-foot waterfall, and a TV that rose from the ground like a sped-up video of a mountain being born.

Even though Gretchen had technically started the Lance Gregory Nevin competition when she snuck him the water bottle, after the cops stopped caring, Beth was the one who really ramped it up. By that point, we were eating most of our meals in her and Sarah's driveway so we could keep an eye on the standoff. One evening, over wood-fired pizzas Onkwani made in the makeshift pizza oven he had constructed in Beth and Sarah's yard, Beth cleared her throat.

"Can I have everyone's attention?" she asked. "I have an idea."

All the neighbors stopped talking. The cops stepped to the middle of the road to hear, and Lance Gregory Nevin rolled down his window.

"School lets out in a few days, and we should throw a party. Games, food, the whole works."

We nodded. With all the standoff excitement, it felt like we had been partying nonstop for a month, but, hey, that's life on Buchanan Street.

"And to make it extra fun, let's host it in Vernon and Bahiriya's driveway. That way, Lance Gregory Nevin can participate!"

No one said anything. We glanced at each other. Then Priya spoke. "Sitting in that car day after day must be hard, but he's still a serial killer."

"Innocent until proven guilty," said Lars.

"He originally came here to kidnap Amberleigh and murder Vernon and Bahiriya," said Yue Pheng. "Do we want to condone that sort of behavior?"

"It's not like he's going to shoot anyone while we're all standing there." Beth held up her arms. "Maybe this will help his rehabilitation. He'll get to see how great his intended victims actually are."

We didn't need more convincing than that. That weekend, we carried the grill over to Vernon's driveway and made sweet corn and kebabs. Kurt brought his cornhole boards and set them up so Lance Gregory Nevin could play, tossing bean bags out his driver's-side window. Amidst all the activity, one of the police officers decided to finally end the standoff by sneaking over to Lance Gregory Nevin's car with her pistol drawn, but at the last minute he saw her and fired a few shots into the air. "It's okay, everyone," he said as the officer dashed away and the rest of us crouched, screamed, and covered our heads. "It was just a warning." After dark, we built a bonfire so the kids could burn their workbooks and assignments from the previous school year, and Lance Gregory Nevin tossed his Dairy Queen uniform into the flames. "I'm not going back there anymore," he shouted. We all laughed. No, he wasn't. He definitely wasn't.

☾

Next up was Sasha, who was still furious that she had lost the hot-tub wars. On one of our neighborhood bike rides, she shifted into a higher gear after cresting a hill and asked, "Does anyone know when Lance Gregory Nevin's birthday is? 'Cause I do." She stared at the road ahead as she picked up speed. "June nineteenth."

"A Gemini," said Alice. "Makes sense."

"Please put it on your calendars." Everyone was out of breath except for Sasha. "I'm throwing a celebration. Catered. Semi-formal."

"Gifts?" asked Marissa.

"I'm sure Lance Gregory Nevin would appreciate gifts. He's had a rough month."

The rental company arrived the morning of the nineteenth to erect a giant tent over Vernon and Bahiriya's driveway. The shade was such a relief that Lance Gregory Nevin wept the entire time the catering company unloaded their vans and the string quartet set up in the third garage stall. At 5:00, we emerged from our houses and walked to the party. The guys wore their lightest suits, the women donned short-sleeve dresses. Marissa's featured a slit all the way up her thigh. Lars kept his sunglasses on all night because he thought they made him look like a Miami Vice character. Sarah admitted that she'd never seen the show. Kurt offered to loan her the DVDs.

In addition to the neighbors, Sasha had invited every police officer who had spent time stationed on Buchanan Street, and many of them came. At one point, the sergeant approached Sasha, Vernon, and a handful of us who had gathered at the bar table.

"I want to make sure you understand what you're doing," said the officer. "That kid is a seriously dangerous individual."

"That's not been our experience," said Sasha.

"Do you remember the series of dognappings last year? We kept it out of the media, but we found all the carcasses behind the abandoned hospital. We're pretty sure it was Lance Gregory Nevin."

We nodded our concern, stroked our chins.

"And the reports out of Chicago are shocking. They've found fourteen victims so far. This is nasty stuff."

"Hate the sin, love the sinner," said Vernon.

"Just be careful," said the sergeant.

Over on the driveway, Lance Gregory Nevin had started opening his presents. Alice handed them to him one at a time. He acted like he was grateful for each one, even the dumb gifts that didn't make any sense, like scented candles. "These smell amazing, thank you," he said as he tossed the jars over his shoulder into the back seat.

Sasha felt a tap on her shoulder then turned to find a man with a gray goatee, flanked by his ghostlike wife. The couple had attempted (and failed) to follow the dress code, he in a corduroy blazer and she in a peasant dress. "Why are you doing this?" the man asked.

"Who are you?" asked Sasha.

"We're Lance Gregory Nevin's parents."

"Of course." Sasha gave them each a hug even though they tensed and leaned away. "I'm so glad you got your invitation."

"You need to leave that boy be," said Mr. Nevin. "You don't understand who he is."

"Nonsense." Sasha grabbed two glasses of red wine from the bar table and handed them to the Nevins. "He's been nothing but polite."

"A squirt gun?" shouted Lance Gregory Nevin from the driveway after tearing open another present. "I love it!" He aimed the neon plastic weapon at the people standing around the driveway. "This is going to be so much fun."

Over the following weeks, several others attempted to join the competition. Kurt put a few-dozen hours into the boy's car, tuning up the engine, buffing out the rust spots, and adding a new set of rims. Robbie, who taught at the university, conducted tutoring sessions in math, writing, and career planning. By the time he was done, Lance Gregory Nevin had completed applications for the technical college and three different scholarships. These were all thoughtful efforts, of course, but Sasha was clearly still in first place. Then Bahiriya decided to join the fray.

By that point, it was early August, and what had been the hottest summer on record got even hotter. One hazy evening, the cops fanned themselves with their hats as the neighbors took turns spraying each other with Beth and Sarah's garden hose.

"What does that boy want more than anything?" asked Bahiriya as she wrung out the bottom of her shirt.

"Freedom?" responded Yue Pheng.

"A shower?" said Evan.

"Love," said Bahiriya. "The same as any of us. And no matter what mistakes we've made, don't we all deserve love?"

We couldn't argue with that.

Bahiriya's plan hinged on convincing her daughter Amberleigh that Lance Gregory Nevin wasn't the monster she had initially assumed. None of us witnessed the negotiations. Maybe Bahiriya threated Amberleigh's access to the family's third Escalade, but that's unlikely. Amberleigh is such a kind and understanding girl. She probably saw how Lance Gregory Nevin was becoming one of us, in a way, and she agreed to her mom's plan without hesitation.

Planning the couple's second date took weeks, and Bahiriya spared no expense. She invested in a series of video monitors on wheels that we set up around Lance Gregory Nevin's car, which played footage of the drive from his house to Buchanan Street so he could imagine he was making the trip. After pretending to park, Lance Gregory Nevin honked his horn and Amberleigh appeared, glowing and youthful in a green sundress. She got into his car, we wheeled the monitors back into place, and they pretended to drive to the restaurant, which consisted of a handful of us dressed as carhops (Alice and Priya had helped sew the uniforms). While Lance Gregory Nevin and Amberleigh ate the hamburgers and drank the shakes we delivered to their car, they tried to make conversation.

"What are you doing after high school?" Lance Gregory Neven asked.

"College, probably pre-med," she replied. "What will you do after you leave our driveway?"

"Maybe computers?"

After dinner, they completed one more "trip," this time to an imaginary drive-in movie theater, and this was where Bahiriya cemented her victory. Several of us parked our cars next to Lance Gregory Nevin's, and behind the vehicles we erected enormous backdrops painted to look like a field of moviegoers. Bahiriya hung a screen that covered her garage, on which she played the film *Grease.*

The hardest part of forming relationships is that they never last. No one is as pretty or as funny or as cool as they are right after you meet them. But not on Buchanan Street, and that's what makes this neighborhood special. We've all lived next to each other for years, and we have disagreements, which sometimes turn into fights. People's feelings get hurt. Such things are inevitable. But for some reason, we still manage to engineer moments where we gather, laugh, do our best Danny Zuko impressions, and sing along with all the songs. There's nowhere we would have rather been. There's nowhere anyone would rather be.

At the part where Sandy appears in her black spandex pants, a shriek sounded from Lance Gregory Nevin's car. We turned to see what happened, our mouths full of half-chewed popcorn. Amberleigh emerged from the passenger side, clutching her side, blood soaking her dress and dripping onto the concrete.

"He stabbed me," she said as tears poured from her eyes. "I thought we had a real connection."

At first, no one moved, and you could see the fear on everyone's faces. Had we made a terrible mistake? But we have a motto on Buchanan Street—there are no mistakes, only opportunities. While "You're the One That I Want" played in the background, we sprang into action. Beth, Robbie, and Bahiriya helped Amberleigh inside. Evan called an ambulance. Lars and Kurt ran to alert the police officers who had been watching the movie through the cracks between the painted backdrops. Marissa and Priya unclipped the movie screen from where it hung above the garage. Vernon grabbed one of the tiki torches that lined the driveway and threw it like a javelin into Lance Gregory Nevin's window. The greasy seats and the scented candles went up like a dried-out Christmas tree. Yue Pheng held the driver's-side door closed until Lance Gregory Nevin stopped screaming.

Olivia Jacobson

Upon Recognizing a Man Being Arrested on COPS

My mother comes running, her slippers slapping
against the cold linoleum after my father yells
to come see Robby on the big black-box CRT TV.
My little brother is scooching
across the carpet, his chubby legs poking out
like sausages from his diaper. We're all here
in the dark—the flashes of light
from the patrol car bouncing
off the walls around us, a meditation
on red and blue and red. The camera
cuts to a close-up of a woman,
Robby's girlfriend, maybe, her neon pink
fake nails pressed to her temple, her brow
slivered and left eye leaking. *That motherfucker*
hit her with a shovel, my father says, his white T-shirt
glowing in the reflection of the glass. My mother nods,
unclamps her hands from her swirling lips
and picks up the baby. I was so young,
I only remember the piles of kitty litter soaking
up oil on the floor of my father's shop,
and Robby scooping me up to rest
on his bone-ridden shoulders. Robby is asked
by the officer if he has anything that will poke,
prick, cut, or stick him as he turns his pockets out
and Robby begins to cry. I don't remember
who turns the TV off after this, or if we ate dinner,
or if I was put to bed. Only, I remember

our dog barking at the back door
and my father sighing and cursing
as he got off the couch to let her in.

Mary Biddinger

Everyone Had Low Expectations, Including Us

Kids in my neighborhood took lessons at the community center and it was nothing special. Zero dazzle, no artifice, leotards passed from family to family via mailbox or alley hand-off. A full session of dance fundamentals cost five bucks, and we brought checks or wadded cash or even coins, depending on what sort of jobs our parents worked. My mother scribbled an IOU that looked legitimate even if barely legible. Anna dragged in a mesh bag of apples and the instructor accepted them on par. We took our place on the studio floor and limbered up. Our neighborhood corner granny always attended the holiday dance performance and vowed to stitch us better costumes next year, someone's cornflake crown disintegrating with a spin, a reindeer resembling a tree trunk crouched next to a cardboard lake. Behind the musty blue curtain we dancers passed a bottle of peppermint schnapps pocketed from Albert's mother's liquor cabinet. Its icy burn blanketed my toes with a sort of invisible sand. In the green room, my godmother gathered us to share the story of a catastrophic theater fire back in Poland. Apparently it was the fault of delinquent children drinking stolen liquor and throwing a lit match into a pillow bin, but some of the details sounded suspiciously adjacent to the Iroquois Theatre inferno of 1903. None of us would have a future on the stage, large or small.

Mary Biddinger

Everyone Mistook Me for a Cousin and That Was Fine

In a photo I'm one of several faded children eating pears in the rain. You can zoom in to see the street name, the trees, and some of the women's faces. Blue Avon eyeshadow and unnaturally rosy cheeks, cork-heeled sandals. Waterlogged decorations like streamers and cardboard stars. Our neighborhood corner granny spent the morning stacking a trifle bowl with berries and Cool Whip, drying lawn chairs with a raggedy beach towel. She was no relation to me, but she knew which immunizations I was missing and how I liked my sandwiches cut. When the rain let up, I wriggled onto a picnic bench between Ewa and Maeve. My godmother appeared with a damp rag yet wiped nothing. Told everyone a story about a runaway summer lamb from the village of her youth. Pitor and Monika kicked a rotten spaghetti squash like one of the ugly rubber balls we had to play soccer with in gym class. Stan from the corner bar muttered about the dank mines he worked for as a child, and there we were damaging vegetables and rocking the picnic table like punks. Music from the street pulsed along with a passing train. I stepped into the house, corner granny's bathroom rug pink and soft under my feet, rose-scented soaps the shape of scallop shells. I washed my hands twice and dried them on towels the size of doll blankets. In the kitchen, a woman asked me where *my grandmother* kept the matches. I did not correct her.

E.C. Gannon

Levittown

In the empty space of this suburbia,
we throw racquetballs at the neighbors'
satellite dishes without reason.
We skateboard around and
aroundandaround the cul-de-sac,
hoping to scrape knees or bruise
elbows. It doesn't matter how much
it hurts. We smoke the butts of discarded
cigarettes, sigh disappointed sighs
when we taste only tobacco. We carve
our initials into the imperceptible, grass-
covered edge of every picket fence
in sight, knowing no one will ever
realize we had been there or care.
We lie on our backs on perfectly
mowed lawns, hoping someone,
a mailman or middle-aged walker,
will wonder if we're all right.

Erin MacNair

Our Town Is Painted Purple and Blue

Sir Raleigh was Metal; I was Punk, allies on the same side of *fuck you*. Everyone called him Sir Raleigh after the one-step-above-no-name smokes he rolled into his muscle-taut T-shirts like a greaser, hair teased into golden fuzz above his pock-marked face.

I pulled up outside his dad's rancher perched above the freeway, a king's view of the semis racing by below. Rainbow arcs of bent rebar lined the steep drive—a decorative touch—random shit strewn everywhere: hunks of metal and wood, a broken awning, garden chairs with rubbery slats pulled free of the aluminum tubing, now encrusted with ice.

"Dad's gonna be pissed I'm late." He hauled himself out of my decrepit, band-stickered four-door sedan, slamming the heavy door. The night had dragged as we'd finished painting the last sets for *Our Town*. A shadow lurked in the doorway, past the frozen scrolls of an aluminum screen door not needed in a midwestern January. Sir Raleigh took a deep pull of his smoke before chucking the butt in the culvert where it sizzled in the grey slush.

"Well. Your shit car wouldn't start, so." I shrugged, flicking my long hair over one shoulder and trying for a laugh as if my idling deathtrap was better. No way would I attempt the slippery driveway, get any closer to what I'd already imagined lay in wait inside that shack. I'd seen his bruises. *Just fighting dudes after school*, he'd said, as I'd raised my eyebrows. I would've heard about it, had his back. No teachers noticed? But half of them didn't know his real name.

Sir Raleigh would often slam me against a locker, roaring into my ear with hot smoke-tinged breath—a declaration of some sort. People thought we were fucking. We let them believe whatever they wanted.

He leveled his eyes with mine.

"You don't know where I live. And never have, if anyone asks." His words burst into little clouds of cold.

"I got you, dude," I said, looking down at my hands, flecked with blue and purple paint.

Sir Raleigh nodded and slowly turned away, sneakers punching through the drift of snow that had obliterated the path upward. The shadow retreated from the doorway. I pulled away, not looking in the rearview mirror, hands shaking as I lit a smoke.

Erin MacNair

Queen of the Hill

Atop this irresistibly teetering mountain of snow, plowed into one corner of the back parking lot behind the Shop-N-Go, you zero in on your enemy: a hulking collegiate couch surfer smelling of patchouli, Marlboro Lights, and some overpowering pheromone that makes you think of goats. Ignore the jingling of wallet chains and rows of earrings as he taunts you, the perfect rip of his jeans harboring a knee wrinkled like a shriveled face. Cringing against the sub-zero wind, you narrow your eyes at his blatant hypocrisy: those boots cost more than any faux gutter-punk could rustle up flipping eggs at the Sunshine Shack—for sure his mom bought them.

Don't lose your balance on the icy precipice; you must never underestimate him or his tall friend on your left, arms outstretched like a bear ready to topple you. There will be some unseen exchange between them, some look or small nod like when you're at a show and they see someone they want to fuck with. Stay alert.

Remember, this one refuses to lose, at anything, ever. Carrying himself like the Prince of Persia with his painfully beautiful cheekbones and his superior knowledge about every question you ever had. You smirk at the memory of someone whistling out of their pickup at his ass, his long wavy hair, not realizing he was *all dude* and peeling away when they did. The trouble you got into! But those bruises quickly faded. Push your matted bangs aside with one sopping mitten, the strands of hair frozen together from a recent snowball bullseye.

There it is—the sudden lunging.

Revel in this moment, Queen. Dare them to upend your throne, kill or be killed—there are reputations to lose—or almost lose: yours teeters at the edges of *whore* and *slut*, especially with these two, everybody knows, but in below-zero weather, nobody's pants are getting unbuckled. Drop to your knees and swing a leg outward; send the Prince rolling down the packed chunks and into the slush of defeat.

Watch the tall one lurch forward—all jingle-jangle and bubbling laughter; he loves you, a little, he said so once just after. Give him a shove so he'll slip and fall hard on the frozen perch, head facing your crotch. Think about pushing his face down, see how he likes it—but you're still a lady, somewhere underneath those hard edges you pretend to have. Grab his woollen hat with the ironic 8 ball on the front and throw it into the freezing wind. Upend the patriarchy, ha-ha!

Feel for a moment the sudden surprise of hands gripping you from behind, the lightning-fast, quick-footed Prince snatching your coat and flinging you into the air, much harder than is necessary, an unmerciful exercise in gravity's pull.

Land hard, arms and legs splayed like a cat who's lost all its lives in one swift blow. Hear yourself wheeze, gasps clawing your windpipe with thin needles of icy air. Realize there is no air inside you, just nothingness. Also, you've clearly broken your back on a rock or a can or a piece of garbage frozen into the ice on the pavement where you've landed fifteen feet below, the pain searing and absolute. Hear the boys raucous cackling from atop the ice-pile, hazy and glowing like a blue secret, backlit by a fluorescent streetlight. Beautiful, even from this vantage point.

Shut your eyes. Pretend to be dead.

Wait to see if they notice. They don't. Inhale a small trickle of air, finally, through your nose, and hold the tears just under your lids. Clasp them there long enough to almost freeze your lashes shut before ripping them apart. Raise a hand to them in surrender. Hear their hurrahs, peals of laughter, and the clicking of a stolen lighter.

Think *good idea* while pushing your frozen body to sitting. Apparently you aren't paralyzed for life. Once again, you aren't broken in any visible way. Reach for your crushed smokes deep inside your navy peacoat. Light the one that is salvageable, pulling off the filter and sticking it into the mountain, a toxic spike, proof you were here. Blow delicious, poisonous smoke from your chapped lips. Search the stars for any discernable meaning. Find none.

Nora Maynard

Union Square Park

I look at Marketplace a lot, although I never buy anything. Today I saw a listing for a jar of tears. The seller wrote, *Don't ask if it's still available because if this listing is still up, it's still available.*

I wasn't looking for tears in any quantity, but I did want to know who was selling them. Their name was just a pair of initials, and their picture was just a jar.

I see the same people day to day, even fewer since my wife left. My coworkers in the office. Clients over Zoom. The guy at the dry cleaners who always pulls up my account by phone number, even after I remind him of my name. I often notice a woman walking a shih Tzu near the Starbucks weekday mornings and I sometimes nod at her.

I knew that the type of person offering to sell a jar of tears would likely be a crank, but maybe they'd be some kind of downtown artist doing some kind of project. A pale young woman in a tiny studio or a rich recluse in a gigantic loft. New York could be like that. I was hoping I could meet them at their door, maybe catch a glimpse. But then they wrote, *How about noon today at Union Square?*

The price was one dollar. It wasn't an amount I could pretend to haggle over.

How will I know you? I typed.

I'll be by the statue of Gandhi. I'll be holding a jar.

I left my desk and got on the subway instead of getting lunch. I had a dollar folded in my pocket. I'd chosen it over a few worn ones because it looked clean and crisp. I was wearing one of my favorite shirts, the one my wife used to say brought out the blue in my eyes. It was sunny out, summer still, pink flowers blooming in raised beds by the sidewalk. People out with babies and shopping bags and dogs.

I went up to the statue of Gandhi in its little fenced-in garden on the far side of the park. It was noon on the dot but I was the only one there, except for a teenage couple on a bench making out. No one holding a jar. I stood for a while, but I felt I was a little too close to the kids, so I got moving. I kept feeling for the dollar in my pocket as I made my way around the statue's wrought iron fence.

I neared the side closest to street. A black sedan with mirrored windows was idling. Wealthy recluse? I stopped and waved, but it just took off.

I felt a little sweat trickle between my shoulder blades, dampening my shirt. I checked my phone. No messages. It was 12:04.

I was back at the bench now. The kids were gone and there was an elderly couple in their place. They were both wearing canvas sunhats, nearly matching, except the woman's had a long loop that fastened under her chin with a sliding bead. Something about that loop, and the way the man held her hand so gently, choked me up right then. It was hot and I needed to sit down.

I crouched on a paving stone in the shade near Gandhi's feet. I pulled up Marketplace on my phone, but the listing was gone, along with the messages. Was this a prank? Someone who wanted to see what kind of person would buy a jar of tears?

I bet my wife wasn't spending her lunch break taking the subway to meet strangers in Union Square. I put my face in my hands.

Then I saw it. Beside me, under a low bush, was a clear glass jar, sealed but empty, glinting in the sun. I lifted it to my chest and held its hollow warmth close.

Cate McGowan

The Neighbor's Left Ear

The neighbor showed up on my porch with her left ear in a Mason jar. She said she found it in the freezer next to a bag of frozen peas and her dead husband's wedding ring. The ear bobbed in cloudy liquid, a tuft of hair curling off the top like a sleeping cowlick.

"I think it's mine," she said, shaking the jar. The ear thunked against the glass.

It didn't seem impossible. Her long hair curtained her face, masking her left side. The ear was smallish and freckled like her, though pallid, like something left too long in the cold. But she was so spacey, I wondered if she'd even know if she were going through life sans a body part.

I let her in, and we sat in the kitchen, staring at the jar.

"What'll you do with it?" I asked and thought, but didn't say, you can't just reattach something that was sitting next to the waffle fries, frozen alongside items of disappointment for who knows how long.

She ran a finger along the jar's condensation ring. "What would you do?"

I hesitated. What would *I* do? Keep it? Press it to the walls at night, listening for the house's secrets locked inside? Instead, I said, "I'd plant it, maybe. See what grows."

Her laughter snagged in the air like it caught on a splinter, and she swirled the jar, her gaze lingering on the spiral of cartilage as it spun through the briny liquid.

Two days later, she returned, her hair tied back, both ears intact. Her fingers brushed the left lobe absently as if mourning unnamable things.

"I think I *will* try planting it," she said, soft but sure.

I watched through the window as she crossed into her yard, movements deliberate, reverent, as though burying not just flesh, but some piece of herself she hoped could grow back.

Cate McGowan

Come to Say

The giraffe showed up on a Tuesday. It wasn't the first time something bizarre happened in our cul-de-sac—last year, a flock of feral chickens nested in the HOA president's bushes—but a giraffe was, frankly, pushing it.

I was pouring coffee when my neighbor Sandy called. "There's a giraffe in your yard." Her voice had the clipped edge of someone used to being unimpressed.

"Sure," I said, assuming this was a dig about my yard flamingos. Sandy hated my flamingos.

"No, really. It's chewing on your mailbox."

I shuffled to the front door, still in my mismatched socks, and there it was: A giraffe, wobbling around like a badly rigged marionette, trying and failing to find purchase on the concrete. It had already knocked over my mailbox, which was now lying in the flower bed with a cheerful tulip sticking through its flag.

"It's definitely yours," Sandy said when I stepped outside, her face smug and arms folded across her monogrammed button-down.

"How can a giraffe be mine?" I asked, sipping my coffee, waving it away like it was some kind of joke.

"Well, it's not mine," she said, as though that answered anything.

The giraffe gave me a mournful look, its head tilting slightly. It blinked those huge lashes, the kind only mammals with unfair genetic advantages can grow, and I swear, it sighed. So cliché.

"Fine," I muttered. "Come inside, I guess."

It ducked through the doorframe, dislodging a chunk of siding with its horns, and ambled directly through the three-story-high corridor, the one with all the windows (it's only selling point) to my high-ceilinged kitchen, where it bent its absurdly long neck to inspect my fridge. Sandy followed into the hallway and gasped. Scandalized.

"You're not really keeping it, are you?"

"What do you expect me to do? Call Animal Control?"

She pursed her lips. "That's exactly what you should do."

But by then, the giraffe had discovered the leftover cheesecake on the bottom shelf, and, well, that was the end of it.

WISH YOU WERE HERE

by C. Zhang

.-. --- ..-.

-.-- .... - .- -.-

12 . 06 . 2025

ONE DAY, LATE AFTERNOON IN THE SUMMER,
I HAD A NAP ON THE COUCH AND
DREAMED ABOUT YOU.

I DREAMED I'D FALLEN ASLEEP ON YOUR
BED WHILE YOU WERE WORKING ON A SET OF
PROBLEMS AT YOUR DESK.

AND WHEN I WOKE UP,

IT WAS THE NICEST FEELING
IN THE WORLD.

I FELT SO SAFE AND
INEXORABLY COMFORTED,

LIKE EVERYTHING WAS GOING TO BE OKAY.

NOTHING WAS OKAY, OBVIOUSLY.

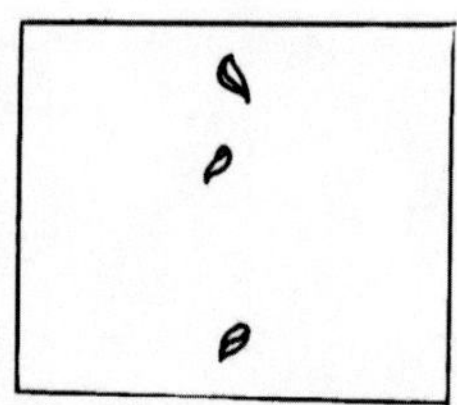
YOU NEVER ENDED UP COMING BACK
TO ME.

BUT I LIKE TO PRETEND THAT IT WAS A VISION, SENT FROM
AN ALTERNATE UNIVERSE'S VERSION OF YOU —— TELLING ME THAT,
SOMEWHERE, OUT THERE, EVERYTHING IS GOING TO BE OKAY.

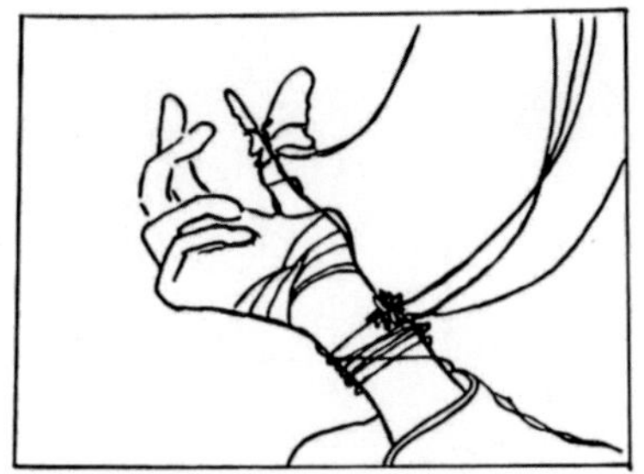

I THINK THAT, WHEN I LOST YOU,

I KIND OF LOST EVERYONE.

AND THIS ISN'T TRUE, BUT SOMETIMES IT FEELS LIKE IT IS.

I LOST MY LITTLE HOME.

I MISS YOU SO MUCH I FEEL LIKE
I CAN'T SURVIVE FEELING SO SOFT
ON THE INSIDE, ALL THE TIME.

WHAT SCARES ME THE MOST IS THAT
MAYBE YOU NEVER LET ME KNOW YOU, AFTER ALL.

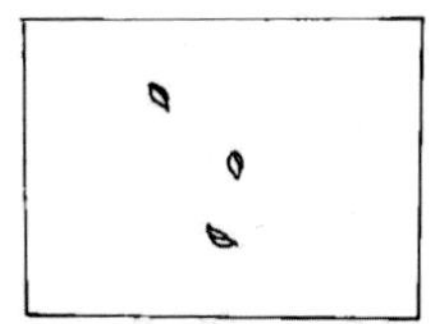
BUT THAT'S MY FEAR TALKING
I WON'T LET IT WIN. I DO KNOW.

I STILL THINK YOU'VE GOT GOLD
INSIDE YOU.

I'M WAITING FOR THE DAY
WHEN YOU REALIZE IT, TOO.

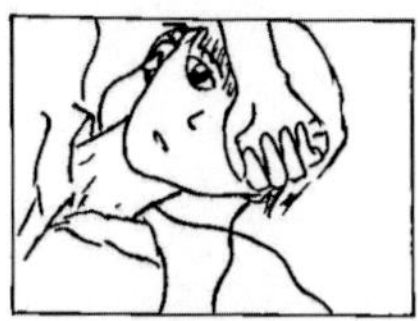
I WANT TO FIND YOU, BUT
I DON'T WANT TO HAVE THAT
CONVERSATION,

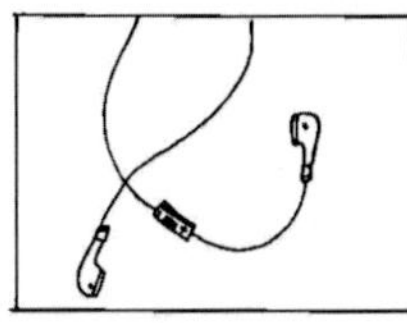
IF I DON'T GET TO
HAVE YOU BACK FOREVER.

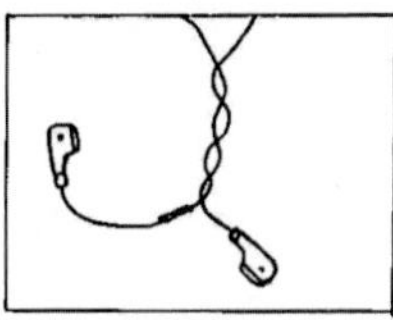
IT'LL HURT TOO MUCH.
I WANT EVERYTHING OR NONE OF IT.

I'M GREEDY.

YOU HAVE NO IDEA
HOW ANGRY I'VE BEEN

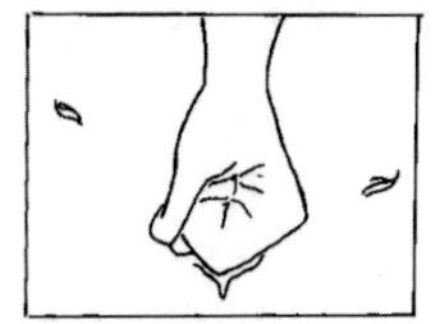
AT YOU.

BUT IF I ONLY HAVE
SO MUCH SPACE TO SPEAK,

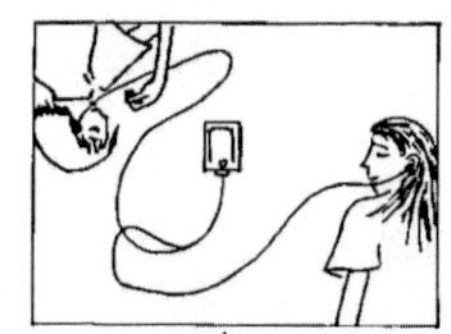
I DON'T WANT TO
GIVE YOU MY ANGER.

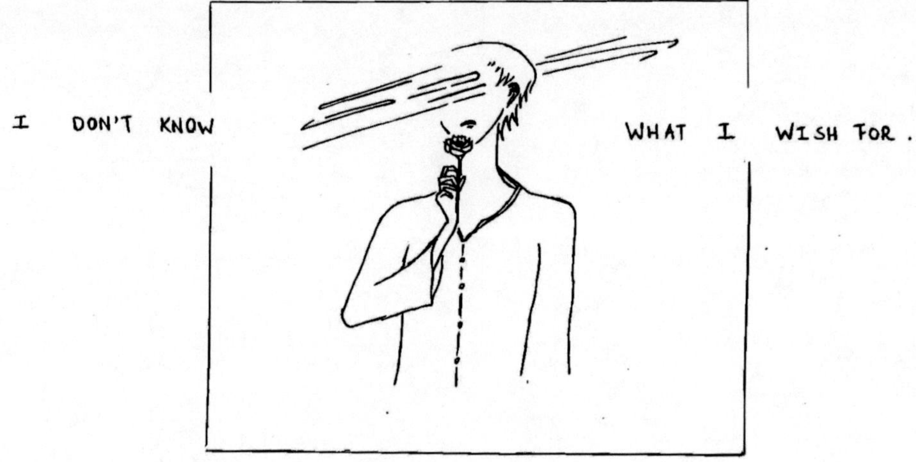
I DON'T KNOW
WHAT I WISH FOR.

I JUST WANT YOU TO KNOW THAT
I'VE KEPT ALL THE LOVE YOU GAVE ME

LIKE A SMALL JAR OF OIL
IN MY HEART.

I CAN USE IT TO LIGHT
LANTERNS, LIGHT FIRES.
IT WILL NEVER BURN OUT.

YOU MADE ME BRAVER, BRIGHTER,
THAN I EVER THOUGHT I COULD BE.

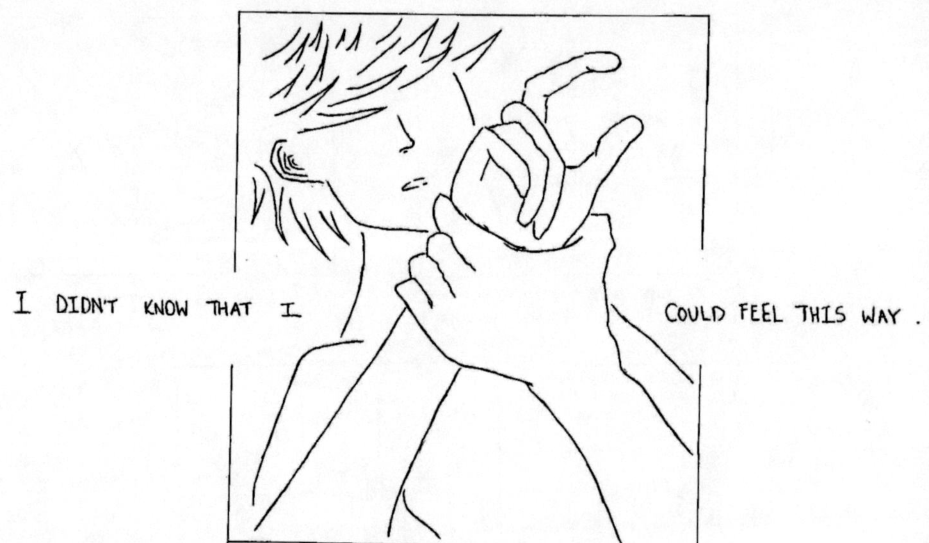
I DIDN'T KNOW THAT I
COULD FEEL THIS WAY.

THERE WAS A WHILE, WHEN I FELT SO BROKEN ABOUT LOSING YOU. I FELT LIKE I DIDN'T KNOW HOW TO SMILE ANYMORE.

BUT THEN I REALIZE I HAVE TO PROTECT THE PART OF ME THAT LOVES YOU.

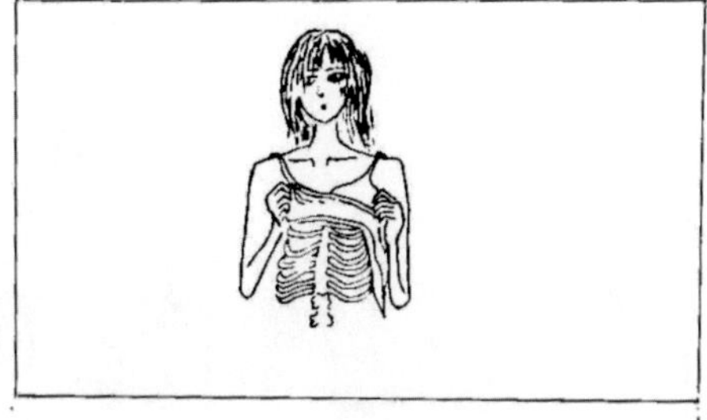

BECAUSE IT'S THE SAME PART OF ME THAT LOVES LAUGHING, LOVES LIVING, LOVES SUNLIGHT AND OLD STORIES.

IT IS MY FAVORITE PART, THE MOST INTEGRAL PART, OF MYSELF.

YOU LOVED MY HAPPINESS LIKE IT WAS YOUR OWN.
I NEVER, EVER WANT TO LOSE IT.

I'M GOING TO PROTECT WHO I AM FOR AS LONG AS I CAN. FOR US.
SO YOU CAN STILL RECOGNIZE ME, THE DAY WHEN YOU WANT TO COME BACK.

OTHERWISE, HOW WILL YOU KNOW HOW TO FIND ME?

Svetlana Litvinchuk

Warbirds

I.

In Kyiv my uncle speaks
into his telephone
as bombs sail overhead.

The barrage intensifies
on a bed of promises
dusted with rare-earth
minerals.

Peace talks dangle—
a carrot on a stick,
before the world's mouth.

With rumbling stomachs,
humanity prepares for sleep.

A rocket lands on a home
while, in the next room,
his daughter dreams of Europe.

My uncle dreams of an empty sky,
therefore, he cannot sleep.

Across the Atlantic, I do not see
the rockets dazzle the sky
here where the war doesn't reach
our windows, only our wallets.

Citizens reach into their pockets,
turn them inside out
like empty stomachs, fresh out
of compassion.

My uncle says
they have learned by now
to sleep through every boom.

II.

Every season is the season
for war.

Grass claws the Earth, screams
through the restless thaw
as Washington churns,
its flames licking the horizon.

The clang of a neighbor's
trash can lid foreshadows violence.
It is the artillery, the shells,
the finality of the ground.

Even as we believe we could never
be next, soon the war will arrive.

Somewhere in the world,
a hunger roams,
a hunting beast—
it sniffs out anywhere
where emptiness grows.

We do not quiet
the famine growing
within us.

And so, it is
already here.

III.

Late winter and early spring
are bitter enemies,
snuffing each other out.

The frantic fervor of songbirds,
the cacophonous corvids—
they are harbingers.

Listen closely—the birds
are already sounding
the alarms.

We are so hungry.

Soon we will eat
our own money.

Umma Habiba

War and Peace

On the nights the hills don't lull me to sleep
I go out
And trace wars on the corners of the refugee camps

War is just the opposite side of the peace coin
The hills scream my name
At the end of the night
Their green tongues invite me to suck
Their breasts invite me to suck
My eyes that stayed awake through the night
Could hardly see now
The fingers in my feet dwarf after strolling through the night
I wait for the fingers to grow again
Sitting on the back of the buffalos
War appears from beneath the clothes
And ask the hills to surrender

I open my mouth for the goodbye kiss
Only to find that the hills have fallen already

Translated From the Bangla by Quamrul Hassan

Lindsay Li

American Étude

Pop open a can, take
        a sip. I'll trade you
a can of Coke

        if you believe
in what you are
        fighting to untangle.

My American Dream
        is an American
dreaming of gold

        laced sweetness. If
you add the hyphen,
        we are not so fully

ourselves. I want
        a house of our own, running
water, pre-packaged

        corner store sandwiches.
Reheat for one minute
        thirty. *What*

are you looking
        forward to doing
in this country? I still remember

her response: *I want to*
try American
hamburgers. We eat them

every day because
sandwiches are below us
and everything else is

too high on the shelf.
I miss my mother,
but she's singing

back at home. I miss
my cousin but he's back
cheering on another

government. Propaganda
is a nice word until we don't
realize it's not. I had

a nightmare I cut off
my tongue at the dentist—
cherry soda, blood canals.

This saccharine dream
decays the less we resist. I'll speak up
until stage fright kicks

into the spotlights
of seven billion eyes
gone through the TV

like static. The bubbles rise
too fast for you
to even say *stop.*

Melissa Llanes Brownlee

I Going Do It Bumbai

Starscream screams and I join in, shrieking my defiance at Megatron and his bossy-bitch-ass ways and I want to fly, zoom zoom, be the bad guy and drain energon cubes from the earth and my sisters yell at me to clean my goddamn room and I tell them I going do it bumbai and they screech as loud as Starscream and I bow my head to their wisdom but I no like it and I put my clothes in the laundry basket and my toys away and make sure my room is perfect for wen mom gets home because any one of us can get lickens if the house isn't spic and span wen she gets home from work and the rice isn't washed and cooked for dinner and I think I wish I was flying through the sky fighting Autobots and transforming into planes and blowing up any place I like, like my mom's bank or my dad's hotel, and I remember the movie I saw where everyone in his hotel got run over by lava and I laughed and laughed at the stupid tourists even though they never say it was my dad's hotel but I knew and I wanted them all to burn to a crisp because they deserved it.

Melissa Llanes Brownlee

I Dream I'm a Tahitian Dancer

My sisters dress me up, let me wear their dresses, their flowers in my hair. They line my eyes, darken my lashes, fill my lips. I am pretty. They let me flounce, let me preen. I shake my slim hips, like a Tahitian dancer, drums and gourds tapping. They clap and laugh, they let me dream until mom comes home, her hands ripping clothes, flowers, hair, *no get mahus in my family, you stay wait until your father get home*, her hands pulling me into the shower, scalding water scoring my skin, searing my face. I cry and she punches me in the eye screaming *you bettah not cry or you really going get it,* scrubbing me raw. Dad comes home, sees my blackened eye, swollen mouth, and red skin, mom screaming at him *your mahu of a son wen wear his sistahs' clothes and makeup and he was shaking his mahu ass.* Dad sighs. I lost my tears in the shower and hiccup, waiting for the belt that always comes. My sisters are hiding in their room, keeping quiet, knowing that at any moment the belt could be for them, and I stand up straight and accept what will come. Dad looks at mom, resigned. *Get da belt, boy, you know you not supposed to wear your sistahs' clothes, you know you not supposed to act like a mahu* and you go get his army belt from the closet, next to his fatigues, and you give it to him.

Cameron MacKenzie

Strangers

The night ended with Daisuke and I on the porch of the rented house trading stories in pidgin English about our grandfathers. We agreed that the men who had fought in that war were the best that either of our countries had to offer, and we toasted the dead as we looked out across the bay to the lights on the Island of Oshima.

Earlier in the night we had all been pushing for Daisuke and Yoshiko to sleep together in the back bedroom. *We are friends*, they said, laughing at first, then more sternly as the night went on. The whole group, both Japanese and American, agreed that it seemed like a natural pairing, both of them surfers, both beautiful and tan and easy with one another as they sat shoulder to shoulder, eating yakisoba off styrofoam plates. Out of their earshot, we hypothesized that they had gotten together at some undefined point in the past, but that it had ended badly. So comfortable as friends, it could be that they found themselves to be strangers on the far side of love—had become brittle and harried by their new expectations, ashamed of one another, and ashamed of themselves. We concluded that they had worked to win back this uneasy friendship, still shot through as it was with delicious strains of unrequited, impossible sex.

All of us got quiet in the den, imagining the two absent surfers and their abandoned, illicit love. And where had they gotten to anyway? No one seemed to know. We sipped our drinks as we stared out the picture window, and in the sudden silence I looked over to Rachel where she sat on the couch. At the way her muscles bunched in her legs as she pulled them up beneath her. Rachel saw me looking, and she smiled, and she slowly shook her head.

Cameron MacKenzie

Downshifting

I told everyone I would drive. I'd been out at the winery with my parents since noon and I'd had I don't know how many glasses of this crisp and clear stuff from the north of Italy that made me feel like I was walking inside of a big shiny bubble, but it was autumn, the day was sharp, and as I cranked my dad's gray VW and pulled out into the road, the asphalt lolled out its tongue like it was ready to sing.

My parents immediately passed out cold in the back seat, and it wasn't until I was a few miles outside of Middleburg that I picked up this little blue Audi behind me. He came out of nowhere, planting himself right up on my bumper, flashing his lights. I sped up a little. He backed off for a minute, then revved his engine and ran up on me again. I peeked in the rearview to get a bead on the guy, but all I could see were these huge sunglasses like two black holes in his face. I looked at my folks asleep in the back. I looked at the road in front of me. I slowed down. I rolled down the window. I stuck out my hand, and I waved the guy on. The Audi pulled out, dropped a gear, and roared up beside me. That's when I slammed on the gas.

This was out in horse country – white fences, low oaks, dappled sunlight. I didn't know the road at all but I felt good about the VW. I felt good about the stick shift and the V6. My dad's car looked like a soulless sedan but I knew how it hugged the road. And I knew he'd never gotten out of it what I could.

When I dropped my foot to the floor, it was like the Audi knew it was coming. He didn't look over and he didn't drop back. Boom. Blind turns. Stone fences. Trees on the right and then on the left, and me and the Audi are running hard, up and back, cutting one another off by inches, passing over the double yellow, squealing tires, hitting fifty on the curves and seventy-five on straightaways. The cylinders whined and barked as the Audi and I moved up and down through the gearboxes but, other than my own breathing, it all seemed very still. No horns. No more lights. We caught air over the rises – a float and a chirp and a wiggle as we touched back down.

After a while my mother sat up and opened her eyes.

"What's going on?" she said.

"I'm racing," I said, downshifting hard into a turn.

"Well," my mother said, lying back down, "just do your best."

Andrew Graham Martin

Miracles

I got invited to speak before Congress, but when I got there, they were not welcoming to me. I thought maybe the senators would be interested in the fact that I had a dog who could talk. But turns out they just wanted to mock me. Politicians were reaching across the aisle for the sole purpose of busting my balls. That was a phrase I learned: "reach across the aisle." Another thing I learned: There are no senators in Congress. At least not the one I was in. There were only congresspeople there.

Whoever they were, they did not seem to care much about the point at hand, which was that at precisely 11:58 p.m. on November 6 my English setter, Roxie, achieved the capability of producing human speech. It started out with basic vocab, like how a baby would do. Pointing things out around my apartment with her wet nose held stiffly forward and her right paw bent dangly at the knee. "Television," she said. "*Hustler*," "Spaghetti."

We got into it pretty quick. My old man always used to say I wouldn't be able to keep my trap shut even if it were welded. If this didn't prove him right, I don't know what would have. Here I was witnessing a miracle, and only three words in, I already found myself taking issue with some of her appraisals.

"Not spaghetti," I said. "Tortellini."

"Spaghetti."

"Tortellini."

"Spaghetti."

"Spaghetti is over there. That was lunch. This is tortellini. It was dinner."

"Dinner."

"Yes, good. It's all cheap, but that doesn't make it the same."

I'm lucky she's patient. You have to be, when it takes a dozen spins around the carpet to find your bed. Roxie speaking confirmed something to me that I'd always known about her, which was that she was forgiving of my uglier tendencies. Like, when she was a puppy and I'd take her on walks, and I'd mutter to myself about this piece of shit, and that piece of shit, and how dare that lady give me a look for walking in the road, et cetera. And Roxie would turn back to look at me with her molasses eyes and they were just so pure and free of judgment it made me reconsider getting so aggravated with strangers, at least for the short little while until we got home and I saw some jackweed using my driveway to turn around.

There are roundabouts all over this part of town, jackweed.

Anyway. Why was I before Congress? I don't know. You don't care. That's not the interesting thing here.

One congressperson with white hair and eyes that looked somehow pinched (you'd know who he was if I could describe him better) really took full advantage of his moment in the sun to rip me a new buttonhole. I never knew someone could get so worked up over a miracle.

"OK, son," he said. "You wanna trot in here and make a mockery of your country?"

"No."

"You wanna give me a little lip?"

"Certainly not."

"You wanna disrespect a hallowed institution?"

"Uh-uh."

"Do you—ain't he supposed to be calling me 'your honor?' Or something?"

Shushed murmuring. Hands over mics.

"I guess I was thinking of something else," he went on. "Anyway. If this really happened, where's the proof?"

"Right here. Talk to her yourself."

At this point, Roxie spoke up, and she was just as patient with this ignoramus as she is with all of us ignoramuses. The moment all the papers ran with, of course, was the exchange she had with the congressperson from Arkansas, where he told her she seemed like something cooked up in one of Jim Henson's Workshops, and she replied that if that were the case, she was owed backpay on some royalty checks. And everyone in the room laughed, and the congressperson's cheeks went red as a clown's nose, and that moment drove the news cycle for a couple days.

That's another phrase I learned: "news cycle."

At this point, with Roxie well known and on the covers of magazines and being cast in soda commercials and such, you'd think she got too good for me and moved on. But she didn't. I almost wished she had. But she was just as good and loyal as ever. It got annoying, I almost got to hating her for it. Like her sticking around and being so decent to me was simply meant to highlight my own inadequacies or something. I don't know. Jesus. She was just always so patient. And thoughtful and unjudgmental in her views. Both before and after she talked.

What creature stays pure even when they get this miserable little gift called speech given to them?

She spent the rest of her life with me. Taking interviews over the phone, regular trips to Hollywood. Visited the Dalai Lama once. I came with her. The man smelled like cardamom. He was double jointed. That's something else I learned: The Dalai Lama is capable of bending his thumb so far back it can goddamn near touch his wrist. Roxie got a real kick out of that, wagging her tail and standing up on her hind legs, nudging him with her snout to do it over and over again.

When Roxie trotted out back to take a leak, I took a moment to ask His Holiness what this particular miracle proved to him. He seemed confused by the question.

I've just never been good with people. Not like Roxie. Even when she passed away, her paw in my hand, hooked up to machines, she looked at me like I was something of value, which I most certainly am not. But when I was around her she made me believe certain impossible things were possible, if just temporarily. Here today, gone tomorrow.

There I go, using clichés. Roxie never used clichés.

Justin Taroli

No Groups This Week—Please Check Back in August

The letter said "coverage termination," but it didn't say for how long or who I was supposed to call to make it go back. Just a list of steps. Step One was to go online. Step Two was to make a new account, even if you already had one. Step Three was to upload documents. I didn't know what kind of documents. I tried my school ID, but it's from two years ago and has a sticker over my face because someone in homeroom thought that was funny. I peeled it off, but the sticky part stayed.

Miss Carla used to help me with this stuff. She had a folder with all my papers in it, one of those thick blue ones with the little string closures, like you see in court shows. She said she was a "coordinator." She also said, "Don't call me Miss" because it made her feel old. But then she left. Her emails started bouncing, and the guy on the helpline said she doesn't work in this region anymore. They call it a "region," like it's a battle map.

My mom doesn't know what to do, either. She's got her own letter that says she makes too much money now, even though she still works at the checkout lane in the same store and we still have the same broken microwave. She said not to worry, she'd figure it out, and then she cried in the bathroom for forty-two minutes. I counted. I didn't tell her I was standing outside the door, because that makes her feel weird, but I didn't want her to be alone.

I'm supposed to see Dr. Mather next week for my regular. He writes things down during our visits—mostly stuff I say—and asks questions like "Do you feel safe at home?" which always makes me feel like I'm saying the wrong thing even when I'm not. He once said I had an "excellent internal vocabulary." I wrote that on my shoe in Sharpie so I wouldn't forget. It's still there, under the dried gum.

I didn't tell Dr. Mather about the letter. I thought maybe if I didn't say anything, he'd still see me. I even picked out a shirt that wasn't stained, one with the little dinosaur patch on the chest. I used to think it was a raptor, but I looked it up and it's a compsognathus, which is smaller and not as scary. That felt more right.

The clinic is three bus stops away, plus a little walk past the car wash that plays loud salsa music even when nobody's there. I like that part. The walk. It gives me time to think about what I'll say. I always rehearse things in my head—how to sit, when to smile, which answers sound normal but still true. It's hard to do both.

When I got there, the front-desk lady with the big silver earrings looked at her screen and said, "Oh ... hmm. Looks like there's been a lapse." I told her I didn't fall or anything, but she didn't laugh. She said the appointment couldn't happen without insurance, unless I wanted to pay out of pocket. I don't know where the out-of-pocket money comes from. Maybe there's a pocket somewhere in the building and you put a dollar in and get a doctor back. I tried asking, but she was already calling the next person.

I sat in the lobby for a while anyway, just in case someone changed their mind. They didn't. I watched the fish in the tank and counted how many times they circled the plastic castle. Fourteen. Then I walked home.

That night, Mom made macaroni with ketchup and didn't talk much. She had a Band-Aid on her thumb from opening a box wrong. I asked if she wanted help doing the online portal-thing, and she said she tried it already but the page kept timing out. She said "timing out" like it meant something bad, like the whole world is just trying to time us out right now. I didn't say anything. I just stirred my macaroni until it turned pink.

Later, I sat on the floor and made a list of things I used to do that I'm not sure I can do anymore:

- Call Dr. Mather.
- Get new shoes from that place where they measure your feet.
- The library tutoring thing on Wednesdays.
- Go to the thing with the gym mats and beanbags (Group C, with Aisha and that one guy who always forgets his name).
- Miss Carla.

I tried calling the number again the next morning. The woman's voice was different but still wrong. She said there's "nothing to be done until the next cycle." I asked when that was, and she said they couldn't say exactly. Then she asked if I had a "support system in place." I told her I have a mom and a dog named Lasagna who eats paper towels. She said okay and hung up.

Sometimes, I wonder if they do that on purpose—make it hard, I mean. If you make something too hard, most people will stop trying. Not because they're lazy but because they get tired. There's a difference. I get tired, too.

I still went to Group C the next Wednesday. I figured maybe if I just showed up and didn't say anything, nobody would notice. Sometimes, if you act like everything is normal, people believe you. It's something I learned from TV.

The beanbag room is in the back of the rec center, behind the glass doors that never close all the way. The carpet always smells a little like wet socks. Aisha was there already, stacking those foam blocks into a pyramid. She's good at eye contact, which is something I'm still practicing. She smiled at me and said, "Hey, you weren't here last week." I didn't know what to say, so I just said, "Neither were you." Which is true.

We were about to start, when the man with the clipboard—Matt, I think, or maybe Mitch—walked over and crouched next to me like I was sitting in a tree or something. He said, "Hey, buddy, I think there's been a change in your service eligibility." He smiled like it was a joke, but it wasn't. "Did your mom get a call? Or a letter?" I told him we got both.

He nodded like that solved it. "Okay, so, unfortunately, we can't let you stay today. Not until everything gets sorted out." I said I was already here. I said Aisha already saw me. I said I didn't even use the beanbags yet. He looked sorry but not sorry enough to let me stay. I asked if I could just sit on the side—no participation, just observation. He said he'd get in trouble. Then he gave me a coupon for a smoothie place I don't even like. The smoothie place smells like vitamins, and the straws are paper.

I walked home slower than usual. I tried not to cry, because I was wearing a hoodie and the tears get caught in the lining. When I opened the door, Mom was on the phone, pacing in little ovals around the coffee table. She didn't see me. She was saying, "I work forty-eight hours a week, and we're still barely scraping by," and then,

"He's not some number on your goddamn spreadsheet." Her voice cracked a little, and I thought, If I walk into the kitchen right now, she'll stop talking. She always does that—like her words are secret. So, I stood there, behind the door, and listened to my mom beg.

She said, "You can't just take things away from people who need them. He didn't do anything wrong." The person on the other end must've said something stupid, because she repeated it like she couldn't believe it. "Insufficient documentation? You've had our documentation since he was ten." Then quieter: "No, he doesn't have a caseworker anymore. You people keep leaving."

She hung up without saying goodbye. She just stood there, staring at the plastic fern in the corner, like maybe it would turn into something else if she looked hard enough. I walked into the kitchen and opened the fridge so she'd hear it and know I was there. She said, "Hey, baby," without turning around.

I ate some string cheese and pretended not to notice anything.

The bus was late, which wasn't unusual, but it still felt rude. The schedule taped to the side of the shelter had been peeled back by weather or fingers—only the word "Sunday" was still visible, and today was Thursday. Or maybe Friday. I wasn't positive. My phone said Thursday, but sometimes it gets confused if I don't plug it in all the way.

A man in a neon vest stood a few feet away, staring into a crumpled paper bag. He looked like someone who had places to be but didn't believe in being on time. A girl with bright red headphones scrolled fast on her phone, her thumbs twitching like bugs. Nobody was talking.

I sat on the metal bench with my legs crossed the way Miss Carla used to say not to because it looked uncomfortable. She never understood that uncomfortable is sometimes better than nothing. Uncomfortable is still a feeling. Nothing is just blank.

The ad on the bench back was for something called "ClearWay." A big smiling family in beige shirts. The words said: "Find Clarity, Find Care, Find Freedom." I stared at the dad's face. His eyes were shiny like he'd never once used a microwave without the turntable. I wanted to draw a mustache on him with my key, but I didn't.

The bus showed up in a rush like it was embarrassed. I didn't get on. I let it open and hiss and wait, then I shook my head at the driver and waved him past. He didn't care. He barely looked. The doors folded shut and the bus groaned forward, leaving a gust of warm engine breath behind.

I stayed on the bench. I wasn't really waiting for the bus. I just wanted to sit in a place where people went places. To pretend. I had my ID in my pocket, the one with the sticker damage, and the appointment card from Dr. Mather's office even though they wouldn't let me see him. I kept them both folded together in a little square like a secret badge. Like proof that I existed somewhere on paper.

A bee landed on my knee and stayed there. It didn't sting me. It just sat like it needed a break. We were two living things in the wrong place. I told it, "You can stay if you want. I won't tell." And I meant it.

On the walk home, I passed a lawn sign that said, "We Support Our Essential Workers." It was old, faded from the sun, half tipped in the dirt like the ground didn't believe it anymore. I stopped and stared at it for a long time, not because it meant anything but because I wanted it to. Sometimes, I look at signs and pretend they're speaking to me, like God used to do in the Bible. If that's blasphemy, I don't care. It helps.

I thought about the lady on the phone, the one who asked if I had a "support system in place." She said it like a checklist item. Like: oxygen? Check. Blood? Check. Support system? Check. But nobody ever asked me if the system was worth supporting. Or if it ever supported me back. The truth is, it's like trying to sit in a chair that isn't really there. You fall slowly at first and then all at once.

I don't think Mom knows how tired she is. I don't think she lets herself know. She keeps pressing her face into the world like it's something soft when it's not. Sometimes, I want to tell her she can stop. That it's okay to say, "This isn't working." But I think she thinks that would make her a bad mom. It wouldn't. It would just make her.

When I got home, the kitchen light was off, and Lasagna was asleep under the table, with one paw on an empty bag of shredded cheese. I didn't turn on any lights. I went straight to my room, took off my shoes, and sat on the floor.

This is what I do when I can't make sense of anything: I line up my coins. Pennies first, then nickels, then dimes. Not for the value, but for the sound they make when I tap them on the baseboard. Pennies have the softest sound. Nickels are more serious. Dimes are sharp. It's like music for the part of my brain that doesn't like music.

I tapped each one three times and then made them into little rows. It's not magic, but it helps. It makes something straight in a day that was crooked. I made a pattern that looked like a ladder. Then I closed my eyes and imagined what it would feel like to climb it, rung by rung, out of the mess, into somewhere clean.

When I opened my eyes, one of the dimes had rolled away and fallen under my dresser. I didn't reach for it. I just left it there. Some things are better off missing.

The next morning, I woke up before my alarm. I didn't sleep much. The inside of my head felt like the back of a junk drawer—too many pieces, nothing that fits. I opened the blinds halfway so the light came in soft. There was a crow on the telephone wire, wobbling like it couldn't decide if it trusted the wire or not. I watched it for ten minutes. It never flew away.

I found the old laminated badge they gave me at the rec center. It just says "C Group—Peer Support Learner" in bold letters, like that meant something. I clipped it to my shirt even though I wasn't going anywhere yet. I sat with it on like armor. After a while, I packed a bag with a few things—my appointment card, the old flyer about HCBS services (even though I don't know what half the letters mean), a granola bar that expired last April.

Mom was still asleep. She works late now—stocking shelves, I think, or maybe she's moved to the register again. She doesn't say. Her shoes are always by the heater, pointed like they're trying to walk off without her.

I left a note that said: "I'm okay. Just trying something. Will text."

It took me a long time to write "just trying something." I kept starting and crossing it out. I didn't want it to sound like a threat or a lie. Just the truth.

I walked back to the clinic. Not because I had an appointment. Not even because I thought they'd let me in. I just wanted to sit there. To be where people are getting care. To remind myself I used to be part of that.

The same woman was at the front desk. She didn't look up at first, then she did. Her eyes narrowed a little, like maybe she was trying to remember if I was trouble. I gave her a small wave. She didn't wave back, but she didn't tell me to leave either.

I sat in the corner by the water cooler. A new stack of brochures had been added to the table. One was about suicide. One had a smiling boy on a scooter with the words "Live Independently, Live Fully." I wondered if they paid the boy or just took the picture when he wasn't looking.

I sat there for forty-three minutes.

Nobody said anything.

I was about to get up—about to call it a failed experiment—when the janitor walked by. He was pushing the big gray bin with all the clunky wheels. He looked tired but not sad. I'd seen him here once before, humming something that sounded like an old cartoon theme. I liked that about him. You don't hum if you don't believe in things a little.

He paused and looked at me—not in a scared way or a pity way. Just ... looked.

He said, "You here for someone?"

I shook my head.

He nodded like that made sense.

Then he said, "Well, you can sit here as long as you want. It's warm in here."

And that was it. He kept moving. The cart clattered against the tile. But he saw me. Not as a problem. Not as paperwork. Just a person sitting in a chair.

I didn't cry, but my throat got tight. Like a door had been opened and slammed again too quickly.

I stayed another hour.

When I got home, Mom was sitting at the kitchen table, holding a piece of paper like it was something fragile. Her eyes looked watery, but she wasn't crying yet. Not really. The table was still sticky from breakfast. Lasagna had shredded a napkin in the corner.

She said, "They're shutting down the rec center."

I sat down across from her. She pushed the paper toward me, like it needed to be seen by more than one person to be real:

"Effective July 31, the Community Wellness Initiative will cease in-person group operations due to lack of sustained funding."

That was Group C. That was the beanbag room. That was Mitch-or-Matt and Aisha and the noise-canceling headphones and the bright paper bins labeled "Go Slow" and "Try Again." Gone.

"They said we could look for a replacement program through the website," Mom said. "But it's the same site that never loads."

I didn't say anything.

She rubbed her eyes and said, "I'm trying. I know it doesn't look like it. But I am."

I nodded. Not because I doubted her. Just because I was afraid if I opened my mouth, something would come out that sounded too big.

I stood up and went to my room. I didn't line up my coins this time. I didn't need order. What I needed was change.

I opened the drawer under my bed—the one with the weird mix of things: expired bus passes, a drawing Aisha made of me as a penguin, a broken flashlight, an envelope labeled "FOR LATER." I pulled out the coins and scattered them across the floor. Let them roll.

I took a piece of paper and wrote three words on it: STILL HERE. STILL.

I folded it into a triangle and taped it to the wall by the light switch. Not as a threat. Not as a prayer. Just as proof.

Then I found my marker and went back to the ID badge from the rec center—the one that said "Peer Support Learner." I crossed out "Learner" and wrote "person" in capital letters underneath.

Peer Support PERSON.

It looked dumb, but it looked true.

After Mom went to bed, the apartment got so quiet I could hear the hum of the refrigerator from across the hall. It sounded like a thought trying not to be heard.

I lay on top of the blanket, not under it. I didn't want weight. I just wanted air. My phone buzzed once. I thought it was an alarm at first, or a reminder I forgot to set, but it was a text:

Aisha: Hey. Did you hear about the center?

I stared at the screen for a minute before replying.

Me: Yeah. We got the paper.

She didn't write back right away. I pictured her on the floor of her room, probably with her electric blanket even though it's warm out, her hair braided and unbraided in half sections, like always. When the phone rang, I picked it up on the second buzz.

"Hi," she said. Her voice was soft but not sad. Just real.

"Hi."

We didn't say anything for a while.

"They said we can go to a different group," she said eventually. "But it's farther away. And it's mostly adults."

"I don't care about that," I said.

"Me, neither. Just, the bus makes me dizzy."

I smiled. "You always sit sideways."

"You're not supposed to *face* the window," she said. "It's not a fish tank."

"It kind of is."

She laughed. It wasn't a big laugh. Just a breath, shaped like something better.

"Do you think," she asked, "if we show up anyway, they'll let us sit in the room? Even if it's empty?"

"Maybe," I said. "If we're quiet."

"I can be quiet."

"I can try."

We didn't say goodbye. Just listened to the line until it didn't need to carry anything else. Then I put the phone down and stared at the ceiling for a long time. I didn't fall asleep, but I didn't need to.

Three days later, we went.

We didn't tell anyone. Not our moms, not the guy at the front desk, not whatever office was supposed to be in charge now. We just texted in the morning—no punctuation, just "you coming" and "yeah."

The rec-center doors weren't locked, even though the flyer said programming was suspended. A paper sign was taped to the glass: "No Groups This Week—Please Check Back in August." August was too far. We went in anyway.

The lights in the hallway were half off. The air smelled like old rubber and dust. Someone had unplugged the coffee machine. The bin of fidget toys was still there, half spilled. The beanbag room was open. Nobody had cleared it out yet. It was like the end of a party that never really started.

We sat down without asking. Aisha picked the blue beanbag with the rip in the side. I took the one that always sagged a little too much in the middle. It remembered me.

We didn't talk at first. Just sat. The floor was quiet. Outside, someone was mowing grass too short and too dry.

She pulled a small carton of chocolate milk out of her bag and offered me one. I didn't ask where she got it. I said thanks. We drank them slowly, like we were trying to make the moment last longer than it wanted to.

"This still counts," she said.

I nodded. "It does to me."

She leaned back and stared at the ceiling tiles. "I'm gonna keep coming here until they kick me out."

"Same," I said.

And we sat there. Not learning, not improving, not being assessed or documented or "supported." Just being. Two people in a room no one thought would matter. Two people not waiting to be let in. Already inside.

Ruiyan Zhu

Late Summer

Curved asphalt. Meadow shoulder. Split Grass. Late summer. Splintered wood. Sweet rot. Inside out. Torn sky. Open meadow. Open sky. Crowned cranberries. Glistening bait. Wheeling Toyota. Fallen body. Compass needles. Four directions. What's gone? Hind legs. Vacant nest. Eggs yesterday. Mate yesterday. Warped metal. Soft underbrush. Ticklish berries. Red confetti. Torn flag. Head buried. Tail flat. Legs pitched. Face curled. Outrun survival. Freed sinews. Elbows bent. Bone split. Road edge. Gravel starts. Stitching sky. Body rests. Tomorrow's sun. Scattered berries. Curved asphalt. Meadow shoulder. What's gone? What's gone?

Liz Ahl

Apps

Well before sunrise, a nonstop cacophony
of birds rousts me from shallow sleep,
especially the one song barreling around
in the foreground of the wall of sound,
the hook of the ruckus that snags me—

so, lying there in the still-dark
I download the app that promises
it knows by heart the songs of all birds,
this app nestled now next to the app
that tracks air quality, and the one
that knows the stars, and the one
that pings me if there's a chance
at visible aurora borealis—

and I hit record, then wait for the algorithms
to digest and translate what I can only see
as a scrolling of grey waveforms,
an audio augury of peaks and valleys.

Swainson's thrush is the pre-dawn diva
demanding my attention and adoration
with its *flute-like, ascending spiral.*
Why do I hear the song more clearly
when the singer has been named?

It *breeds in the boreal forest,*
as in *borealis*, as in northern, as in
this spring's grand lightshow of auroras
I slept through, hence the aurora app,
added after the fact to the basket of apps,
each one an egg I have added in spite
of a voice that suggests I do otherwise.

Tomorrow morning the wind
rollercoasting down from the Olympics
and across the fjord as promised by the weather app
will have blown these birds and their songs
elsewhere—and I'll sleep until woken by sun
and by the rhythms of the distant whitecaps
and by this other song: I'll hit record,
wait for the app to help me discern the name
of that particular wind by listening to it
whistle through the trees.

Liz Ahl

Seeing Red

For the second time this week, I've seen
4:41 a.m., the clock's ruby numerals glow
in night so deep it's nearly morning.

If I rose and pulled the curtains, I'd see
a matching shade of red beginning
its slow seep to sunrise beyond the trees.

If instead, I turn away from this red hour,
I might retreat to the dark rooms of sleep,
though even there, a pulsing red awaits:

the very thing that woke me:
a worry's embers, fear's old mercury rising
in the thermometer's glass throat.

Or it's the Mars in me, volcanic rage,
the creeping magma of some anger besting me,
even in sleep. Or something like sleep.

Restless, half-in, half-out, I could choose
one path or other—close my eyes or keep
them open; not a real choice. Red or red.

Devan Murphy

My Church

My legs are covered not with hair but sticks; they *tum-tum* hollowly when I walk, like wooden wind chimes. A tiny chapel made of wood is nestled in between my thighs from birth; the tiny bell dongs when I walk. I walk slowly to keep quiet. I spend much of my time alone in the forest. In the forest everything sounds like *tum-tum-tum-tum-tum-tum-tum-tum*.

Devan Murphy

The Tongue

I've finally hooked a fish but she begs to be set free, or kissed. Swinging back and forth on the line, she says:

> *I am a witch. I slit the tongue of this fish and ate it, and then I shrank and took the tongue's place. Now I speak for the fish. I hid behind these lips for weeks to escape my enemies, but when I wanted to get free again I discovered I couldn't reverse the magic without a kiss from a beautiful woman. Kiss me, or at least set me free so I can swim away.*

"How do I know you're telling the truth?" I say. "Look in my mouth and see," she says. I look inside the fish's mouth and sure enough there is a tiny woman glued to the spot where the tongue should be. I can't tell if she is pretty or ugly but I give the fish a peck on the cheek. "No," she says, "kiss the lips, and use your tongue." "I don't want to." "Then I will be a fish forever," she says forlornly. I sigh and remove the hook from the fish's lip and pucker up. I kiss the fish on the lips and slip my tongue inside the fish's mouth and lick the little woman. I feel her tiny tongue lick me back. The sensation is oddly pleasurable, and I kiss the fish for a long time. I begin to think I may be in love, maybe with the fish, or with the witch, or with kissing. The hour passes. The sky becomes orange. I begin to realize no magic is happening, the witch is still a tongue, she has not grown. At last I draw back from the fish and say, "Why has nothing happened?" "Wait, just wait," the fish says. We both wait for several long minutes. The fish stares at me. Its eyes are very human. I wonder if they were that way before the witch took control of the tongue. Now the sun has died. I can no longer see the fish or its human eyes. "Just wait," says a voice in the darkness.

R. Allen Abshire

Butterfly Sausage

I asked the American girl for a third date so she can help me catch butterflies for sausage. I picked her up in my white Korean SUV with Chinese bamboo nets cluttering the back. She shimmied in a sundress decorated like the Japanese flag. We searched through the backs of beaches near My Lai and captured or killed 347 ruby and sapphire-spotted lepidoptera. I plucked the liquor-puckered moths from the sack and her eyes asked why. No good eating, I said, and my smile manufactured in her a laugh that made the butterflies dance.

When there were enough in my collection pouches that the desperate, beating wings lifted the cloth to a near-steady hover, I let her drive, since she was nervous about how many Dutch beers I had impaled and ravaged. I watched her eyes from the side of my sun-scorched mug and I couldn't wait to feed her.

In my work room I smoked a hand-rolled spike of Virginia rough-cut lung duster. She called someone avuncular with her antediluvian Finn-phone. The wind rustled the wobbly plastic antenna so that she kept needing to unlace her hair from it. What's for dinner, she asked, and I reminded her the purpose of our entomological escapade: butterfly sausage.

I removed the long poster board containers and dragged out a big sheet of what she mistook for a map of South Africa. This'll be the casings, I proffered, all organic and approved with high marks by several Thai culinary academies. I fed the slippery hose nose from my meat grinder into a vaguely-slick length of edible plastic. That was where she shuddered, right when she hung up and told me her brother had been arrested for his preaching in Cambodia. She let the phone carry some distance down the length of her torso and the joint of her elbow snapped it back at an odd angle.

Her face was rouged and her mouth hung twitching in a convulsive sine curve. Her eyes grew when I took the collection purses and fired up the rented Canadian government meat grinder, its coggy metal wheel spanning only six inches. I removed my satin gloves like a duchess in a British black-and-white period piece. I selected a fine crater-speckled Eye of God butterfly and held it closely for inspection. She let out a gasp as I fed it to the humming wheel.

Her voice fell out of sync with her lips then the vocalizations, after a syncope, whistled in Brazilian Portuguese. My blank eyes met and held hers, as I tickled more half-dead insects into the grinder.

She knew it was one of the few tongues I hadn't mastered, so I couldn't understand.

Her exhalations were semi-understandable gibberish that I convinced myself was banal. I shoved more butterflies into the blades and they stopped spinning. The red light on the control panel grew verdant and ripe for plucking. She saw me lick my upper lip and pat my tummy but she didn't smile. I depressed the switch and the casing filled up slowly like a birthday-clown animal balloon.

There was a thud and I saw she was no longer whispering but had dropped the heavy cell. She approached and nearly retched. I asked again what happened, what the voice on the call had said. She said I had to stop and I apologized, clarified I was being too nosy, that was fine. I didn't mind when people kept things to themselves. I always did the same, in an odd day-to-day or hourly oscillation into the roles required by employer, family, government, strangers, and cotton candy spinners at the volunteer church fair. The casing grew as the ground-up cache emptied and the light metamorphosed to red again.

I twisted and knotted the long end and she stood, staccato notes gurgling out like a curse or some kind of transcendental prayer.

I clipped the link of warm pink sausage. She said, what have you done, holding her arms akimbo. I knotted the long tube into several small butterfly sausages. I convinced her to close her eyes and I draped the sausage around her neck and placed my hands on her upper arms.

I tilted down to her and she held her breath for a long time.

I asked, after her lungs re-inflated, did she feel it, did she know what she could do?

She opened her eyes, looked at me, and began, ever-so-slightly, to float.

Chella Courington

The Sand Mountain Poultry Plant

I spend eight to twelve hours on greasy cement killing chickens. Sometimes day shift, sometimes night shift. The killing never stops. But I don't kill them with my hands like Grandma who swings the bird 'round till the neck pops. No, I stand at my machine, in bloody whites wearing a hairnet. Splattering blood every five seconds, my machine chops off the head. Fresh blood that tastes salty and sweet. It bothers me at first, but the pay's good.

What disgusts me is the line chief. A six-foot-two asshole named Walter ("Don't call me Walt") Johnston Bragg III. His fancy name can't save that redneck sack of shit. I'm poor, probably poorer than Walter, still I have manners and treat people like I want to be treated. With respect and common decency.

Shortly after I start working the line, Walter says he's kin to General Bragg who fought for the Confederacy and has an army fort named for him. I look the general up in the library and find out he's awful. I tell a few line ladies and one of them probably tells Walter because that's when he starts in on me.

During break one day, he says he knows when a girl's on the rag. Claims he can smell her. A week later, he tells me he broke up with his last girlfriend cause she bled too much. "I can't trust any of God's creatures that bleed that much and don't die." He makes me feel dirty. That night I scrub myself with my bath brush so hard the water turns pink. At the end of the shift the next day, he follows me out to the car. Says he dreams of me. Likes to taste me in his sleep.

I don't tell him my dream where the hook curls through the back of his head and his blood floods the floor, but I tell Charlene who works the line beside me. He did the same to her. And Nancy. And Meg. But it was worse for Babs. He came up behind her, wrapped his arm across her breasts, and shoved his hand down her jeans and inside her panties. When he pulled out his hand, two fingers were red. He sniffed them and said, "I told you so."

It's not like we killed him. Though we cut him up pretty good.

Brett Hymel, Jr.

Finger Food

When I was pulled from my grave and reanimated by Carl, necromancer and back-of-house manager at the Lenox Avenue Chili's, I was grateful for another shot. The modern age was full of wonders: discount margaritas, the Marvel Cinematic Universe, unlimited Internet pornography. My heart exploded in the seventies; I had missed half a century of innovation. So yes, I worked sixty-five hours a week and lived in a tin shed Carl had built behind his own ramshackle shit-fiesta of a peeling plaster bungalow, but this seemed a small price to pay for extra years. Being dead wasn't terrible, but it was kind of beyond human comprehension. The closest I could get to describing it would be soft, round words that shimmer in your ear: *Bourbon, human, absolution.*

Me and about seven other guys Carl had dug up hung out in the kitchen, reheating frozen mozzarella sticks for Triple Dippers all day long. "Don't you want to hear about *human*?" we'd ask Carl. "Don't you want to know about *absolution*?" and he'd go, "Tell me about *no tickets in the queue* and then we'll talk about what happens after."

The Chili's had that glow—you know. Walls the deep burgundy color of blood, dim elegance approximated by the faux Tiffany lamps at each booth, and the sizzle-sweet scent of fajitas wafting through the air. It was a ruse, those fajitas. We had a water bottle that we sprayed on the metal plate to create the steam. Maybe people didn't care—discount margaritas discredit reality, I guess.

We were zombified, shambling corpses. You've got to remember, some of us had been dead forty, fifty years by now, so yeah, there were some fingers, some earlobes falling into dishes. We couldn't catch them all. We'd crouch behind the swinging door, gray eyes in the porthole as some poor schmuck uncovered Mike's index in his Caesar salad.

"Excuse me, ma'am," the schmuck would say, "I think there's a finger in my Caesar salad." Waitress, Tess—it was always Tess—would roll her eyes and go, "Yeah, sir, this is fast-casual Tex-Mex chain Chili's. You're going to get a body part or two in your meal."

"I'll just eat around it, then," the schmuck would mutter, embarrassed for making a fuss. We doubled over behind the porthole, laughing about finger food.

Yeah, I watched a lot of Internet pornography, but I also found out what happened to the world. We lost the Vietnam war—minor bummer, no surprise. Reagan won in '80—major bummer, no surprise. My wife lived until ninety. She died last year. She remarried after me; that was surprising. I didn't meet her in the afterlife. Personhood doesn't really exist beyond the body. How do I explain it? *Beneficence.*

My nose fell off in the Bloomin' Onion and the scent of fajitas faded, and with that, some of the world-magic. I didn't know what I was doing here. I was tired. "Mah nobe," I said, and Carl said, "It's not a Bloomin' Onion, they're Awesome Blossom Petals, do you want me to flip my lid completely?"

ICE came and raided our Chili's and Carl snuck us out the back door. "Why are we sneaking out?" we asked, "We were born here. We were here before you were. Our ancestry sings through the empty air of these graveyards, our blood feeds the soil."

"No papers, they ship you out," Carl said.

"Ship you out where?" we asked. "Where would we even go?" but Carl just shook his head, like it was too much to say.

After the magic left, we remembered how much of it was sweat for someone else. All day long we would labor, leave our bodies in the meals, return to our tin shacks too tired to shampoo our rotting, fetid hair. Yeah, we watched a lot of Internet pornography, but we also YouTube'd a political education. We came to realize that maybe we were the grease that kept the wheels turning and not just some big inconvenience to Carl's pasty ass, so we stopped him early one morning and said, "Look Carl, us zombies are thinking of starting a union." He didn't say anything, just grabbed a knife and cut himself real long in the palm, right along the lifeline, red blood miming a frown.

He tilted his head back, said some "Lorem ipsum dolor" type shit, and we all disintegrated, turned to dust right there in the Chili's back-of-house.

I wanted to tell him something, wanted to say, "Really, dude? This is the world you've created? One in which you'd kill us before you'd offer us even the faintest shred of kindness?" but you don't ever get the last word when you die. All you get is *beeswax, fusion, circumlocution.*

JI Daniels

Macarons at the End of the Party

I do not know where to begin, so I will start at the end.

Like most introverts, I love people. I just find them stressful and would rather spend my time alone. Some people are surprised by this: I'm alright in public, I teach at a university and stand in front of my students delivering lectures, answering questions, engaging in dialog and debate. I go to parties with my peers, and I chat amiably with the people there. The introverts know that this comes at a cost, that I feel myself coming apart, like I am a ball of string that can only be whole at home. To be away requires spooling myself, an act of love that feels like a literal unravelling. When I am away, and diminishing, I think longingly of my bed and of my computer and of my study that holds my books, and of not having to make small talk with a single other person. As I edit this chapter, I am visiting my in-laws with my wife, but despite the presence of my body, I am really away from them, huddled into myself, on the computer, typing words, deleting others.

This is the hard part of living for people like me. We love people too much to stay where we are happiest. We want to be connected, and to share moments, and to laugh and to give laughter to the people we care about. Just because I have difficulty with the stress of these interactions doesn't mean that I don't benefit from them. Just because this makes me feel uncertain about myself and the people around me, doesn't mean that I'm not willing to try. Even on this trip, I will put away the work, and I will come upstairs and mingle with my wife's family because I have chosen to make them my family too.

This is how an introvert ends up as the last person at the party.

In a food processor, pulse 110 grams almond flour, 155 grams confectioner's sugar, and the zest of one lemon until it comes to a fine powder. Sift this a few times, and discard any big clumps. Oh, and draw some one-and-a-half inch circles on parchment paper that fits on two baking trays.

In your electric mixer's bowl, add ninety grams of egg whites (around three eggs' worth, but weigh it carefully), fifty-five grams granulated sugar, and a quarter teaspoon cream of tartar, and mix together with a whisk attachment on low speed, slowly increase the speed to medium-high until stiff peaks begin to form, around five to seven minutes.

I'm not always the last one, but it's too often the case. If you can get me to a party, the hard part is done. I will bring something tasty and bask in the kind words of people that try it. I will find a person I know and corner them. I've been practicing, I've studied up on interesting topics, I'm ready for this.

When you have stiff peaks, add in one to two drops of yellow food coloring and ¼ tsp lemon extract. Whisk to combine for another minute. Then add the dry ingredients to the meringue and fold it in with your spatula. Don't whisk it, but scrape down the sides into the middle, raise, and then back out to the edges, pressing the mixture to the side of the bowl. Do this twenty to thirty times, until the mixture is smooth and shiny, and when you drop a small spoon sized dab of the mixture, it will hold a peak for a second before relaxing back into the batter. Scoop the mixture into a pastry bag with a large circular tip and pipe into the one-and-a-half inch circles on the parchment. When you are done, smack the trays on the counter to remove any bubbles in the batter. Let this sit on the counter for half an hour. Preheat your oven to 300 degrees.

I pour myself a drink and really get to chatting. We discuss our recent lives and the things that are driving us. At some point I manage to work *Anna Karenina* into the conversation, though I swear I will stop doing that at some point. Someone else comes over and the conversations continue. I refill my drink and offer some to other people. We move onto the politics of work, the politics of the country. The group disbands, and I get some food and another drink. I find someone else and catch up, and soon there is a small group of people huddled together, talking about nothing. There are jokes.

Julius Caesar goes to the bartender, holds up two fingers and says, Five beers, please. Someone brings up how sad they were when they learned that the Vesuvius masturbating guy wasn't really captured in the throes of self-pleasure. Someone hands around their phone with dogs on Instagram eating carrots, captioned with the text, "cronchy" every time they bite down, and this consumes us for some time.

Your macarons should have a skin on them by now and will have settled. If so, it's time to bake them for fifteen, twenty minutes, until the shells harden. Rotate the macarons halfway through, just as you would rotate through people at a party. Let the shells cool completely.

There are more drinks, of course. Eventually, you and I are sitting together on a couch somewhere, really connecting. This is why I am here. I like jokes and drinks and snacking food, but I really crave that moment when I can sit and really get to know you. When there has been enough bullshitting and substance intake for us to let down our guard and really connect. When I am looking in your eyes and listening to your heart, I can forget about what the President has done, or what some legislature is up to, or the latest exploits of billionaires seeking validation. I can pretend that the world is not coming down around our ears while we scream into the void for distraction. I am whole, connecting, I am tied to you, and you are tied to me. I want to hear about your struggle, and I will tell you something of mine. I want to tell you how much I love you, and how important you are to me, and the only way to do it is in this moment, disarmed, a little drunk, and obviously way too careless. Somehow, it is two in the morning, and I am blinking my eyes at the clock, not even realizing we had passed into the next day.

Time for the filling. You can make a lemon buttercream for this, but I prefer a curd. It's not quite as sweet, and it packs more flavor. Cream three teaspoons room-temperature butter in an electric mixer, and then slowly add three tablespoons lemon zest and a third cup sugar. Mix until light and fluffy, just a few minutes. Add two eggs, one at a time until fully mixed, then one-eighth teaspoon salt and one-quarter cup lemon juice. Pour this into a small pot and cook over medium low, stirring constantly with a silicone spatula until it becomes a thick, creamy, luscious curd. You're going to keep stirring until it comes to 170 degrees, never boiling, and when it does, immediately take off the stove and pour into a heat proof bowl. Let this cool completely in the fridge.

Nearly there. Now we are down to the last handful of people. Five of us or so. I should probably go, but much of the time, this small last group feels as intimate as a one-on-one conversation. We are truly meeting each other in this space. Where it might feel like too much of a burden to confess something to a single person, a tiny group of intimates feels safer. If one person does not understand what you are saying, someone else will. We work through our neuroses and our desires, and we let the veritas of vino speak through us. There is a community that is coming together here. We plan a hike that will never be realized, and a brunch that will be. We find common ground on a thorny issue.

Put a decent little dab of filling onto one macaron cookie, and then cover with another one. Voilà. These are light and crisp and airy and tart and sweet and perfection. They'll keep in an airtight container for a few days, but they rarely last long at all. This recipe doesn't even make two dozen, and your friends will eat them up. They may even forgive you if you linger.

And then the problem. People are leaving in earnest, because it is late and they are tired, and they don't want to burden the hosts. Sometimes it happens nearly invisibly until I am the only one left. I will help the host clean up, wanting to be useful and not recognizing this as a sign that the party is over. Or I will watch each leave-taking with jealousy, wondering how people can simply stand up, thank the host, and excuse themselves. I don't want the evening to end. I don't want to go back home. I don't want this connection to be severed even though I do want sleep.

This is the point where something happens. Good or bad, it cannot continue like this. Sometimes I can finally say my shaky goodbyes. Once, I made a friend: we drank peaty scotch all night and talked about books and games, and we lingered, and we bonded, and then it was more than a decade later. Once, a brilliant poet complimented me on the body I had sculpted to get into my costume, and she squeezed my arm with her hands. I made light of the compliment and told her it was all for show, and she told me that it was working. We were down to the last few people filtering out of the door, and I thought to myself, Hmm. Her partner was lying on the bed ten feet away, but I had the impression it might be more opportunity than problem. When the other last guest asked me if I wanted a ride home, I balked. Do I regret this? I still think about it, but the hour was late, and it is better not to complicate things with people you know. A lesson I have only ever partly learned. I took the ride. Another time at another party I got to wrangle the heroin addict back to his meager and depressing apartment and prop him on his side.

I do not know what I should do, is what I am saying. Sometimes I feel I have lingered too long, but then I keep getting invitations to stay. Sometimes it feels like the night is young and then I realize I am being ushered to the door. I do not know if my hosts are just waiting for me to kiss them or if they'd sooner I kiss their ass on my way out. I am only here because I love them, and I don't know what to do with myself. Still, I have managed to keep some friends. Still, I have managed to get an invitation now and then, and if I can pry myself from my basement computer, I will bring you these cookies, and I'll be there longer than you'd think.

Hayden Park

Symphony of Everything

The week before I turned eight, I learned the name for the noise.

Not the noise in my ears—that was just the sound of blood—but the noise in my head. A static that wasn't a sound, but a feeling, a texture. Like rubbing velvet the wrong way in the dark. A room full of televisions all on different channels, but with the volume off. Just the flicker. Just the relentless, strobing, silent chaos. The doctor used words, of course she did. A woman made of beige, her office the color of waiting. She said, Attention. Deficit. Hyperactivity. Disorder. The words were big and important. They had a weight to them, like stones in my pocket I was meant to carry. I was seven years, eleven months, and three weeks old. I had been climbing things. I had been forgetting things. I had been humming when silence was required. I was told that the brains of children and adolescents with ADHD are, on average, three to four percent smaller than the brains of children who don't have it. A fact I held onto. Not with sadness, but with a kind of secret pride. Something was different, quantifiably so. My brain was smaller, denser, maybe. A small, dark star, instead of a gas giant.

We can start here: a neurotransmitter. A chemical messenger. Dopamine. It is involved in mood, working memory, attention, decision-making. It helps regulate emotional responses and take action to achieve specific outcomes. Or, if you want it said plainer, it's the thing that lets you do the thing. The kick. The spark. In the ADHD brain, the dopamine pathways are, let's say, idiosyncratic. Disrupted. The transmission is faulty. The signal drops. Imagine you're trying to call God, but the reception is bad. Imagine you are trying to tell yourself, do the homework, but the message gets lost in transit, eaten by the static, and instead you are counting the number of books on your shelf, all 237 of them, and then you're looking up the history of the Dewey Decimal System, and then you are reading about Melvil Dewey's bizarre personal life, and then you are three hours deep down a rabbit hole that started with a single, simple command. *Do the homework.* The task is a cliff face. My brain has no rope.

But the piano is different. So is the violin. An eighty-eight key universe, a four-stringed cosmos. My fingers find the notes, the patterns, the logic. The music is a structure, a scaffold I can climb. When I play a Bach Fugue, the world makes sense. There are multiple lines, a conversation between hands, but my brain, this supposedly deficit brain, can hold all of them at once. The left hand a steady lament, the right a frantic, glittering reply. It's a kind of hyperfocus, they say. A symptom. But in this room, with this wood and these wires, it's a gift. My brain, that small dark star, lights up. The televisions in the room all switch to the same channel. I can sit for four hours, unmedicated, and trace the intricate architecture of the sound. I don't need to be told to focus. The music is the focus. It pulls me in. Gives the chaos a shape. A purpose.

Writing is the same. Here, on this page. The words are notes, the sentences are phrases. The noise doesn't stop, but it harmonizes. It becomes a kind of music itself, a strange, discordant symphony. I can follow it, I can lead it. I am the conductor of my own weird orchestra. It is the only time the conductor is not asleep at the podium. That's what executive function is, they say. The conductor of the brain's orchestra. My conductor is often on a smoke break. He's union, probably. Works only when the passion is high, the stakes beautiful, the project a burning house of my own design. He's not interested in taking out the trash, or remembering to email the teacher, or sitting still in a chair while someone speaks in beige.

It's the "H" in ADHD that got me, mostly. Hyperactivity. A word that tastes like trouble. Not the running and climbing that you think. It's not just external. There's an internal restlessness that doesn't have a body, no legs to tire it out. My mind paces. A caged animal in the zoo of my skull. It translates to other things. Including, but not limited to: An over-eager tongue. Blurting out an answer in class before the question is finished. Interrupting a conversation not out of arrogance but out of a desperate, panicked need to get the thought out before it dissolves, a sandcastle in a rising tide of other thoughts. You see the look on their face. The flicker of annoyance. The subtle re-angling of their body away from yours. You are too much. That's the feeling. You have spoken too loud. You have vibrated too fast. You have shared too much of the weird, obsessive thing you learned about last night. They say that in girls, the hyperactivity is often quieter, more hidden. They might fidget quietly, their minds wandering while they appear serene. I wasn't a quiet girl. My "H" was on the outside. It was in the constant, rhythmic tapping of my fingers on my desk, a silent drum solo only I could hear. It was in the way I had to stand up to do my homework, walking in circles around the dining room table, reading a history chapter in motion. Stillness was a kind of pain, a suit that was too tight. I'm learning, now, just how much society values a person who is the exact opposite of me. Who has mastered the art of pausing. Of behavioral nuances. Of listening without formulating a response. Of the calm, slow exchange of managed thoughts. My thoughts are not managed. They are a stampede. And my mouth is the gate, left swinging open. Their words are like candle smoke, dissolving as soon as it appears.

Here is a numbered list for you, a way to make order. A form I can follow.

DSM-5 diagnostic criteria for inattention. These are the bones of my childhood:

(a) Often fails to give close attention to details or makes careless mistakes in schoolwork, at work, or during other activities.
(b) Often has difficulty sustaining attention in tasks or play activities.
(c) Often does not seem to listen when spoken to directly.
(d) Often does not follow through on instructions and fails to finish schoolwork, chores, or duties in the workplace.
(e) Often has difficulty organizing tasks and activities.
(f) Often avoids, dislikes, or is reluctant to engage in tasks that require sustained mental effort.
(g) Often loses things necessary for tasks or activities.
(h) Is often easily distracted by extraneous stimuli.
(i) Is often forgetful in daily activities.

DSM-5 diagnostic criteria for hyperactivity:

(a) Often fidgets with hands or feet or squirms in seat.
(b) Often leaves seat in classroom or in other situations in which remaining seated is expected.

> *(c) Often runs about or climbs excessively in situations in which it is inappropriate.*
> *(d) Often has difficulty playing or engaging in leisure activities quietly.*
> *(e) Is often "on the go" or often acts as if "driven by a motor."*

This is not a biography. This is a clinical checklist. And yet, it is not even a checklist. For me, it is the most personal poem I have ever read.

One of the theories: It isn't a deficit of attention, but an inability to regulate it. A dysregulation. I can pay attention. I can pay so much attention to a single dead leaf on the pavement that the entire world falls away. I can spend six hours researching the migratory patterns of Arctic terns. The problem is, I can't choose what deserves the attention. The leaf is as loud as the lecture. The terns are as important as the taxes. The "selective visual attention system" has faulty wiring. I notice everything, all at once. The hum of the refrigerator. The tag in my shirt. The memory of a conversation from three years ago. The distant siren. The ache in my left pinky finger. It is a democracy of input, and all the candidates are screaming.

Emotional control. Part of the executive function suite. The ability to tolerate frustration. To think before acting or speaking. Imagine your emotions are a volume knob with no numbers, spinning freely. A small slight feels like a catastrophe. A moment of joy is a supernova. The frustration of not being able to start a task, of seeing the mess in my room and feeling a paralysis so profound it's like being encased in amber—this is not laziness. It is a kind of emotional drowning. A daily agony that looks, from the outside, like a character flaw. The world says, *Try harder.* The brain says, *I don't know how.* The shame that follows is a poison.

And then, the meds. A small white pill. I remember the first day; I was 14. I swallowed it with water and waited for a thunderclap. A change. An hour later, the world just … quieted. The televisions turned off. All of them. A silence so profound it was its own kind of noise. I could do the thing. The simple thing. I could sit down and do a page of math homework from start to finish. And I cried. I didn't know why at the time. I was just a kid. But I think I was crying for the version of me that had been trying so hard, swimming against a current I didn't know was there. I was crying with relief. But now, at seventeen, the quiet feels different. Sometimes it feels like a smoothing out, a sanding down of the interesting parts of me. The part that would stay up all night writing. The part that found joy in the chaotic symphony. The unmedicated mind is a wild garden. The medicated mind is a neatly trimmed lawn. And some days I want to be a lawn. I want to be able to do my taxes and get my driver's license and navigate a social gathering without a three-day recovery period. But other days I miss the garden. I miss the strange flowers that grew there, the weeds, the feral life. I have to decide, every morning, what kind of person I want to be. The one who can function, or the one who can create a world out of the noise. And who am I without the noise? This is the question that keeps me up at night. Is this me writing this, or is this the absence of a thing that I am? Is the art made from the disorder, or as a way to fight it? And if you cure the disorder, what happens to the art?

A confession: I am afraid of silence. The external kind. I have to play music, turn on a fan, something. Because when the world outside gets too quiet, the world inside gets too loud. The televisions flicker back on, one by one. The restless pacing begins. Maybe this is not a piece about a disorder. Maybe this is a piece about a sound. The sound of a mind that doesn't stop. A symphony of everything, all at once. A brain that feels like a poem that is ripping itself open, trying to find a form, a key, a moment of rest. Trying to make sense of its own beautiful, ruinous music. And sometimes, just for a moment, on a page, or at a keyboard, it does. And it is enough.

Dell Lemmon

Crystal Crying

The doctor told me
I had an abdominal mass

according to the ultrasound
and I should speak with

Crystal about scheduling
a follow-up MRI

to find out more.
But when I called Crystal

and told her my name,
she started crying.

"I get headaches,"
she said weakly to which

I replied, "I am so sorry."
But she only cried harder

and excused herself
for a moment while I thought,

"This is not a good sign."
It felt as if Crystal was crying

for me, because I had such
a bad diagnosis. But Crystal

had her own problems. Still,
I appreciated her crying.

It reminded me of all
the angels crying for Jesus

when he died. Not that I
am Jesus, but I have tried

to live a good life, or
what I think is a good one.

Crystal does have some
angel aura about her,

so maybe that's why
I got all biblical.

The best crying angels

I ever saw were in Padua,
Italy, painted by Giotto,

perhaps the first celebrity
artist, because he reduced

his images to the most
essential parts of the narrative.

And he depicted those inner
psychological states so well,

creating universal truths
about human experience,

such as those crying angels
circling the crucified Christ

against a bright blue sky.
You never saw such sad,

tortured creatures. Their faces
twisted and distorted in agony.

I was surprised they could
keep flying with all that grief.

Alyssa McIntire Start

Recovery Triptych

I. *A Questionnaire*

In the past twelve months have you consumed alcohol alone before noon had a post-drinking lapse in memory used alcohol to cope with stress found yourself unable to stop at just one drink had a friend suggest you cut back on alcohol destroyed your relationship with your best friend been kicked out of one or more bars snuck shooters of Pink Whitney into a Marvel movie reached for the olive oil in the cupboard only to grab the Grey Goose next to it drunk texted your great aunt peed in a still-full Biggby cup been called a lush by your mother had to look up the word lush gone to a party and pregamed your drive home disregarded the other night drivers swerved to avoid a shadow taken an exit ramp onto the highway cried upon realizing you made it out unscathed

II. *A Ghazal*

I say *the flavor* when the counselor has us go around and name our favorite thing about booze.
Twelve sets of puffy eyes stare, and I add that I mostly drink artisan beer, not booze.

The counselor says my new flavorful hobby is jellybean-eating. I picture holding a Jelly Belly
variety pack at Brass Ring Brewing, green apple on my tongue instead of my barrel-aged brews.

Next session begins with the counselor belting out, *hopped up out the bed, turn my swag on*. Singing

Soulja Boy songs in the mirror each morning hypes her up, helps her stay clean from booze.

Nobody's got more swagger than someone who has a good time without drinkin and druggin,
my counselor says before urging us to recall the relationships we've left bleeding and bruised.

Ever since restriction (home, court, counseling, 7-Eleven for gas only), I relish in radio
and traffic jams on the way home while ignoring three memorized billboards for booze.

In the morning, I don't hit snooze in favor of an early a.m. start. I sing a duet with my sleepy
reflection until Dad gives my door a quiet-down knock and I shout, *Sorry, I'm giving up booze!*

III. *A Wave*

She floats easily in saltwater,
occasionally submerging one cheek
or the other to lap it up. Her body bobs
until it is no longer body but water,
until she is the ocean pissing where
she pleases because she is piss
and salt and plankton.

She bathes in her own growing swells
and waits for crash.

When she wakes,
there are no waves, only people
insisting there are far better pastimes
than swimming and maybe she should
consider hiking though her body
longs for sea.

She takes comfort in knowing somewhere
a domesticated chimp returns to its feral nature
and rips a pacifier from an infant's lips.
A baby reverts to moments after birth,
starts sobbing hard
as waves breaking on shore.

Molly Akin

Dead Doe at Chapoquoit

A woman warned us
don't let the kids see

we went anyway

a quick look
was enough
for the girls

sad they said
and skipped
off to waves

I stayed

her hooves
stilled into surf

water lifting
a gash
revealing
ochre sand
below her
damaged belly

it felt important
to see

on this day
death
was beautiful

before tides
dragged her
into the sea

Jeff Friedman

A Bird in Hand

There were two birds in the cedar bush, singing a pretty song. The bird in my hands scratched my palm and occasionally let out a burst of wild song. "Let it go," my wife said. "I'm taking it home to heal it," I said. "It's not injured," she said. We stood under a two-hundred-year-old plane tree, whose outer bark was peeling. "When I picked it up, it made no effort to fly away. How do you explain that?" "Too trusting," she answered. "Its wing is damaged, look for yourself." She peered into my hands, then looked at me. "You're crushing its wings, holding it too tightly," she said. The birds in the bush stopped singing. I opened my palms slightly and peeked in. The bird's beak pinched my nose. "What did you expect," my wife asked, "gratitude for picking it up?" "Why are you still with me?" I asked. She shook her head. I opened my hands to show her that she was wrong. The birds in the bush began singing again. The bird in my hand fluttered its wings. "It's not going anywhere," I said, just as it flew away.

Cheryl Pappas

Morning Bus

The driver adjusts his fan. His shirt billows over his thin frame. *Hello, Carol. Good morning, John. Hello.* People read their phones.

A swallow swoops in, bouncing into shoulders, into glass. People swoosh it away, screaming *Get it out!* The bird careens toward the back, where there is an old woman with waiting, cupped hands. The swallow nestles inside her bony nest. As the woman walks to the front, the only sound is wings flapping. She's been waiting for this moment her entire life. On the street, she kisses her cupped hands, and lets the swallow go.

Kim Chinquee

Landfall

Dogs drop onto the island—a bubble of flowers and pastels: yellow, pink, and blue. Long carpets of green. Shapes soft and round and pregnant, a few pointed, sharp. The sky is a balloon. Butterflies flutter, birds sing, bees buzz. Owls hoohoohoo. Dogs run in all sizes: big as cows, some squirrel-like, some are almost human: brown and orange, black and white, some striped in red and purple. Some have fur, some hair, all of them groomed proper. Some are long necked like giraffes, some bodies stout like donkeys, some heads like the alpacas at the farm owned by my cousin, where I once rode my bike to, holding a three-day old cria bigger than my rescue. Creatures romp. They sniff and roll and play. Tumble, their limbs tangling, angling, their paws toying with the ocean. Everything smells clean. The water hums. It rolls. With my wings I rise, finding the meteorologist. He says earth is a bargain. He howls, shows his canines. Admits he's a wolf.

Susan Fuchtman

Disappointed by Gravity

I twin my shoes on the sand and slip off my swimsuit cover-up. Warm water creeps over my toes, baby waves tumbling in, foaming ripples of sparkling laughter.

It's early, but already the beach is littered with walkers, paddle-boarders, swimmers, children playing water games. On a small hill, a bearded man nods in a lawn chair as if he kept vigil through the night.

Together we are drawn to our ancient womb, where restless ancestors emerged from the deep.

Last night, I floated on my back in the hotel pool, sighting Sirius, Mercury, Saturn, the stars in Orion's belt, all held aloft in the inky sky. Thin, frothy clouds drifted over an almost full moon. When at last I climbed out, heavier with each step, my body was disappointed by gravity. I shivered in the dark.

Today when I slide into the warm ocean, she embraces me. I am buoyant, light. My arms are powerful on the flat water, and I breathe every other stroke. Then every third.

I finally understand why I have these extra layers of fat and the gills I'd mistaken for wrinkles. Before long I don't need to breathe at all; the water gives me everything I need.

Adrianna Sanchez-Lopez

Shark Teeth

After my class tour of the aquarium, I had just enough cash for a plastic set of snap-on shark teeth. My teacher clicked her tongue at my find, asked if I brought money. When I showed her my five-dollar bill, she asked, "What about lunch?" Earlier that day, the morning still dark as I prepared for my trip, I saw how my mom wore her exhaustion like a thick winter coat. I told her the school would provide packed lunches, sure my friend Kendra would share. She exhaled a sigh of relief and told me to pack my brother's Pringles, just in case. Sleep-hardened yellow in the corners of his eyes, he glared at me when mom turned and reached for milk. He drew his index finger across his neck and mouthed, *Dead Meat.* I flipped him off then pocketed the five dollars my grandpa gave me for my birthday instead, not thinking much about lunch. I was seeking something else: a set of needle teeth. Forever teeth. The kind that grows back even when they break.

I shrugged at my teacher, my shoulders pointy in my oversized blue hoodie. Another hand-me-down from my brother. I was supposed to be wearing the same black shirt with our school's logo as everyone else, but I was always cold. I curled my fingers around the fraying at my wrists, dug my thumbs into the holes my brother had created. Shark teeth in my fist, I felt satisfied with my decision.

I handed the cashier my money and didn't wait for change. I didn't bother with cleaning or rinsing. I pressed the artificial teeth into my mouth with salty thumbs. The click of plastic against enamel reverberated in my temples. Hot saliva pricked at the hinges of my jawbones. I widened my mouth, clamped down on air. So much delicious air, stale with classmates' bodies and crumpled dollar bills. The cashier smiled, showing the shiniest, whitest teeth I'd ever seen. I smiled back, the first time I'd revealed my new teeth.

The thing about those teeth was that they really did make me feel full and steady. When Heri bumped my shoulder on his way out of the gift shop, I didn't even flinch. I barely noticed him and saw how he lost his cool when I didn't fall forward or wince. I hissed through my shark teeth, said, "G'day," and skipped my way to the meeting spot our teacher had made us repeat fifty-two times that day. I glided my mouth side to side, practice for finding my prey.

At lunch, Kendra asked if I wanted one of her nuggets or some fries. But I was too busy thinking about my heightened senses now that I had new teeth. I could almost see Kendra's nose hair, cherry-almond Jergens in her pores. I balked and said, "Sharks don't eat winged beasts. I have *hunter's teeth*." I consumed another helping of air, pointed to my mouth. I lifted my chin and ahhhed like I was in a dentist chair. "See? I'm a predator of the sea."

Kendra rolled her eyes, turned her back to me, and dipped her nugget in ranch. She chewed, swallowed, loudly slurped Sprite from her straw. "Don't you care what anyone thinks?"

I gulped more air.

During lunch, I learned how to be a way-finder, invisible particles guiding me like stars. I tasted my way to the bus, vats of dusty, reused oil dissipated to exhaust and rain-soaked pavement. When Jason and Ashley and Heri spit laughter at me as I walked by, the air wet with their cruelty, Kendra stared at her hands. My best friend pressed her back to the small window and put her chunky black boots on the seat next to her. I lifted my chin to them all, revealed my shark teeth. Fools. They thought they were the predators, when, really, they were prey. I sat in the back, right beside the words EMERGENCY EXIT, and bit down hungrily on the faint taste of urine mixed with Cheetos and Corn Nuts and unwashed hair.

My sweaty thighs stuck to the leather bus seat. I peeled my skin free with my fingers, ran my tongue across the tips and then my new bite, hopeful my own blood would seep into the porous, calcified knowing of each ancient tooth. I pressed my face to the glass of the emergency exit, grazed my tongue against the condensation ever so softly. I ate particles of air and water, listened.

What I heard made me realize the city made my classmates more hungry than usual. Their games of family turned to games of exclusion. Heri was the father, Ashley the mother. Jason excitedly accepted the role of son as more classmates rose to their knees and pressed their bellies to their seatbacks, desperate to be part of a family. I was tracing the second E with my tongue when I heard Kendra say, “Can I play?”

Heri inhaled and smiled. I heard it. I tasted it. On his exhale, he said, “Sure.” A pause. And then, “You can be our black lab.”

I slowly turned around, just in time to see Amy’s pupils widen. She grinned, “Yes! You just need a collar ….” She sifted through her backpack, pulled a roll of red-and-purple Fruit by the Foot from her bag.

Kendra reached for her imagined collar, hesitantly. Like it might burn. Her eyes had that soft look they sometimes get when her parents fight or when Amy teases her at school. Eyes like a puddle and one stomp in their center and her brown irises would ripple away.

I unhinged my jaw, snapped my shark teeth around the sugar lingering in the air. The sound of my bite ripped through the bus.

Jason jumped then to make up for his slip in confidence, shouted, “What? Got something to say?”

Kendra shook her head, said, “She didn’t say anything. She’s just … being her weirdo self.”

Her voice was solid, strong. But I saw her soft eyes. I could taste them, salt and terror. Tears pooling in the corners like the rose petals her mother pressed into her evening tea. Heri laughed first. Our teacher stirred from half-sleep, shooshed us, and closed her eyes again.

“There’s no place in this family for freaks,” Heri said, laughing awkwardly and looking at Jason to join.

Kendra hung her head. Amy, Jason, and Heri laughed, saying other things I didn’t hear. Because I was thinking about electroreceptor organs that I’d read about in the books at the library. I was thinking about how long sharks have been sharks. My shark teeth made me wise, helped me see their game of family for what it was. My new receptors allowed me to sense the shift in the bus before the idea of the game even occurred to them. I peered into the distant sea of classmates and duct-taped leather seats until I met the bus driver’s gaze. I could see the white lines of the highway in my periphery, but in the rearview, all I saw were his chestnut eyes, watching me. Then I blinked twice and slapped the red emergency handle. I leaned forward, mouth agape to welcome outside air. It wasn’t like our air back home that tasted of fireplaces and dirt and, on the coldest days, the clearest, deepest blue. No. It was violent and metallic. Urgent air that flattened my skin against my face and dried my shark teeth to the root. Air that made me hunger for the first time that day.

Red lights flickered on and off; an alarm screeched. The bus driver cursed and turned on his signal, trying to pull the bus to a stop. Classmates' voices rose and trembled. Our teacher snored. Jason hid behind his seat. Kendra wailed and Amy stood. "What's your problem, freak face?"

I ran my tongue along my shark teeth, rewetting each jagged point, getting sharper with every gulp of air. I bared my bite. Ready to hurt. Ready to break. Plastic teeth no longer, they were fused to me. And no matter how many times they snapped, I knew they'd grow back, stronger.

Mark Budman

An Occurrence at Owl Creek Farm

The grandfather, known to his grandkids as *Deda*, stops by the farm stand and kills the car engine. His grandkids in the back chatter with his wife in Russian. That is the language of the country *Deda* and *Baba* come from. It's dying now, just like America, just like the rest of the world. There is no emergency room big enough to contain them all.

The last words *Deda* hears before closing the car doors are, "The angels in heaven protect us from harm." That was *Baba*. She always comes up with something evocative.

Deda puts the Versaflo Hood Assembly with Inner Collar and Premium Head Suspension on his head. It's an ancient one, going back to the middle of the twenty-first century.

Better than nothing.

He has been shopping at this farm for years. He likes the name, right from the First Civil War, except for the farm instead of the bridge. For the last few weeks here, the family was lucky. No one caught any viruses. And no one assaulted let alone shot them.

Deda wants to buy a gun, but *Baba* is against it. She says that *Deda* would hurt the family before he hurt the attackers. *Deda* is angry. He can afford to buy even the newest laser gun, let alone an old-fashioned and reliable pistol.

"The laser gun is good for the environment," he keeps arguing with *Baba*. "No lead, copper, and zinc from spent ammunition."

"But imagine if the kids get hold of it."

"Can I buy at least a flak jacket? I mean, may I?"

She shrugs. He interprets that as a yes. So he wears it when he's outside.

Last time at the farm, *Baba,* who speaks to the grandkids only in Russian, reported afterward that when *Deda* was in the store, the kids asked why he was there for so long. She said, "*On platit,*" which means "he's paying," but the kids understood it as "*on plachet,*" which means "he's crying." They all laughed. And *Deda* told them a fairy tale about another *Deda* who, a long time ago, planted a turnip for his grandkids. It grew so big that *Deda* couldn't pull it out. Up came *Baba,* and she pulled at *Deda*'s waist. No luck. There came two grandkids, and they pulled, too. So, there was a whole line of people pulling at each other, but the turnip still stayed in the ground until a little mouse came and pulled at the last person in the line.

"That means don't belittle any kind of help," *Deda* explained the moral of the story.

"Did you give the mouse a treat?" the grandson asked.

"It wasn't me," *Deda* said. "It was a different *Deda*. So, I don't know. Probably he did."

"What was it?" the granddaughter asked.

"A bit of the boiled turnip. Very healthy."

Now, *Deda* comes back to the car with two paper bags full of veggies and fruits in his arthritic hands. Halfway through, he faces a man with a pistol pointing at *Deda*'s chest. He seems kind of young. Round eyes, thin mustache, pointed ears. No Versaflo for him. At that age, *Deda* was an engineer, inventor, and a short-story writer.

"Give me your wallet, old fart," he says. He sounds nervous. Maybe this is his first robbery.

How quaint. Couldn't he come up with a better pickup line? The new generation has no imagination.

Deda puts the bags down. Strangely, even to him, he's still not afraid. He reaches for his wallet. Credit cards don't work anymore, and inflation is rampant. So, the wallet is full of paper bills. A fat wallet.

The man fires his gun. He *is* nervous.

At that point, *Deda*'s imagination goes into overdrive. One of several things might happen now:

1. If *Deda* is lucky, the pistol jams and *Deda* takes a big fat turnip and hurls it at the assailant's head while he tries to reload his pistol, and *Deda* escapes, albeit without the bags.

2. If *Deda* is lucky, the pistol fires, but *Deda's* guardian angel in heaven fires a laser beam from his finger and shoots down the bullet, and *Deda* escapes, albeit without the bags.
3. If *Deda* is lucky, the pistol fires, and while no angel intervenes, a little mouse bites the robber's foot, he misses, and *Deda* escapes, albeit without the bags.
4. If *Deda* is lucky, the pistol fires, and while no little mouse intervenes, *Deda's* flak jacket stops the bullet, and a good Samaritan shoots the assailant, and *Deda* escapes with the bags.
5. If there is justice in this world ... no, there is always justice in this world. If there is justice in *this particular place and time*, the bullet will ricochet from the turnip (justice doesn't care about the laws of physics), strike the assailant's gun, and force him to run away.

That is, if *Deda* is lucky and if there is justice in *this particular place and time*. Lucky people don't cry in or outside stores, but they pay for their luck in the currency that even the fattest wallet can't contain.

Susan Blackwell Ramsey

Kalamazoo Defends the Rhotic R

Together, nasality and rhoticity explain why Midwesterners
have been said to sound like pirates with head colds
—Edward McClelland, How to Speak Midwestern

Here we don't pahk cahs in yahds. We're sure
    Bob's lodge apahtment is Barb's large apartment,
so why say *ah* as if some balsa stick
    depressed our tongues? We're depressed already.
By February even our auras are gray.

Midwestern voices live just south of the sinus,
    like treed cats, choosing cheekbones over throats
for sounding boards, and we don't notice, but

when an R shows up after a vowel
    or at the end of a word, it just feels rude
to ignore it, to pretend it isn't there,
    to shun it as if some tater tot
hot dish with baseball cap and fanny pack
    had tagged along on our tour of Versailles.

In flyover country, discourtesy's discouraged
    so maybe our sharp Rs rise from what's repressed,
cold car in the morning starting hard.

So what if we sound like chainsaws, like chipper-shredders?
    If we sound provincial, then let's be provincial.

Kalamazoo Defends the Rhotic R

Let's own it, celebrate the rhotic R,
    little throat-burr in our collective throat,
the roar of snowblowers chewing through four-foot drifts,
    the crunch of glacier gravel under tires
turning into driveways, dinner ready,
    the motor of a small cat home and warm.

Heather Paul-Tillery

The Women in Boats

—after Ashley Capps

outside my home / a headache
of daisies / yesterday
there was a green field

now flowers so impossibly close
together / like so many faces
on a boat

over each stem / a bead
of dark knowledge
at the center / all eyes
looking inward

knowledge is / a black pearl
the immigrant / the women with petals
of children

I have been thinking / of the women
who have been made smaller /
the women / who arrived on boats
in shackles / the women /
with ribboned feet

Sean Thomas Dougherty

In a time

The secret police are rounding up immigrants in Chicago and for some reason I am back in Tetovo teaching that class to the children who survived the civil war, Albanian and Macedonian children. The secret police are disappearing anyone who speaks Spanish in the projects, snatching them off the street as the wind blows cold off Lake Michigan, and I am back teaching the children in their spare English to write what they know of each other, suspicious they are of those whose fathers killed a relative or two, in the brief war when neighbors walked to the house next door and shot them. And the sound of gunfire rang over the red-tiled roofs and the hills outside Tetovo, and these children are telling me of things like they can't wait for winter and there might be snow, or the girl who writes of her grandmother, a man came to the door, and her grandmother answered, and a man came to the door, and her grandmother, head wrapped in a scarf the way both Albanian *mamajas* and Macedonian *babas* might and a man came with a machete, and my *mamaja* or did she say her *baba*, the girl wrote, stood in the door, and she said his name, and said I remember when you were this tall, and asked how is your *majica* or did she say *majca*, and said come in and I will feed you. And that is where the poem ended. For what happened next could not be said. And in Los Angeles, entire families have been taken, and in Chicago, a woman was shot down in the street, but I am back in Tetovo as the girl finishes her poem, in a time not long after war, in a small room in a small town in a small nation, and there was silence in the room, after the words of witnesses, where none of them for a moment were strangers, and then there was applause, though it felt more like praying than applause, and a few of them began to weep.

Sarp Sozdinler

Wholery

It's my duty as a mother to come up with words for him, words for feelings he can't quite explain. *Wholery* is a noun I recently wrote in his notebook, something I defined as "becoming one with someone else." In his world, each word can also mean other things depending on how it sounds. *Coo?* means "May I?" on a good day, while *coo* with a downward inflection means "I can't." He can't express "stop" because he doesn't know how to stop. *Bubbas* is another word I devised after his first day in class, plural for *bubba*, a substitute for the scorn one feels toward an absent parent. Every time he feels sad, *bub* becomes *bub-bub* becomes *bubbins*, sounding like pointy little rocks in the cave of his mouth. Kids his age are more prone to having not-feelings for their not-parents: not-rage and not-joy, all melding into one big nonentity in the slime of their minds. Today, the words I write in his notebook—*unwittery*, *sheol*, *kickaroo*—are like a recipe for an infantile disaster. They prompt him to become someone he's not, a bully instead of the bullied. In the principal's office, I find him scouring a dictionary, possibly searching for words that were born and died on the other side of the planet, like his father. When he notices me, his face scrambles in distaste as if I'm some new word he can't define. *I'm sorry*, I want to say, but my words feel oddly foreign on the back of my tongue. I'm sorry that I couldn't find the right words when you needed it most. I'm sorry that I had to lie my way out of most anything. I'm sorry that I left you in need of something to latch on when you were born—a nipple, a mother, a feeling—craving *wholery*. I'm sorry, I'm sorry, I'm sorry.

Lindsey Godfrey Eccles

Tap, Tap, Tap

Your fingers jab at the hatch like an adolescent monkey's. Gorged on flesh, I fill the airlock as a snail fills its shell, and time spirals into this moment of rebirth. You've trapped me, you think, and you'll dispose of me, you hope, but I am not troubled; I will not die, cannot die, have not died. My billions of cilia twitch to your tap, tap, tapping and imitate the signal, transferring it to the void. It's a game I play to pass the time—a paradox because for me, time doesn't pass.

The ship's built mind clicks and clacks as you struggle to override its better judgment. You don't know what you're doing; in opening the outer hatch you might also open the inner and join me in oblivion. The ones I ate—beings that were, are, will be, wriggling and jostling my insides—they believed in a god, pilgrims all. Perhaps you too believe, and perhaps your god brings comfort and strength, but even as you struggle to destroy me, you're wondering how I arrived without a vessel. No protection, no support, no propulsion. The truth is, I need no ship. Animal, vegetable, mineral; I am all. I speak in symphonies and proofs, forests, and constellations. I am smaller than an atom, larger than your universe, and snug in this compartment of yours. I am the snake that eats its tail, and soon you will die, my dear.

Or no? I swim in the river; you cling to its banks. A cloud, you pass over the landscape of time. A boulder, you block my view. And now, yes, an impossibility unspools. You've released a flood of integers, tickling and sparkling in exact sequence, and the ship's built mind is changed. Locks spin. Hatches release. I quiver; soon I will fill the emptiness between the stars. Shall we travel on together, you and I? This moment is a pit with no bottom. I fall; I transmit, frantic fingers, my fingers, tap, tap, tapping past planets, past galaxies, past all that was, and is, and never will be. I taste terror as if you were inside me or

I inside you, my molecules your molecules, your molecules mine. I am giddy as a young thing. I have questions. Like a child, I am nothing but questions.

What are we?
What have we been?
What will we become?

Jeff Harvey

Hollow

After another day of online shopping, Helen pops into Gilbert's Butcher Shop for ground beef to make Phil a burger even though he moved out last year. While she waits to order, Gilbert drops a pig carcass on the countertop. He slices it open with a handheld saw and the organs look like an image from a textbook.

Gilbert's thick muscles and freshly shaved head lure Helen around the counter to stand next to him. His turned-up nose exposing several hairs no longer puts her off. She pushes her hand inside the pig's stomach. The intestines feel firmer than she expected, and warmer. Dripping in sweat, Gilbert glistens. He must have had some beach time; his arms are golden and his cheeks rosy. Helen asks him if he'd gone recently, and he grunts, "Not likely."

A woman announces over the intercom they're out of ground beef and Gilbert looks at Helen and smacks his lips, "Anything else?" He butchers another pig, and Helen waits to touch the heart.

Lauren Fath

What Is Gold

While the house was under construction, my mom pulled me out of my second-grade class early on the day the cement mixer rolled in to pour the driveway. With my sister, just two then, propped on her hip, she led me around the wet concrete to the edge that abutted the backyard—or the flat expanse of dirt that would soon become it. She told me to put my hand down, and pressed my small fingers, one by one, into the cold, grainy concrete. She did the same with my sister. And then, with a stick she'd pried from the mud, she carved each of our names under our hands, along with "1987." At the time, I didn't understand that this house wouldn't always be ours. But my mom did—before we had even moved in, I suspect. Before she had hung the first round of Christmas garland on the bannisters that winter, before spring arrived and my dad planted pear and willow saplings in the yard. The house wasn't even ours yet, that October, and maybe, just maybe, with the fresh concrete still on our hands, she already mourned its loss.

The house sits between a small, man-made lake and a forest of creaky oak trees in a subdivision on the outskirts of Fort Wayne, Indiana. The lawn, thanks to my dad's diligence, is broad and green, shaded by pear and willow trees whose size now testifies to the house's age. My dad and I used to wake up early on Saturday mornings, trying to scramble outside first and lay claim to the riding lawnmower, then drive for hours across the two acres, carving broad, even rows in the grass. Whoever showed up second was relegated to the push mower. These were our signs of victory over the house: coming in with ankles stained green, and even after taking our shoes off, leaving a trail of grass blades across the kitchen floor; rubbing aloe gel on our pale faces to ease the heat of sunburn and manual labor.

These small battles are the ones I will miss, now that my parents' house is no longer theirs. They closed the deal in 2008, selling it to a younger couple from northern California. I suppose I shouldn't say "they," because my mom couldn't do it. My dad told me the story on the phone that night, just a shade of irritation in his voice.

"She said she wouldn't sign away our family house," he repeated when I didn't respond the first time.

But I found my mind wandering as he talked about having to get a power of attorney to sign her name, having to attend the closing without her. I wondered silently why my mother had held so steadfastly to that house. I hadn't called it "home" since 1998, when I left for Evanston, Illinois, to attend college. And even at the time I did live there, my resentment toward the house was unwavering. Maybe it's because the larger battles, the ones that couldn't be fought with a lawnmower and pair of hedge pruners, stretched far beyond what I understood, at the time, about nostalgia: We look back on things fondly when memory is our only way to access them. Perhaps, in the words of Robert Frost, "nothing gold can stay," because nothing gold ever was. What is gold in hindsight was not, necessarily, at the time.

Indeed, during my teenage years, there always used to be some complaint lodged against the house. Mostly, its expense was cause for my parents' constant worry. I recall the foreboding nights when my dad sat down at the dining room table—a table that never seemed to get any use, otherwise—and, with a look of determination, or maybe frustration, maybe worry, pay all the month's bills at once. It was always at night, after dinner. I'd come downstairs from my bedroom, my adolescent hideout, and find the only light on to be the one in the dining room. In an eerie yellow halo sat my dad, writing with a tight grip and hard stroke, his characteristic neatness, all capital letters. I knew not to bother him when he was doing this. I could hear his sighs, see him run a hand across his forehead. I felt guilty for being part of his burden, and the house became an easy scapegoat.

Everything soon turned into the house's fault. I came to see it as I suspected my dad did: as the source of my family's problems—though they extended beyond money. I see now that money was not the biggest problem; it was just the most visible one. And somehow the house was the neediest of us all: Over the years, it demanded a new air conditioner, a new furnace and kitchen appliances, repairs to a leaky living room skylight. Its roof shed shingles whenever a storm approached from the west, as if to scornfully deny us the protection it was supposed to offer.

Despite its shortcomings, my mother seemed to have a blind allegiance to the house—in a way that I deemed unacceptable. I maligned her humble attempts at home decor: ceramic angels that fluttered in the kitchen window box, fake plants that gathered dust on bookshelves. It was always immaculately clean, the house, thanks to my mother's neatness, but its contents seemed old and dirty. This was especially true of the toys my mother kept stored in the basement. "Why is she keeping *those*?" I always wondered with an admittable scorn. High school age by then, I was far too old for a toy kitchen set, a plastic dollhouse, books by Richard Scarry, a life-size Barbie head whose hair hung in tangled clumps. But there they were, the toys, staring at me with their unfocused, painted-on eyes, reminding me of something I couldn't understand or didn't want to. And despite my protests, my mother refused to let them go. And now I see that it wasn't the toys, themselves, that she wanted. Already, she was aware of the finality of the past, and how time would, too soon, grip the present and fling it toward that unused corner of the house.

Try as I did to deny the house would ever be gone, its loss has become an unforeseen test of my memory. Its absence now calls into question, for me, whether anything can be remembered as it was. Perhaps only my mother knows, because only she, in all the silliness and sentimentality I accused her of, knew to miss what wasn't yet gone. So she held on while she had it, to that house, to the last of what would soon be flung backward, to what she, from the beginning, already harbored a certain nostalgia for.

And now it is gone. Now, I remember the smell of fall leaves in the front yard, damp and crisp, slightly musty. Now, the sound of the high school marching band practicing just a few blocks away in the stadium, and how the white glow of the lights on game night reached all the way to my bedroom window. And, now, the way that house, in summer, absorbed all the humidity July and August could muster. With its windows open, the night air carried in the smell of still lakewater and the sound of moths all aflutter, diving toward the light. These are gold.

On the day the house was sold, I lived in Chicago. There, it rained while my father signed his name. Walking home from the subway after work, I smelled the petrichor of the past: a mix of moss and wet concrete, how it used to sit so stale in the air. I smelled it, then (perhaps just the city sewers letting off a little steam?). I recalled how I used to sit in the garage and watch summer storms roll in, turning the sky chamomile. How the water on even our small neighborhood lake picked up speed, and I swore I felt a breeze come off of it just then; though maybe it was just the wind off Lake Michigan moving through the streets, spurred by the rush-hour hurry. And there she was, too, my mother, moving around the house, closing all the windows before the hard rains came.

Nathan Fako

Playing Pretend

The smell of tar became Nevada dust
as we crossed the old bridge over Bunkerville Ditch.
Brown dirt, khaki rock. Hell, even the river was brown.

At this point I can't remember what we thought we were doing,
but that desert felt like a door to where we could just be
brothers without all our history.

What is that expression about glass
houses, and throwing stones?
It goes you shattered me, Jacob,

or goes nowhere at all—besides, we hadn't
taken aim at each other for years. And we had to
stop because you hurt your shoulder

chucking one of the rocks too hard.
I wish we'd gotten smoother stones and skipped them,
or scrambled down to touch the water.

That'd make for a better story. Why am I always looking
for a better story? Say we hugged it out

on that little hill overlooking the Virgin River.
Say I flipped a nickel into your likeness on the muddled water,
then dove in after the long-drowned boy.

Polly Buckingham

In Wildfire Smoke

Jill planted the seed
that took her to the mother giant

by way of a ladder in the sky
made of pea blossoms

and hummingbirds.
From the woodchips of my garden

floor, I watch her
polka-dotted pants disappear

into the smoke, her bright
red jelly sandals

like the eye of a phoenix.

Dustin King

Hummingbird

The one true God is the hummingbird
not the sun, not a celestial body
obscured by another celestial body.
Not the reflection of lightning across the dark sea
when I sit alone on a beach
surrounded by sand crabs.
God is not a sandcrab.
God could've been an elk or cougar
but not now, not for us.
Your God, *our* God has a sweet tooth
and a tongue as long as Her body
uncoiling in a cascade.
God is not a grandmother,
even if God *is* a quiet moment
or memory I can't quite reconstruct.
God bathes in the splash of a splash of a raindrop.
I never confused god for myself
most days.
I never confused god for a lover or drug
just the confusion that followed
beating invisible wings at an impossible rhythm.
God is the shape of the air in the space
the hummingbird vacated.
The hummingbird is shadowless but not soundless:
It's everything else that goes quiet
as Her heart thumps 1,200 times a minute.

George Singleton

Can You Use That in a Sentence?

Why couldn't it have been dysentery? I knew that one. Some of the others got easy things, like polio or measles. They got cancer, eczema, psoriasis, endometriosis, rubella, those kinds of ailments. I don't know how things work out in most spelling bee competitions, but we seemed to be stuck in the "health calamities" section of words. One little girl right before me got mumps. Who can't spell that? I didn't know that I should've spent more time poring over a book of medical terminology, as opposed to the dictionary. This kid with a bad cowlick from two towns over got an easy melanoma. I'd made it through six rounds of the statewide spelling bee when I got diarrhea.

My parents were in the audience, of course, as was my youngish seventh grade English teacher and her husband. We'd carpooled down to Columbia, the state capital. "Don't let Pinebark Middle down," my teacher kept saying to me as I sat in the backseat between her and Mr. Waymer. My father drove the speed limit, one hand on the steering wheel, the other holding a cigarette. My mother wore her favorite dress, the one she wore only to funerals. In my mind I went over words I feared might come my way: serendipitous, and cacophony, and malodorous. I said to my teacher, "Yes, ma'am," more times than I ever did in the classroom. She wore a dress, too, and it seemed to creep up her thighs every time my father stepped on the accelerator. I kind of had a thing for Ms. Waymer. In class I sat on the front row, only because she played these albums once a week of Shakespeare things, and she set the record player on the floor and bent straight over in front of me. For a long time I thought that seam in her pantyhose was her actual vagina.

"Can you use that in a sentence?" I asked the judge, who was some kind of bigwig at the University of South Carolina's library. He wore a bowtie. I didn't trust him, for my father told me to never trust a man in a bowtie. He said that there are paintings of the devil wearing a bowtie, but they kept them out of the public eye.

The judge said, "After Connie ate at the all-you-can-eat Golden Corral, she had to run into the restroom because she feared she might have diarrhea."

I stared at him. None of my competitors giggled, which, later on, surprised me. I said, "Are there any alternative pronunciations?" because Ms. Waymer instructed me to always stall so I could think.

He said, "No. *Diarrhea*."

I said, "Diarrhea," and counted on my fingers. I thought, Does it have two Rs? I thought, Isn't there an H in there somewhere? And then I completely blew it by spelling the word without one of the Rs, and missing the H altogether.

I got the buzzer, and the next girl—from Charleston, who went to one of those white flight private schools—got ptomaine. It wasn't the easiest word, but I knew how to spell it because I'd suffered from ptomaine a year earlier after eating at a *Golden Corral*.

I sat back down and didn't look out into the audience. I didn't want to see my parents' disappointed faces. My mother'd said earlier that, if I won the South Carolina Spelling Bee and went on to the Nationals, it might mean a complete scholarship to college. She said that if I won on the national level, I might be able to study in England or France.

I ended up not getting big scholarships. I did okay. I got my degree in plain philosophy. I didn't go to grad school. When people ask me what held me back, I say, of course, "Diarrhea."

My parents divorced. Ms. Waymer divorced. People with bowties overtook the government. My wife kisses me every morning. On Sundays, we sit at the kitchen table and do the crossword puzzle.

Aasiya Mirza Glover

But No One Asks Where the Pieces Go When They Fall

Well, I left my arm on the floor of the office bathroom. By that point, I'd just gotten so tired. Constantly picking up and cleaning up after myself took a real toll on my mental health. The stress was starting to get to me. My therapist said I should give myself some grace. Check my inner self-recriminations, watch my language, my descriptions of events. So, this time, I left my arm where it fell. On the floor of the office bathroom.

It was also physically harder to put up my mess. All the pieces I kept losing. I thought maybe losing them would free me to send all my energy to what was left. Maybe one day I'd just be a floating brain running on the same energy, and I'd be then (as I'm not now) a certified genius. Maybe it wasn't worth it, but I liked thinking about it.

You, of course, really took offense when I said that. As if I were saying you were stupider because your energy spread out in your gently growing weight. We don't have a single unit of energy that gets used up, you said. We're not plants that need to be pruned.

Well, I said, shrugging and turning back to sewing the left arm of my shirt, I don't know how you think you can know that.

Because, you said, furious. I'm a scientist.

I raised my left eyebrow (the right one had been one of the first parts to go). We both knew what I meant. You were an astrophysicist. Not even in the same solar system.

You need to stop reading the news, you said, for the hundredth time.

That, I said, clenching the shirt between my legs and pulling the thread taut with my teeth before I bit it off, that is impossible.

The elevators shone with headlines on the tiny screens above the heads of coworkers and strangers whose eye contact I avoided each morning.

And anyway, I said, it's not psychosomatic. It's not the *information* that does it, it's the fact of it happening.

You opened your mouth and I knew I should let you speak; I was always running over you. It was an ongoing struggle I perpetually lost. But I cut you off anyway, because I need things out before I can think them. So I said, even if it were the information, the information's already in there. I know what I know, one more death, one more arrest, one more interrogation. It's not the accumulation that does it, it's well, this *knowledge* I carry with me.

You snorted, shifted on your right thigh so you could angle yourself out the window and away from me.

Do you like it, I said, raising my new top to show you my work. I was proud of it. I've always been a bad sewer, and this was a passable job at a hidden seam. You looked back at me, still jutting your hips in my direction and your shoulders out the window. You began to cry, nodded, and looked away again.

Well, I said, shrugging. I like it.

I folded it slowly with my left foot and right hand and then picked up the next shirt.

What? You asked over dinner that evening.

What, what? I answered, not looking up.

You waved vaguely at my face. That. Your face.

I released the tension in my face, after taking a moment to notice it and find it, just as the online yoga instructor had said.

I don't know. Maybe I should have picked up my arm.

And taken it where? And done what with it, exactly? You don't owe them. Let them clean up after you, given what they've done.

Your indignation exhausted me.

They've just silenced me. That's all. They're not signing the death warrants.

I could feel your anger, your skepticism, your caveats and criticisms, your *footnotes*, crawling through my hair. I shook my head like a sleepy dog and went back to my noodles.

Later that night, as I packed my leftovers for next day's lunch, I said, It's not the company that cleaned it up anyway.

You were next to me, putting up the dishes.

It's a contracted custodial service. It was Yvonne. That's who probably cleaned up my arm. If she was working that night.

I put my Tupperware in the fridge and watched you close the dishwasher door. I didn't know if you'd heard me.

Brushing my teeth, in my tank and shorts, I watched the rippling of the various holes in my skin as I twisted and tilted and grimaced and spat. It's good, I said for the thousandth time, they don't bleed. You were walking by the open bathroom door and expelled a sharp blast of breath. You kept walking to our room.

You don't grow back, you said to me in bed as the rain punched our window.

We don't know that. It's not over yet. I haven't had a chance to grow back. We're still in it.

I smiled. I felt I had made a very profound point. One with just a little bit of hope.

You've never done this before, though. You pressed up from the bed and perched on your elbow, trying to glare me into self-conscious misery. The world has always hated you, you said, and killed you and arrested you and interrogated you. But this—you fluttered fearful fingers over my uncorked shoulder—never happened before.

Maybe it did, though, I said, staring at the ceiling and thinking about the clumps of hair I regularly pulled from the shower drain.

Do you think it's the silence, you asked, for the ten thousandth time.

I closed my eyes.

When I woke in the morning, another neighborhood was gone and my ears were sitting delicately next to each cheek on my pillow.

Jessica Klimesh

All My Old Selves

In my closet hanging pristinely, as though it had just been washed and ironed, was a body that looked just like me. Or what I had looked like at one time.

When had I hung myself up? Time was a blur, but it must have been right after my mother died.

I pulled the body off the hanger, wondering if it would still fit.

I undressed and slid my fingers over my skin, searching for zippers, snaps. I finally found an opening, and slipped out of one self into the other.

My old self was too snug in places, while oddly loose in others, but I decided to wear it anyway, to run some errands, get coffee, see if anyone noticed, if they'd say, "You look different. Did you get a haircut? New glasses?"

It didn't take long, though, before I couldn't stand the chafing. Clearly I had outgrown my old self.

My mother had always told me to get rid of things I no longer had use for, had chided me for keeping a sticker book from elementary school and a thread-worn blanket I still cherished. She'd wave her arms and scoff. *Just get rid of it.* But this was also the person who'd buy three of the same shirt if she liked it well enough, sometimes in different sizes, and who had left me boxes and boxes of possessions to sort through when she died, boxes that now sat in my basement. I hadn't opened them yet. Couldn't bear to.

I folded up my ill-fitting self and stuffed it into a plastic bag. I took it down to the basement and set it next to my mother's boxes. To deal with later. But I could hear her exasperated voice. *Just get rid of it.*

In my head, I argued back. What if I lose weight and it fits me later?

I missed that old body's confidence, the way she exuded joy. Oh, how I missed me! I decided that if I could just lose five pounds, maybe ten, my old self would surely fit again. So I hit the gym, ran laps, cut out sugar. But after a few weeks, when I tried on my old self again, it still didn't fit comfortably.

Just get rid of it.

With my mother's voice echoing in my head, I took my old self to Goodwill. I made small talk with the associate as they wrote out my donation receipt.

"Do you get many of these?" I asked.

"Some," the associate said, "but we generally just end up recycling them. They never fit right. It's not like jeans."

An ache of nostalgia washed over me. "I think maybe I'll keep it then," I said. The associate nodded, handed the bag back to me.

At home, I hung my old self back up in the closet and just sat on the bed and stared at it, trying to imagine who I used to be, assessing the differences, past and present. It took a while, but I finally saw it. Something akin to heaviness. The weight of grief.

Just get rid of it.

I trudged down my basement steps, took a deep breath, and finally opened, one by one, my mother's boxes. All her earthly belongings. I found some expected treasures—school photos, report cards, an old stuffed bear I'd called Foo Foo.

But there were some unexpected ones as well: baby teeth I'd assumed the tooth fairy had taken, a lock of hair from my first haircut, a slew of Mother's Day and birthday cards I'd handcrafted and given to my mother through the years.

But also in the boxes, to my surprise, were all of my old selves. Me as a baby. Me as a three-year-old. Me from kindergarten. Me from sixth grade. Me as a senior in high school.

My mother had saved everything.

Dan McDermott

Silver People

We meet for the first time while walking between brick buildings that hide the sun. Deanna is twenty-two and I'm thirty-three. She says when she's thirty-three and I'm forty-four we should meet back in the alley and celebrate. She wears silver stretch pants, silver hair, tinfoil boots and gloves, silver makeup on her face, ears, and neck, a men's suit jacket and sunglasses dipped in silver paint. I live in an apartment at the end of the alley near Fountain Park, and Deanna tells me the same is true for her.

When we reach the park she takes her perch atop the old rock monument.

We plan a date.

"I won't be able to talk for a couple hours," she says.

I say farewell by gripping her silver elbow.

She takes the crouched stance of someone examining a bug in the grass and freezes her lips in an adorable silver pout.

"The tin girl," says my sister, Phoebe. We're at a café in a part of the city where everything besides coffee is more than we can afford.

"Deanna," I say. "*Dee* like the sting of a *bee*."

Phoebe asks if sex with the tin girl is a kinky experience.

I tell her I don't have that kind of information, but the idea is intriguing.

"Condoms and an oil can," she says.

"And no kissing in the rain," I say.

"Rust," Phoebe says.

Phoebe is two years older and two inches shorter than I am but still tall for a woman. She goes out with men who punch and drink and likes the idea of dating someone silver for a change.

"What about your old girlfriends?" she says. "All those cheaters."

"A silver person might be different," I say.

"A trail of tinfoil and paint," Phoebe says. "Catch 'em silver-handed."

"She's an artist," I say. "Artists are honest about their feelings."

"Depends on your definition of artist," my sister says. "Some cat-burglars are artists."

I arrive for our date and Deanna is silver when she answers the door. On the subway she assumes the posture of someone running through the wind and people leave tips in her silver top hat.

We go to a rooftop party full of silver people. If forty people are there then thirty-eight of them are silver. Some look naked beneath silver body paint. One is wrapped in silver string like a mummy. I make eye contact with the other non-silver, a woman who appears to be the mummy's date, and she points in recognition, as if to say, *If this gets weird, you're the one I can trust.*

Deanna introduces me. The silver people have nicknames like Tron, Krull, Voltar, Larz, and Newt.

Larz is father to an elementary school daughter. "I'm a parent first and a silver person second," he says.

Newt is maybe four feet tall and wears a duct tape suit. "You're here with Devo?" he says.

I look to Deanna and she nods her silver face, confirming that, yes, indeed, I am here with Devo.

Silver string Christmas lights hang from coat racks, weave through metal railing. A collapsible table holds silver cups, silver cookies, cans of silver beer and bottles of Sambuca.

"I wanted it to be a surprise," Deanna says.

I tell her Devo was my favorite band in middle school. I saved my allowance and ordered one of their flowerpot hats from a catalog.

She says the two aren't related. "It's an abbreviation. For *devolution*." She says the silver people are dissident. A society made of steel.

Devo stands on a chair and claps her tinfoil hands and thanks everyone, especially the non-silvers, for coming. She thanks Tron for donating the rooftop space, Krull for supplying the booze, Voltar for crossing three states to attend.

We stay for two hours and do many shots and on the subway back to her apartment she's a statue of a soldier with a bent arm and ridged hand fixed in salute. She makes eight dollars and thirty cents in tips.

This is how it works, she tells me. Little bits all the time. Long sessions in the park on weekends and holidays.

She takes my hand and drags me into her building and up to an apartment with silver appliances in the kitchen, silver comforter on the bed. She tells me to wait and goes in the bathroom and turns on the shower and returns minutes later looking pink, and sheepish, and perfect. She dives into bed and slides her naked body beneath the silver blanket.

"You getting in?" she says.

"Your hair's still silver," I say.

"Yeah," she says. "Some of it's permanent."

Hanna Reynditskiy

Dollface

Nowadays, I tell anyone who asks the truth.

When I was twenty, I wasn't as honest. Part of it was due to age, though most of it was owed to the silly notion that one day I'd become an actress.

An even sillier notion: If I didn't schlep off to Los Angeles, my career as an actress would fail to begin, my life stalled, so that I could do absolutely nothing but dream.

This was a couple years after the Rodney King riots. My father, who had watched the televised scenes—cars set ablaze, wreckage spilling out of disemboweled shops—said, "No chance." Los Angeles was out of the question. We lived in Modesto. I was two years out of high school, worked part-time as an office secretary, and spent my free time watching old movies. Old videotapes, to be exact.

The fact that I spent my time alone, locked, as my parents enjoyed saying, like a hermit in my room, a dim light flickering beneath the doorsill, was, to my parents, highly unusual. They summoned their criticisms when we sat for dinner. I stayed up too late! I was wasting my time! Why didn't I *do* something? Wasn't there someone from the office I'd like to date or at least spend time with, even just a friend? I could go to the movies with them, they insisted, knowing this was not something I'd do. That puzzled them the most. An aspirant who doesn't bother with the theatres. Who'd rather watch the antiquated, the dead.

Oh, but I wanted to do something. Here, I would turn the argument back around: If they would only let me go to Los Angeles, then I could shuck the old and replace it with something greater. I'd come crawling out; I'd make something of myself. Besides, this was really my father's idea (he would laugh), not mine.

They could not force me to stay, I told them.

"The door's open," my father said, sitting hunched over his plate, slicing into his chicken thigh.

Throughout that summer, I made an effort to assert, usually around dinnertime, that I really was going to leave, that I must be believed. And my father, always one step ahead, would say, "I see you've packed your bags." But of course, there were never any bags.

This continued into fall. A dying mosaic overtook the streets, and the leaves lay discontented over our lawn. Time was shedding in our driveway. It was this observation that led me to finally pack my bags.

My mother plodded into the kitchen early the next morning, too tired to notice me at the table. She gaped at the full pot of coffee, swayed, rubbed her eyes, and, turning round to see me, stiffened, caught her breath. Why, this was strange. Waking up so early. So eager. And for what? Work? Was I coming around?

"I quit," I said.

"You what?"

Then it was my father's turn. He was frantic, having been woken up by my excited mother, plodding into the kitchen in his tartan pajama pants, red in the face, not so much upset as he was rattled. *You what?*

I led them to the front door. There, stationed like two good soldiers, were my suitcases, their handles pulled into an upright salute. Before my father could say anything, I threatened to call a cab.

He stood there for a while, his tongue scoring the groves of his teeth, looking at the enlisted luggage. Finally, his shoulders drooped. Fine, he said. Fine. But first, I had to promise. Promise that when things go south—*if*, I corrected—fine, if things go south, I'd come home.

We drove to the bus station a week later. It was dawn, and a soft rain fell around us. My mother sat passenger, and I sat in the back and watched the vanishing road. The dark curved into nowhere. We were silent, tired from a poor night of sleep, and the wipers cut across the windshield every now and then like a drowsy metronome. Then the rain thickened. The farther we drove, the harder it came down, and by the time we got to the station, the rain had turned relentless and cold, and the wipers were kicked awake, frantically cutting the waterfall that blocked our vision. Water sloshed down the windshield in outrage.

My father let me and my mother off at the front, but even then the rain got us. Rain puddled in our shoes, and we stood under the station canopy while the rain beat down and my father ran across the parking lot. He was soaked through when he got to us, and we stood together, shivering. The bus slept against the curb, and we watched torrent upon torrent clash against its long, metallic spine, rain lifting off as a silver fog.

It must have been ten minutes before the doors opened. All three of us stepped in with the excuse that my father had to hoist my luggage onto the overhead rack, that my mother had to say her final goodbye. Her goodbye included a checklist of everything I carried with me. While she spoke, ironclad pellets rained down from above. Did I have the addresses and telephone numbers I needed? Let's see: There was the police department, the YWCA, the medical clinics. And the address for the apartment I'd rent out in Studio City. And the emergency envelope she had me tuck inside my bra, which she now hinted at with a light touch to her own chest. "Make sure you know how to get there before you get off," she said.

"And call us if you need anything," said my father.

Then we said our real goodbyes.

The bus groaned to a start and, heaving, began to pull forward. It was an eight-hour trip to Hollywood, and when I got off I'd need to take another bus to Ventura Boulevard. From there, I would walk up Vineland Avenue, over the dry concrete riverbed, and find the apartment my father and I leased, unseen, over the telephone.

As soon as we got out of Modesto, the rain let up and the sun tipped out from behind a few leftover clouds. We drove down through the Central Valley, a flat, sweeping land skirted by the coastal ranges to the west and the Sierra Nevadas to the east. It's the same land for miles. Golden pastures giving way to hypnotic rows of cotton and bursting almond trees. Foothills rising in the distance, dotted by cloistered scrublands. We passed through the Grapevine, climbing up Tejon Pass onto the steep highway. We were tilting backward the whole way up, rising higher into the mountain until finally the Interstate flattened out. Then we had to catch ourselves on the backseat before us to keep from falling forward. And with that, we descended back into the flat, sprawling land, the same land, though it was now called the San Fernando Valley.

Along the highway were outlet malls, billboards, construction cranes, all the typical city topography. Santa Clarita became San Fernando and San Fernando became Burbank. Without looking at the road signs, it was difficult, if not impossible, to tell when one city poured itself into the next, when one chain-link fence gave way to another, fortifying a derivative home. Pushed against us were mountains blanketed by green and gold chaparral. They seemed to shift around, moving from the outskirts to the horizon line, as if they were anxious to leave the terrain. We hurled toward them, and when they saw us advancing, they stepped out of reach.

The world outside the window was a dull, concrete place. Even the palm trees looked sickly. Their needle-thin bodies were weathered by the weight of their heads. There was a certain haziness around us, a persistent gloom. I thought it was the window—dried rain and sediment—and I breathed on the glass and wiped it with my sleeve. Nothing changed. I kept at it until someone across the aisle woke up from their nap and regarded me with an accusatory eye.

This gloom, I'd come to find out, was the notorious smog. Up on Griffith, some weeks later, I would point to the red flood laying stagnant across the city floor. I had to ask what it was. The lady I stopped shot me a bewildered expression. "It's the smog," she said. "Don't you know about the smog?"

Studio City looked the same as everything else did. It was dark by the time I arrived, and the red and green lights swung over the wide, cracked asphalt, giving a luminous glint to an otherwise drab place. Rush hour was long gone, yet traffic persisted and the cars sped through stop signs without the slightest concern for order. There was a great deal of noise, and I stepped into it, dragging the luggage off the bus and down onto the sidewalk. Then the bus pulled away and joined the noisy, erratic push forward, and I stood half frantic, alone for the first time.

I followed the directions the landlady had repeated over the telephone the day before. She wouldn't be there, but the unit would be open for me and the keys would be stashed inside one of the kitchen drawers. The problem was, I couldn't find the right building. I knew what to look for: a wrought-iron gate and a two-story building with the number 1150 stamped to its forehead. But all the streets looked the same. Each had a narrow road and was flanked by suspiciously low telephone lines. The only source of light came from the buildings themselves, from lit windows and wall fixtures. The latter cast murky orbs of light onto the concrete. Cars lined the sides like a set of gilded molars.

No matter which direction I went, the numbers seemed to jump out of place, number 1150 somehow always skipped. I turned the same corner and figured I must be walking in circles. By the third lap, my knees had gone weak. I was tired of lugging the suitcases behind me. I threw my luggage down and sat on the curb.

Where was I? Underneath a tunnel? Inside a stomach? The orbs could be eggs incubating inside the hollows of pavement, and the cars a set of monstrous teeth clamped shut, the curb a cold, slick tongue. The street stretched down into an eternal esophagus. I was to be digested, processed, spit out. The street welled, undulated, glinted, and threatened to swallow.

And then it stepped forward. Across the street right before me was my building. The 50 had fallen off, leaving an impression of color where it had once been, and the wrought-iron gate that I'd been directed to look for was a skinny thing, barely taller than my waist. I could have screamed. But I pulled myself up, wiped the wet from my eyes, and thought about how stupid I was. I must have passed it multiple times over.

The next couple days were unmemorable. I met the landlady, did the remaining paperwork, called my parents, and unpacked my bags. The unit came furnished, which, although morbid—the previous tenant had broken his lease due to a death back home—was nice. It was by no means perfect, though. The floorboards were buttered by a layer of unknown adhesive, and the cabinets were either stripped bare or caked with bone-white paint. The furnishing too was sparse and ragged. It included a sunken couch, a standing lamp, a small table with a set of folding chairs, curtains for the front-facing window, and a twin bed pushed into one of the corners.

The complex itself was a two-story building—broad, like a typical motel. The outdoor staircase was the only way to access the upper units. It had wide and weak steps, and the metal frame reminded me of an outstretched slinky. The gate fenced everything in, though it was clearly more for show than security. Behind it lay a dismal overgrown lawn halved in two by concrete.

As I said, those first days were unremarkable—except for one strange thing that happened. At the time, I wouldn't have called it that. Curious, perhaps. Funny.

My neighbors were quite guarded. I hardly noticed anyone coming or going, and when I did, it was a closing door, voices in the apartment over, footsteps on the stairs. It took seconds to cut across the lawn and about the same time to mount the stairs. It was not standard to loiter, and those who smoked did it either inside their apartment or directly outside their door. It was even less common to see a stranger. So, it was a surprise when I saw one standing idly around.

It was morning. I had just closed my door. There were a few errands I needed to run, and I was looking for a job. I hadn't thought anything of the stranger, a woman, who stood right outside the gate, except that it was odd, unexpected. She had her head down and was flitting her fingers over the railing, across the gaps, never touching the rail. She looked around my age and was, perhaps, a little taller than me—I was 5'5"—dressed in a puffed blouse and loose-fit jeans. If she saw me, she did not make it apparent.

She was, at that time, just another person. To put it bluntly: She was not the slightest bit interesting. If anything, she was timid. When she finally looked up, she glanced around with a flickering nervousness, a bird's hesitation. If she had just touched the gate, it would have opened. But she flitted across the gaps instead. It would have been easy to forget about her. But I felt sorry for her and was leaving anyway, so I went to let her in.

"H-How kind of you," she said, stepping through.

I learned that she was a prospective tenant and was scheduled for a studio tour. Her name was Nora Gilbert. I took her to the landlady's office, a small space tucked behind the mailroom. The landlady herself was an older woman with a graying bob cut, and she was closing the door behind her when we met. "This makes it easy," the landlady said. I wasn't sure what she meant. She waved me forward and we climbed the stairs. She gestured for me to open my door. I realized then that it was my unit up for tour.

"What a wonderful place you've got," Nora said. She stood buoyed, her hands clasped together, looking restlessly around my apartment. A small tremble moved across her lips. It seemed she was marking off a private checklist which included the things she approved of and the things she'd like to change. I wanted to tell her that the furniture was not mine, that I had just moved in a few days ago, that this—here, I would gesture to the entire studio—was not a good representation of who I was. When she turned to me, I prepared for a question about the furniture. "Are you an actress?" she said.

"Me?" I said, and she looked at me with a little pressed smile. "Yes," I said. "Well, not really. An aspiring one, that's all. How did you know?"

"Why else come to Los Angeles," she said, and at this, her hands unclasped, her chest deflated, so that she seemed suddenly bored by her own aphorism.

"Are you?" I asked.

"Am I what?"

"An actress?"

"Can't *you* tell?" she said. She was smiling a little differently now; it was a small, coy smile. She had her earlobe pinched between her thumb and forefinger. I didn't know what to say. I thought for a moment that she might be testing me. Then she laughed. "Sorry. I-I've been putting on a little show." She thanked me for the tour, asked a couple more questions regarding the unit, said again that she thought the place was nice, and left.

Not long after, I took a job at the Warner Brothers' cafeteria. It was an opening, a foot in the door. I considered myself lucky.

To get there, I had to go through the studio backlots, through the residential facades and accented brick. The streets were wide and empty, and sometimes a golf cart would stop and give me a lift and take me all the way to the end. They'd drop me off where the road opened to a forest of umbrellas and thermoplastic picnic tables. Behind it was the small unassuming building in which my days were spent.

The influx came around lunchtime. Golf carts loitered around the counterfeit forest. Doors burst open the second they closed. Men came in, loud and boisterous, and behind them their beautiful consorts, laughing, slinking. They were in their own world, circling the cafeteria, surveying the salads we packed in plastic shells. The glass partition divided us. I watched them self-consciously, adjusting my hair net, waiting to be of use.

It was an open secret that us cafeteria girls wanted to act and so, occasionally, the casting directors would take pity on us and chat about open calls. *We're looking for a mid-sized brunette. Know any?* We were supposed to laugh and say, *Who, me? I haven't seen anyone like that in years.* But that was on the rare occasion. For the most part, I took specialty orders and restocked iceberg lettuce. One handsome face after the other would pass by, unnoticing, and I stood and let my imagination take hold. Here was a handsome man, looking up, looking my way; here was that wild look, a face choked with absolutes. *Here's looking at you, kid.*

The first large purchase I made was a Toshiba television set that came with an integrated VCR player. I'd brought my favorite films with me from Modesto, all classics, all on videotape, and I spent my nights watching them on repeat. Ingrid Bergman's *Notorious*, Joan Crawford's *Mildred Pierce*. I knew them by heart. When Joan spoke, I spoke with her. When Ingrid moved, so did I.

I would do this until I fell asleep. There was something ritualistic about it, even soothing. For a good night's sleep, I needed to escape into someone else's life. And most of the time, it helped. I slept soundlessly. I didn't dream, or at least I didn't tend to remember my dreams. Strangely, there's only one dream I remember from back then, a dream that's become more of a memory now, about a corridor.

It was a long, endless corridor, and it had nothing at the end of it. I remember it being pitch black. I had to use the wall, which was smooth and glassy, for guidance. I didn't know if I could reach the end, but I kept going nonetheless, feeling my way down. Somehow, I knew someone was there, obscured behind the wall. Someone watching me. For a moment, it was only me watching—watching from a different vantage, as you can sometimes do in dreams—then a voice echoed down the empty passageway.

Hello, Doll.

Perhaps I can remember the dream because the voice had pushed itself through the fog of sleep. Because when I woke, I could still hear it. It was a woman's voice. Deep and melodic.

Then a knock sounded and I screamed.

"Are you all right?" a voice called. It came from behind my door. I didn't say anything, and after a moment, the voice spoke again. "Hello?"

I don't remember exactly what time it was, but I remember it was well past midnight. It could have been close to dawn. I stripped back the bed sheets as quietly as I could and slunk to the door on tiptoe.

I had no desire to know who was standing outside my door, but now I was too jumpy to keep still. I pressed carefully against the small circular lens imbedded into my door.

It was a woman. The night sky was drawn to her by the effects of the fisheye, and she hugged herself and glanced around nervously, as if distressed by the strange, distorted world curving around her. She wore a red, slim-fit pencil dress that showed her bare shoulders, and she held her arms against the cold—and I had absolutely no idea who she was.

There were only two explanations: Either she was drunk or she had lost her keys. She had to be a neighbor, and now, thanks to her impairment, she was at my door, thinking it was her own, hoping her roommate or whoever it was that lived with her would wake up and let her in. If I kept quiet, she might realize her mistake and leave. "Doll," she said, "I know it's late, but I'm freezing out here. Please. Open the door."

Doll. But how could she have known? It had to be a terrible coincidence. Though what a coincidence it was.

When she reached to knock again, I opened the door.

"Thank God," she said, stepping through the doorway. She kicked off her heels and threw herself onto the sinking couch. "It's freezing out there," she said again, this time giving a dramatic little shiver and rubbing her arms. She did this frantically then gave up all of a sudden, dropping her hands and leaning forward to cup her chin in a propped palm. She became impersonal, almost aloof. Then, in a quiet voice, as if to reprimand, she said, "I could really use a blanket, you know." I handed her my comforter, and she fiddled with it, rising in a mock levitation to get it around her. "Much better. Thanks." Now that the blanket was caped, she smiled and leaned back, extending her legs in a fluid, trained way.

There was no better way to say it, so I went ahead and said it outright. "I'm sorry, but do I know you?"

"I believe so," she said. She sounded hurt. "I looked at your apartment a couple months ago. Maybe you don't remember me. My name's Nora. I really thought you'd remember me."

I took a long look at her then. She looked nothing like the person she referred to herself as. I remembered that "Nora" had reddish-brown hair the color of a bay horse and a forehead that was wider than average due in part to a receding hairline. She had short teeth and close-set eyes. Her face, too, was a little rotund, with a small chin and rosebud lips. This "Nora," the one before me, had entirely different features—wide-set eyes, full lips, a broad chin—and her hair was lighter, too, fringing on blonde.

"There's no way you're the same person," I said. I almost laughed.

"Don't be silly. Of course I am."

"Well, *Nora*. You look nothing like you did in October."

"That's crazy," she said, smiling. "Just crazy."

I cleared the table to make room for coffee. I was fully awake now and unnerved, and because I was unnerved, I couldn't kick her out. In any case, she had passed a sort of threshold walking in, and we both knew it. So, we drank and talked, and she told me about how she had just come from a party. She had intended to go home with a man she met there, had even gotten into his car, but the minute he revealed he was not the so-and-so producer he said he was, she jumped out the passenger door and waved goodbye with a genial "Thanks for the ride!" She thought she would be stranded out here in Studio City but then remembered my apartment.

"And it's such a nice one, too," she said, looking around. "I really should get my own place. Do you mind?" She fingered through her purse and pulled out a gold cigarette case. It had the letters "N.G." engraved on it. I shook my head. Smoke soon ribboned the air.

"Why don't you?" I said. She was silent and held the cigarette aloft. The air bittered underneath it.

"I hate being alone," she said finally. Then she sighed and took a drag. "There. I said it. I hate being alone. I know it's pathetic. But that's the truth."

"It's not pathetic."

"It is. And you know why?" She tapped her cigarette, and a few specks of ash dropped onto the table. "Well, it doesn't matter why."

"I don't like being alone, either," I said.

"But you are, aren't you?"

I considered this. I called my parents regularly and was surrounded by people at the cafeteria.

"I don't know," I said. "I don't think so."

"Everyone's alone in Los Angeles," Nora said dismally. "At least, everyone who's been here long enough. Oh, don't look so worried. It'll happen to you too." She gave me such an odd look then, as if she were suppressing some great joke. Then she broke out into a laugh, a real laugh, and it zigzagged around the room in jovial spirit. I began to laugh, too—she had sounded so serious! But it was a joke, a deadpan irony, and the spirit took me by the arm and whisked me into good humor. Then our joy was cut short by a high-pitched cry, and there she was, with her mouth downturned, sobbing.

I sat dismayed. She let go of her cigarette—it sat burning out, its embers fraying into a collapsed gray—so she could cover her wet face. She sat like that for a while. I brought her a roll of toilet paper and brewed another pot of coffee. When I brought our mugs, she uncovered her face and crutched her limp head in her arms. Sharp, unflattering shadows hung across her skin like small black sails. She suddenly looked different.

"I'm sorry," she said, choking a little. "It happens sometimes. I get into these kinds of moods."

"Don't worry about it," I said. We watched her dying cigarette. After a while, she rummaged through her purse and pulled out a fresh one.

This time, I watched her face. Her nose seemed more crooked, her skin more pale. Her face more obtuse. That full mouth shrunk into a thin blade. But lighting, especially poor lighting, could do that to any face. New smoke rose in eddies under the harsh fluorescence. And there sat Nora, the same Nora who came to tour my apartment a couple months back.

You may have guessed it already. Is that our Nora Gilbert?—yes, she's the same one you've seen in the theatres. The same one you've seen walking down the carpet at the Met Gala. Here, I mean, as you mean, the latter Nora, the bombshell exemplar.

In the 90s, she was still unknown, a nobody. We both were. She liked to say we were "in it together," and I suppose that could have been true.

Over the next few months, Nora visited now and again. She always came after midnight from a party, and I stayed up just for the chance she'd come by.

Most nights I spent alone. If I got too tired from watching rentals—I started watching rentals for the sole purpose of staying awake, since the unfamiliar jolted me—I'd read *A Practical Handbook for the Actor,* and when I got tired of that, I'd make coffee. I'd try not to get too excited when someone came up the stairs or when the wind knocked a branch against the window. Because it was only on a whim that she'd come by.

When she did come, there was hardly an indication that she was there. Even with the restless night, the sirens bellowing on and off again, the occasional uproar and shouting, I'd listen for her. I could hear my neighbors but not Nora. She'd come up noiselessly, watching her step, and, when all was quiet, call out from behind the door. *It's me. Open sesame!* Then she'd whisk in, throw off her heels, shimmy out of her ivory pantyhose.

Maybe she liked startling me. It was odd enough how she changed.

Each time I opened the door, I opened to that second version—the glamorous and unblemished—and later, once she settled, she began to look like good old Nora again. It seemed she had a half-life of a quarter hour, though sometimes it took longer. Sometimes, it took her having a shower, changing into my clothes.

It was spring by the time I started to audition. They were, sad to say, unproductive auditions. The trouble was with the casting director: He kept forgetting who I was. It didn't matter how often I said my name, age, weight and height, he kept calling me "Hon-ey." We were all "Hon-ey" to him. All us girls. Some of the other cafeteria girls called him "Whiny" in private. This was because his name was Wayne Morris and he had a staggered, high-pitched voice, almost squeaky, which he often strung out into a songlike meter. When we entered the room, he'd clap his hands together and beckon us with a stupendous "This way, Hon-ey!" He wanted us to call him by his first name. He'd be upset if we called him Mr. Morris.

These were open calls I went to. I would perform reasonably well. I never fidgeted or stuttered, which was a common occurrence in my bracket. And yet, midway through, Wayne would jerk his hand in the air in rapid swats then stand, clapping his hands together. *Not what we're looking for, Hon-ey.* I would be guided out the door with a little push on the rear. Afterward, I'd go sit alone in whichever backlot wasn't being occupied.

During that particular spring, Los Angeles was in the midst of a superbloom. Poppies were everywhere. You could see them from the highways, big bursts of orange quilted into the mountainside. Some even grew on the roadside among the discarded trash. There was, supposedly, a great field of poppies in Antelope Valley. People—

tourists, mostly—would hike up the mountains just to lie in the orange fields. But I never did. The bus ride, which would have neared four hours roundtrip, hadn't seemed worth it at the time.

The lots, however, were exempt from seasons. They did not concede to time, like the rest of us; instead, the elms and oaks were dressed according to the shooting schedule, the foliage painted by hand. If you looked close enough, you could see the brown zip ties clinging to the branches.

"It's the trees that make it feel subterranean," I told Nora once during a visit. She had asked about my auditions, and I talked about the trees instead.

That spring, the trees were completely naked. No directive had been given about which season they needed to match, so they had been stripped bare. If you sat underneath them, as I did, you would see that their branches were thin and fibrous, much like human veins, and that they tapered off into the air. They sunk themselves in sky just as they sunk themselves in the ground, each crown an inverse of the root system below. Each opposite a separate world. The trunk, I told Nora, was the direct conduit into dream, into the polished, untouched facade, where everything remained unchanging.

We had muted the film we were watching to talk. It was nighttime, of course, and the lights were off. We had closed the curtains to ensure complete darkness. The only light allowed was that of the television screen, and though it was a dim light, it flickered faintly across Nora. She bobbed her head as she listened to me.

Sometime after we started the movie, she had reverted back to her ordinary self. Her cheeks had become puffed and ruddy and freckled, no longer porcelain, slim. Her hair had dulled into a flat mess. Her nose and forehead and teeth had regained their usual length. But now, with the bobbing, her appearances skated between one another. Upswing, and she slipped into beauty; downswing, and she looked plain again.

"That's an interesting take," Nora said, bobbing. Then she stopped and looked at me. She was caught between two disparate images. One was wide, in bloom, the other small and confined. It was as though someone had gone through a magazine and cut out several features—taking an eye here, a nose there—pasting them together into one visage. "But when do you know?"

"When do you know what?" I said.

"When do you know you're there?"

☾

More than twenty years have passed since then. It's strange to think about. All that time suddenly gone, ended. No explanation as to how it happened.

And through all that, I've said nothing about Nora. Not a word. When I married, I said nothing, and when I had three children—two boys and a girl—I was even quieter.

Nora became the actress. I saw her everywhere: on highway billboards, in grocery aisles. Nora with her prominent cheekbones, her shapely jawline. Her enticing eyes and petite, straight nose. The camera always caught her mid-laugh and delirious, teeth as white as pearls.

She drowned in her bathtub several years ago. The exact cause of death—whether it was accidental or premeditated—was not made public. Though the general consensus was that she had done herself in.

People couldn't stop talking about it when it happened. Everywhere my husband and I went, every outing, every dinner, people wanted to talk about her. Yes, they had seen it coming, or no, they hadn't, and why had she done it? Everyone agreed it was tragic, though how tragic was up for discussion. Certain friends felt the need to weigh her life and determine the level of sympathy they ought to give. It's always like that when a celebrity dies.

A couple weeks ago, I was in the city for a writers' conference. I had gone without my family and decided to make a little trip out of it and so I rented a car. There were attractions I wanted to see, places I had missed when I lived in Los Angeles. What I did not want was to visit Nora. There was no reason for me to go out of my way to see the grave of someone I had barely known.

Had I not been stuck in traffic during my trip back from The Getty, my plan would have gone accordingly. But as it happened, I had made the unwise decision to drive back on the 405 right when rush hour began. It was bad traffic, too, bumper to bumper. Everyone wanted to go home. I myself was headed back to my hotel in downtown. But it would be an hour or so before I'd get there, stuck as I was. And it was just my luck that I was stuck with the woman I wanted to avoid. For up ahead a few hundred yards was Nora, her face enlarged to fill the whole length of the billboard that contained her. It had not been taken down either out of forgetfulness or commemoration, and her broad face hung above the highway and smiled down on us all. Even when I passed her, she continued to smile at me in the rearview mirror. There seemed to be no escaping her. So, when Wilshire Boulevard came up, I took it and turned onto the next right, toward her cemetery.

The cemetery is one of those reserved for the notable few. It's very picturesque and has its graves spread over a green, well kept lawn. Footstones are set instead of headstones, so nothing rises above the grass but flowers. The grounds are walled off and private, and in the back is a mausoleum. It's there, quilted into stone, that Nora lies. Her crypt, like the ones beside it, has a bronze plaque and pocket vase. At the time, a fresh rose was pinned to it like a boutonniere.

While I was there, a woman, perhaps ten years my senior, was going around tending the flowers. She saw me at Nora's memorial and stopped by to chat. She was the caretaker, and she said it was awfully tragic what had happened. I agreed and said it was especially so, considering the way she had gone.

"I don't believe it, if you ask me," she said. "Not for a second. It's total nonsense."

And did I want to know why it was nonsense? Because there were other rumors going around, things talked about behind closed doors. There was one, in fact, even more absurd than the death itself, and it was about what happened afterward. Apparently (the caretaker leaned in to tell me this), the mortician had to call the medicinal examiner the day after she was brought in. He needed to confirm whether it really was Nora Gilbert lying deceased in his freezer.

"The things you hear," the caretaker said and took the rose and trimmed its stem.

I should mention now that there's something I haven't gotten to yet.

That spring twenty or so years ago was the last time Nora visited. She hadn't given any signs that she'd stop. She simply never came around again. I'd wait up for her, hoping that the wind rattling the door, the steps coming up the stairway, were her. But when I'd go look out the window, nobody would be there.

It occurred to me that she might have died. But I knew that was ridiculous. To think myself so special, as if that was the only reason she couldn't come to see me. What was more likely was that she no longer needed a place to stay. But I suppose it didn't matter how it ended—there's hardly any difference between dying and disappearing. So, after a few months, I quit waiting for her to show.

Soon, it was fall again. A whole year gone. The same beautiful faces floated in and out of the cafeteria, each sunny day a testament to the industry's foresight in claiming Los Angeles. Autumn hardly made herself known. Yet there were dreary days on occasion, and I can remember one of the days that was clouded over entirely. Absent was the brilliant light that shot through the windows; instead, men and women filtered through the gloom and seated themselves at tables that, with the sunlight gone, looked shabby and mundane. All around the cafeteria, small talk was pushed aside and replaced by plaintive nods or short, cursory quibbles.

It was on that day I saw Nora.

She had swept in with Wayne Morris. He was guiding her with his arm around her waist. She had on a tremendous gown that was accompanied by a set of matching silver heels. There were heads turning in every direction to watch her. She was, at that very moment, the kind of woman you'd turn to look at while she walked by and from whom it was impossible to look away.

Wayne pointed to my glass partition, and soon she was wading alone through the dim air. She took her time. She moved as though the floor was liable to crumble beneath her at any moment, and yet she retained a certain elegance, moving one step after another in balletic accord.

The first thought I had was to hide. Duck under the counter and wait until she disappeared. But she came straight for me. I pretended to look bored and readjusted my hairnet. But I felt a sudden dizzying wave come over me and I stopped. My hands, I realized, were shaking.

When she greeted me, she had the funniest look. Something must have gotten into her eye, because she winced and blinked madly while trying terribly to keep a normal expression. It had a wonderful comedic effect, so much so that I wanted to laugh. But then whatever it was that bothered her seemed to have gone, and she gave a weak but friendly smile. She asked, casually, if she could get a turkey sandwich.

My confusion must have been apparent, since she asked if I had heard her.

"I heard you," I said. "You want me to make you a turkey sandwich. What else do you want? Please tell."

She hesitated.

"Excuse me?"

Then I did laugh.

"I didn't know you were so funny," I said. I had not started her sandwich, and I decided then that I would never do a favor for her again.

"I'm sorry," she said. She was beginning to sound annoyed. "But do we know each other from somewhere?"

I looked into her face. It was pulled into itself, irritated and sorry. Her eyes were strained, as though she were trying to remember the impossible.

"You're a better actress than I thought."

"Look. I'm sorry. Really, I wish I had a better memory. But I'm sure if you'd just tell me your name …."

"I'm Nora Gilbert," I said.

"What?" Her expression widened into an incredulous stare. She stood like that for a moment or so, her eyes moving in a restless attempt to see through me. Then she composed herself and smiled. "Well, then, Nora, here's a piece of advice." She leaned in as close as she could to the divider. "Go home."

Sometime after—I can't remember how long—I called my parents. It was late and I couldn't sleep. I'd been tossing around all night, thrusting my head helplessly onto the cool side of my pillow, kicking the blanket on and off my legs. But it was no use, so I got up and went outside and walked to the closest payphone.

Even in the dark of night, there was noise. You could hear the rush of cars, the loud stream of traffic coming off the highways, the paramedics hurtling into nowhere. The payphone was next to a drugstore, and in the distance came a rapid burst of pops, fireworks or otherwise. I pressed against the telephone, and it shivered into my ear, shivering then pausing, then shivering again. It was cold and haughty and eventually it shivered itself dead. So, I started it up again. I punched in the numbers and waited and there was the phone, shivering, and there I was, standing in the center of noise, punching, pressing, waiting, hanging up the greasy telephone and taking it off again. Then dialing again. Then again. Then again.

"Hello?"

It was my father.

"Thank God," I said. "I'm sorry to call like this. I know it's late."

And with that, I launched into a desperate speech on how I had gotten it all wrong. I had never wanted to be an actress. What I wanted was to come home.

My father was silent. If it wasn't for the feeble breath that came through, I would have thought the line dropped.

"Dolly," my father said finally. "Is that you?"

Contributors' Notes

R. Allen Abshire lives in rural Louisiana,where he makes a living selling books and antiques. His writing has appeared or is forthcoming in *Monkeybicycle*, *BULL*, and *The Louisiana Review*.

Liz Ahl's most recent full-length collection of poetry is *A Case for Solace* (Lily Poetry Review Books, 2022), which won the 2023 New Hampshire Award for Poetry. She is also the author of numerous chapbooks, including *A Thirst That's Partly Mine*, winner of the 2008 Slapering Hol Chapbook Contest.

Molly Akin is a writer and nonprofit library director based in Cape Cod, Massachusetts. She is a 2023 recipient of a Massachusetts Cultural Council grant, and her writing has been supported by the Sundress Academy for the Arts and the Fine Arts Work Center. Her chapbook, *Hospice*, was the Finishing Line Press 2024 New Women's Voices Chapbook Competition winner.

Mario Aliberto III is the author of *All the Dead We Have Yet to Bury* (Chestnut Review, 2025), and his short fiction has appeared in *SmokeLong Quarterly*, *Fractured Lit*, *The Pinch*, and other journals. He has a creative writing degree from the University of South Florida.

Connor Beeman is the winner of an Academy of American Poets Award, the 2025 Helen Earnhart Harley Creative Nonfiction Fellowship Award, and the 2022 Mark Ritzenhein Emerging Poet Award. They are the author of the chapbook *concrete, rust, marrow* (Finishing Line Press, 2023), and more of their work can be found in *The Mississippi Review*, *14 Poems*, *Foglifter*, and *Passages North*.

Rebecca Bernard's work has recently appeared or is forthcoming in *Oxford American*, *Mississippi Review*, *The Cincinnati Review*, and *The Adroit Journal*, where she recently won the Editor's Prize in Fiction. She is the author of the story collection *Our Sister Who Will Not Die* (Mad Creek Books, 2022). She is an assistant professor of English at East Carolina University and serves as a fiction editor for *The Boiler* and *North Carolina Literary Review*.

Caroline Beuley is an alumnus of the Bread Loaf Writers' Conference and is currently pursuing a Master of Fine Arts at the University of North Carolina Wilmington, where she works as a publication assistant for Lookout Books.

Her writing is published or forthcoming in *Chestnut Review*, *Cleaver*, *Fractured Lit*, *F(r)iction*, and *Ghost Parachute*, among other venues.

Patricia Q. Bidar is a writer from the Port of Los Angeles area. She is an alum of the UC Davis Graduate Writing Program, where she taught creative writing and earned a Master of Arts. Her work has been celebrated in *Wigleaf*'s Top 50 and widely anthologized, including in *Flash Fiction America*, *Best Microfiction 2023*, and *Best Small Fictions 2023* and *2024*. Her collection of short works was released from Unsolicited Press in December 2025.

Mary Biddinger's poems have appeared or are forthcoming in *Unbroken*, *Thimble Literary Magazine*, *A Dozen Nothing*, *Cherry Tree*, *Diode*, *Great Lakes Review*, *HAD*, *Indianapolis Review*, *Pithead Chapel*, and *Under a Warm Green Linden*. Her latest book is a novella-in-flash titled *The Girl with the Black Lipstick* (Black Lawrence Press, 2025), and she is a co-editor of *A Mollusk Without a Shell: Essays on Self-Care for Writers* (University of Akron Press, 2024). She teaches creative writing at the University of Akron, where she serves as Poetry Editor for the University of Akron Press.

Laurie Blauner is the author of *The Solace of Monsters* (Leapfrog Press, 2016), and a recent novel, *Out of Which Came Nothing* (2021), is available from Spuyten Duyvil Press. Her second hybrid nonfiction book, *Swerve,* was released from Rain Mountain Press in 2025. Her latest poetry book, *Come Closer* (2023), won the Library of Poetry Award from Bitter Oleander Press.

Ronda Piszk Broatch is the author of *Chaos Theory for Beginners* (MoonPath Press, 2023) and *Lake of Fallen Constellations* (MoonPath Press, 2015). Winner of the Willow Springs Surrealist Poetry Prize, her journal publications include *Greensboro Review*, *Blackbird*, *Sycamore Review*, *The Missouri Review*, *Palette Poetry*, *Moon City Review*, and NPR News/KUOW's *All Things Considered.* She is a graduate of the Pacific Lutheran University's Rainier Writing Workshop.

Polly Buckingham is the author of one book of poetry, *The River People* (Lost Horse Press, 2020), and two books of fiction, *The Expense of a View* (Katherine Anne Porter Prize, UNT Press, 2016) and *A Year of Silence* (Jeanne Leiby Memorial Chapbook Award, Florida Review Press, 2015). Her work appears in *The Gettysburg Review*, *Threepenny Review*, *Alaska Quarterly Review*, *Sugar House Review*, *North American Review*, *Spillway*, and elsewhere.

Mark Budman's books include *My Life at First Try* (Counterpoint Press, 2008), *An Accidental American Odyssey* (Livingston Press, 2021), *The Most*

Excellent Immigrant (Livingston Press, 2022), and *Short, Vigorous Roots* (with Sue O'Neill, Ooligan Press, 2022). His short fiction has been featured in *Abyss & Apex*, *Virginia Quarterly Review*, and *Mississippi Review*.

Mary Kovaleski Byrnes is the author of *So Long the Sky* (Platypus Press, 2018). Her work has appeared in *Palette*, *Image Journal*, *Guernica*, *Meridian*, *Nimrod*, *Salamander*, the *Four Way Review*, *Best of the Net*, and elsewhere. She teaches writing and literature at Emerson College, where she co-founded the EmersonWRITES program, a free creative writing program for Boston Public School students.

Luanne Castle's stories have appeared in *Your Impossible Voice*, *Gooseberry Pie*, *Bending Genres*, *BULL*, *The Ekphrastic Review*, *MacQueen's Quinterly*, *Cleaver*, *Disappointed Housewife*, *South 85 Journal*, *Roi Fainéant*, *River Teeth*, *The Dribble Drabble Review*, *Flash Boulevard*, and many other publications. She has published four award-winning poetry collections. Her hybrid memoir-in-flash will be published by ELJ Editions in December 2026.

Kim Chinquee's eighth book is *Pipette* (2022), a novel, while *Contact With the Wild* (MadHat Press, 2025) is also available now. Her collection *Octopus Arms* (MadHat Press) and novella *I Thought of England* (Baobab Press) are forthcoming. She's a three-time Pushcart Prize recipient, edits for *New World Writing Quarterly*, ELJ Editions, and *Midwest Review*, and is a competitive triathlete.

Grant Clauser's sixth poetry book, *Temporary Shelters* (2025), is available from Cornerstone Press. His poems have appeared in *The American Poetry Review*, *The Greensboro Review*, *The Kenyon Review*, and other journals. He teaches poetry at Rosemont College in Pennsylvania.

Chella Courington is a writer and teacher. With a doctorate in literature and an MFA in poetry, she is the author of the novella *Adele & Tom: The Portrait of a Marriage* (Impspired, 2023), five fiction chapbooks, and ten poetry chapbooks. Her debut novel, *Janet Hall* (2024), is available now from All Things That Matter Press.

JI Daniels is an assistant professor of English at Clayton State University and is the author of a novel, *Mount Fugue* (Kernpunkt Press, 2016), and a collection of short stories, *If You Can* (Spuyten Duyvil, 2020). Other work has been published in *DIAGRAM*, *Notre Dame Review*, *Juked*, and elsewhere.

Lynn Domina is the author of three full-length collections of poetry, *Inland Sea* (Kelsay Books, 2023), *Corporal Works* (Four Way Books, 1995), and

Framed in Silence (Main Street Rag, 2011). Her more recent work appears or is forthcoming in *Ninth Letter, the museum of americana: A LITERARY REVIEW, About Place*, and other periodicals.

Sean Thomas Dougherty's most recent book is *Death Prefers the Minor Keys* (2023) from BOA Editions. New poems and essays are forthcoming in *Diode, Midway Journal, Poetry Ireland*, and *Talking River Review*. He works as a carer and medtech for folks with traumatic brain injuries along Lake Erie.

Lindsey Godfrey Eccles has flash in *Fractured Lit, Salamander*, and *Gone Lawn*, among other places, and her fiction has appeared in *One Story* and *Uncanny*. She is a member of the Science Fiction and Fantasy Writers Association and the Horror Writers Association and is a graduate of the Odyssey Workshop.

Nathan Fako (he/they) is a former high school teacher. Their work can be found or is forthcoming in *The Rumpus, West Trade Review, Moist Poetry Journal, Whale Road Review*, and elsewhere.

Lauren Fath is the author of *My Hands, Remembering: A Memoir* (Passengers Press, 2022, finalist for the New Mexico/Arizona Book Awards) and the lyric essay chapbook *A Landlocked State* (*Quarterly West*, 2020). Her work has appeared in *CutBank, Fourth Genre, High Desert Journal*, and the *Tahoma Literary Review*, among other journals. She is an associate professor of English at New Mexico Highlands University.

Blue Fay (he/him) is a writer from Southern California. He has worked odd jobs in concert halls, newsrooms, and, most recently, the prison system, teaching creative writing. He is currently serving as the poetry editor of *Faultline Journal*. He is a graduate of the University of California, Irvine.

Gary Fincke's latest books are *The Necessary Going On: Selected Poems* (Press 53, 2025) and *After Arson: New and Selected Essays* (Madville, 2025). Braddock Avenue Books will publish *The Comfort of Taboos: More Selected Stories* in 2026. He is the co-editor of the annual anthology series *Best Microfiction*.

Jeff Friedman's eleventh book, *Broken Signals* (2024), was recently published by Bamboo Dart Press. Friedman's poems and microfictions have appeared in *American Poetry Review*; *Poetry*; *Fiction International*; *Dreaming Awake: New Contemporary Prose Poetry from the United States, Australia and the United Kingdom*; *SmokeLong Quarterly*; *Flash Fiction Funny*; *Contemporary Surrealist and Magical Realist Poetry*; the last five editions of *Best Microfiction*, and *The New Republic*. He has received an NEA Literature Translation Fellowship and numerous other awards.

Susan Fuchtman's recent and forthcoming work can be found in *South Florida Poetry Journal*, *Flash Flood*, *Short Circuit*, *Reckon Review*, and elsewhere. She lives in Iowa City, Iowa, where she is a board member for PorchLight Literary Organization.

E.C. Gannon's work has appeared in *Peatsmoke Journal*, *South Florida Poetry Journal*, *The Broadkill Review*, *Vast Chasm Magazine*, and elsewhere. Raised in New Hampshire, she is a graduate of Florida State University and an MFA student at the University of New Mexico.

Scott Garson's fiction has appeared in *Electric Literature*, *Story*, *The Kenyon Review*, *American Short Fiction*, *Threepenny Review*, and other journals. He lives in central Missouri and edits the multi-Pushcart Prize-winning journal of flash *Wigleaf.*

Aasiya Mirza Glover's stories have been published in *Catapult*, *Notre Dame Review*, *Fatal Flaw*, *Headland*, and *Damazine*. She is an attorney based in New York, where she lives with her husband, two children, and two cats. She is originally from Brunswick, Tennessee, and a proud mixed American-Pakistani.

Jeremy Griffin is the author of the short fiction collections *A Last Resort for Desperate People: Stories and a Novella* (2012), from SFAU Press; *Oceanography,* winner of the 2018 Orison Books Fiction Prize; and *Scream Queen,* winner of the 2023 Black Lawrence Press Hudson Prize. He has appeared in such journals as *Alaska Quarterly Review*, *Bellevue Literary Review*, and others. He teaches Creative Writing at Simpson College in Indianola, Iowa.

Chelsea Guo is an emerging poet and writer from Lexington, Massachusetts. Her work has been recognized or supported by *The Kenyon Review* and *National Scholastic Art & Writing Awards*, among other places. She reads submissions for *Aster Lit* and *The Adroit Journal.*

Shivani Gupta is a writer, curator, dancer, and overall stage-loving human. Her work has been featured globally in *BBC*, *Forbes*, *Edinburgh Fringe Festival*, *Mumbai Poetry Slam*, *Loyola University Chicago*, *Baby Teeth Journal*, *Ranger Magazine*, *The Well*, and more. She is a current *In Surreal Life* fellow and serves as the Development Committee Chair for the Chicago Poetry Center.

Umma Habiba is a poet and theater activist from Dhaka, Bangladesh. Her debut book of poetry, *Ghashe Ghashe Roktoful* (*Blood Flowers in the Grass*), was published in 2022. She is a development professional and has worked with Rohingya refugees, children with special needs, and the underprivileged indigenous people in the country's hill tracts.

D.E. Hardy's work has appeared in *Pithead Chapel, X-R-A-Y Literary Magazine, Lost Balloon, Flashback Fiction*, among other venues. Her work has been anthologized in *Best Small Fictions* and *Best Microfiction.*

Jeff Harvey lives in San Diego and is the founding editor of *Gooseberry Pie.* His work has recently appeared in or is forthcoming in *South Florida Poetry Journal, Whale Road Review, Ghost Parachute*, and *MoonPark Review.*

Quamrul Hassan is an MFA candidate at the University of Arkansas in creative writing and translation. His poems and translations have been published or are forthcoming in *Copper Nickel, Hayden's Ferry Review, The Malahat Review, Agni, Mantis, World Literature Today, The Los Angeles Review*, among other journals. He is the author of the haiku collections *Spring Moon* (Hassan's, 2011) and *Hyaku Haiku* (Hassan's, 2021). His haiku and tanka have appeared in *Asahi Shimbun, Mainichi, Frogpond, Modern Haiku*, and others.

Rachael Hershon grew up just outside of Boston. She now teaches at the University of North Carolina at Greensboro, where she earned her MFA in Creative Writing. Her work has appeared in *South Carolina Review, Boulevard*, and *Empty House Press.*

Dennis Hinrichsen's work, *dementia lyrics* (2024), was published by Green Linden Press. His new work appears or is forthcoming in *Action, Spectacle, ballast, Blackbird, Midwest Review, Posit, Third Coast, Waxwing*, and *Under a Warm Green Linden.*

Shen Chen Hsieh is an art director working in retail experiential design and brand identity, with a practice in illustration and exploring inner narratives through visual systems.

Sarah Lynn Hurd is a writer and poet living in Grand Rapids, Michigan. Her writing appears or is forthcoming in *New Flash Fiction Review, Fractured Lit, trampset, Flash Frog, Anti-Heroin Chic*, and elsewhere. Her work often explores grief, nostalgia, womanhood, and self-perception. She has a BA in creative writing and English literature from Grand Valley State University.

Brett Hymel, Jr., writes stories for bugs. These stories have appeared in *The Cincinnati Review, Subtropics, Black Warrior Review, Split Lip Magazine*, and elsewhere. His website is www.bretthymeljr.com.

Olivia Jacobson is an MFA candidate at Syracuse University. She is the co-editor in chief of *Salt Hill Journal* and is originally from Sheridan, Indiana. Her chapbook, *On Junkyards*, won the Etchings Press Book Prize for Poetry (2025). Her work appears or is forthcoming in *Watershed Review*, *Shō Poetry Journal*, *Cottonmouth Journal*, *Club Plum*, *The Shore*, and *SUNHOUSE Literary*.

Mitch James is a professor of composition and literature at Lakeland Community College. He is the author of the novel, *Seldom Seen: A Miner's Tale* (Sunbury Press, 2023), and *Young Men, Cry* (forthcoming from Cornerstone Press). You can find his latest fiction in *Lost Balloon*, *Bending Genres*, and *SmokeLong Quarterly*, his poetry at *Shelia-Na-Gig*, and his scholarship at *Journal of Creative Writing Studies* and *New Writing: The International Journal for the Practice and Theory of Creative Writing*.

Dustin King's poems appear in *New Letters*, *Prism Review*, *The Tusculum Review*, *Marrow Magazine*, and other venues. He is a reader for *Sublunary Review* and co-curates the poetry and performance event, *Yodel Farm*. His first chapbook, *Last Echo* (2025), was published by Bottlecap Press, and his second, *Courteous Gringo* (2025), is available from Seven Kitchens Press.

Jessica Klimesh (she/her) is a U.S.-based writer and writing coach whose creative work has appeared or is forthcoming in *Ghost Parachute*, *Flash Frog*, *Gone Lawn*, *Rawhead Journal*, *Claudine*, *BULL*, and *Milk Candy Review*, among other journals. Additionally, her work was selected for *Best Microfiction 2025* and *Best of the Net 2025*.

Ray Kruger is a biracial and transgender writer from St. Louis. He obtained his BA from Lindenwood University in 2025. You can find more of his work in *The Raven Review*, *The Orange Rose Literary Magazine*, *The Lindenwood Review*, and other venues. To keep up with writing updates and to see what he's currently reading, you can follow him @reading_with_ray_ on Instagram.

Dell Lemmon is the author of two books of poetry: *Are You Somebody I Should Know?* (2020) and *Single Woman* (2016), both published by Box Turtle Press. Her poems have appeared in *Brooklyn Poets Anthology*, *Court Green*, *Laurel Review*, *The Broadkill Review*, *Mudfish*, *Cape Cod Poetry Review*, and *Washington Square Review*, among other publications.

Lindsay Li is a Chinese-American writer based in the Bay Area. In her free time, she attempts to unite history with the coming future, goes down Wikipedia rabbit holes, and writes anything that comes to mind.

Svetlana Litvinchuk graduated from University of New Mexico. She is the author of a poetry chapbook, *Only a Season* (Bottlecap Features, 2024). Her poetry appears in *swamp pink*, *ANMLY*, *About Place*, *Flyway*, *Apple Valley Review*, *Sky Island Journal*, *Arkana*, and elsewhere. She is the associate editor and reviews editor with *ONLY POEMS* and is serving as an editor for *Rockvale Review* in 2025. Her debut poetry collection is forthcoming in Spring 2026.

Melissa Llanes Brownlee (she/her), a native Hawaiian writer living in Japan, has work published and forthcoming in *Prairie Schooner* and *Redivider*. She has published *Hard Skin* (2022), *Kahi and Lua* (2022), and her new collection, *Bitter Over Sweet* (2025), from Santa Fe Writers Project.

Cameron MacKenzie's work has appeared in *Salmagundi*, *Blackbird*, *Cleaver*, *Lost Balloon*, and *Michigan Quarterly Review*, among other places. His collection, *All Of Our Sadness Has Been A Mistake,* is forthcoming from Cornerstone Press.

Erin MacNair is a Wisconsinite now living in British Columbia, Canada. Her stories have been published in *Conjunctions*, *The Baffler*, *The Walrus*, *december*, and other journals. She is a Canada Council grant recipient and has penned a collection of short stories, one of which will be featured in *Best Canadian Stories 2026*.

Michael Malan is editor of *Cloudbank*, a literary journal in Corvallis, Oregon. He is the winner of *Meridian*'s 2024 Editors' Prize for Fiction. He is also the author of four books from Blue Light Press, including *Midnight at the Chevron Station* (2025, poetry and flash fiction). His work has appeared recently in *Puerto del Sol*, *Lake Effect*, *Cincinnati Review*, *Washington Square Review*, *New American Writing*, and *Grist*.

Andrea Marcusa's writings have appeared in *The Gettysburg Review*, *Milk Candy Review*, *Ghost Parachute*, *The Citron Review*, *Moon City Review*, and other venues. She is the author of the chapbook *What We Now Live With* (Bottlecap Press, 2025) and a member of the faculty at The Writers Studio.

Andrew Graham Martin's writing has appeared or is forthcoming in *Post Road*, *Bat City Review*, *Okay Donkey*, *SmokeLong Quarterly*, *Cleaver*, and elsewhere. He lives in Indianapolis.

Victoria Martynko is a recent English and psychology graduate of the University of Minnesota. Her work has previously appeared in *The Tower* and *Silly Goose Press*.

Nora Maynard's fiction and nonfiction have appeared in *Tiny Molecules*, *HAD*, *Pangyrus*, *Atticus Review*, *Drunken Boat*, *Necessary Fiction*, *Salon*, *The Millions*, and other journals. She's received fiction fellowships from the Millay Colony, Ragdale, Ucross, Blue Mountain Center, and The Artists' Enclave at I-Park. She's the co-founder and co-editor of *-ette review*.

Dan McDermott's work has appeared in *Ploughshares*, *The Southampton Review*, *Gertrude Press*, *Times Literary Supplement*, *Brilliant Corners: A Journal of Jazz & Literature*, and elsewhere. He earned an MFA from the Bennington Writing Seminars and teaches creative writing at Phoenix College.

Cate McGowan is an artist, critic, historian, poet, and prose writer. Her poetry collection, *Sacrificial Steel* (2025), is now available from Driftwood Press and won its Editors' Pick Poetry Prize; Brill published her collection of memoir essays, *Writing is Revision*, in 2024; Gold Wake Press published *These Lowly Objects*, a novel, in 2020; and her short story collection, *True Places Never Are* (2015), won the inaugural Moon City Press Short Fiction Award in 2014.

Laura Leigh Morris is the author of *The Stone Catchers: A Novel* (The University Press of Kentucky, 2024) and *Jaws of Life: Stories* (West Virginia University Press, 2018). She's previously published short fiction in *STORY Magazine*, *North American Review*, *Redivider*, and other journals. She teaches creative writing and literature at Furman University in Greenville, South Carolina.

Devan Murphy is the author of *I'm Not I'm Not I'm Not a Baby* (Ethel, 2024), a chapbook of prose poems, abstract comics, and short essays about God and loneliness. Her visual art has been featured in galleries throughout the Pittsburgh region. Her writing and illustrations appear in *The Iowa Review*, *A Velvet Giant*, *The Guardian*, *The Cincinnati Review*, *Diagram*, *Anomaly*, and other journals.

Will Musgrove is a writer and journalist from Northwest Iowa. He received an MFA from Minnesota State University, Mankato. His work has appeared or is forthcoming in *Wigleaf*, *The Florida Review*, *The Pinch*, *The Cincinnati Review*, *The Forge*, *Passages North*, *Tampa Review*, and elsewhere.

Kurt Olsson has published two award-winning poetry collections, *Burning Down Disneyland* (Gunpowder Press, 2017) and *What Kills What Kills Us* (Silverfish Review Press, 2007). His third collection, *The Unnumbered Anniversaries* (2025), is out now from Fernwood Press. Olsson's poems have appeared in many journals, including *Poetry*, *The New Republic*, *The Southern Review*, and *The Threepenny Review*.

Pamela Painter is the author of five story collections. Her stories have been included in four Norton Anthologies, *Best Microfiction*, *Best Short Fictions*, and have received four Pushcart Prizes. Painter's stories have also been featured on NPR, YouTube, and staged by WORDTheatre in Los Angeles, London, and New York. Painter is a Founding Donor of the Flash Fiction Archive.

Cheryl Pappas is the author of the flash fiction collection *The Clarity of Hunger*, published by word west press (2021). Her flash has appeared in *Swamp Pink*, *Wigleaf*, *Hunger Mountain*, *SmokeLong Quarterly*, *The Chattahoochee Review*, and elsewhere. She is a 2023 MacDowell Fellow and a recipient of a 2022 Massachusetts Cultural Council grant in fiction.

Hayden Park is a high school senior from Southern California. She is the winner of *The Malahat Review*'s 2025 Constance Rooke Creative Nonfiction Prize and a Scholastic Art & Writing Awards National Medalist. Her poems and prose appear or are forthcoming in *The Malahat Review*, *Slippery Elm*, *REDAMANCY Magazine*, and *Yin Literary Magazine*, as well as in anthologies from One Page Poetry and TulipTree Publishing.

Alan Michael Parker has written four novels, nine books of poems, and a collection of flash fictions and bingo cards called *BINGO BANGO BOINGO* (Dzanc Books, 2025). He has won three Pushcart Prizes, two *Best American Poetry* selections, the North Carolina Book Award, the Fineline Prize, the Lunate (500) prize, and the Balch Award, among other honors. His next book, a user's guide to single-panel cartoons, will be published by Duke University Press. He is the chair of the Department of English at Davidson College.

Heather Paul-Tillery (she/they) holds an MFA from Eastern Washington University. Her work has appeared in *Cagibi Journal*, *I-70 Review*, *Prairie Schooner*, and elsewhere. She currently lives in Spokane, Washington, with her partner and children.

Ryan Pierce is a visual artist and writer based in Oregon. His artwork has been exhibited internationally, and he has been a fellow at the Djerassi, Ucross, and Joan Mitchell Foundations. He currently directs the Low-Residency Visual Studies MFA at Pacific Northwest College of Art in Portland.

Dan Pinkerton earned an MA from Iowa State University and an MFA from Penn State University. His stories and poems have appeared in *Chicago Quarterly Review*, *Crazyhorse*, *Cimarron Review*, *Subtropics*, *North American Review*, *Boulevard*, *New Orleans Review*, *Pleiades*, and elsewhere. His first book of poetry, *Democracy of Noise*, was published by Gray Duck Press (2025).

Susan Blackwell Ramsey's work has appeared in *The Southern Review*, *Poetry Northwest*, and *32 Poems*, among other places. Her book, *A Mind Like This* (2012), won the Raz-Shumaker prize from *Prairie Schooner* and was published by the University of Nebraska Press.

Eric Rasmussen teaches high school English in western Wisconsin, runs the upper Midwest journal *Barstow & Grand*, and handles fiction for *Sundog Lit*. He won *Jabberwock Review*'s 2024 Nancy D. Hargrove Editors' Prize and *Blue Mesa Review*'s 2022 Fiction Contest, with stories also featured in *Third Coast*, *Fugue*, *Pithead Chapel*, and other journals. He holds an MFA from Augsburg University.

nat raum is a disabled artist, writer, and genderless disaster based on unceded Piscataway and Susquehannock land in Baltimore. They're the editor-in-chief of *fifth wheel press*. Their writing is published or forthcoming with *Split Lip Magazine*, *BRUISER*, *beestung*, *Gone Lawn*, and others.

August Reid (they/them) is a writer and artist from Rio Rancho, New Mexico. They received a Bachelor of Arts and an MA in English literature from Arizona State University and an MFA from Northern Michigan University. Their work appears in *Blue Mesa Review*, *Hunger Mountain*, and *Cream City Review*, among other journals. They teach high school English.

Scott Repass has been a bar owner, bartender, teacher, carpenter, and barista. He holds an MFA in creative writing from the University of Houston. His fiction and nonfiction have appeared in *Film Quarterly*, *Literature/Film Quarterly*, *Houston and Nomadic Voices*, *The Heartland Review*, *Fort Necessity*, and elsewhere. His novel, *Last Call Lounge* (written under the pen name Stuart Spears), was co-winner of the 2012 Houston Writers Guild Novel Contest.

Hanna Reynditskiy is based in the Pacific Northwest. She was a Woodfin Fellow in Fiction at the College of Charleston, where she was selected as a recipient for the 2024 AWP Intro to Journals Project prize. Her work can be found in *Quarterly West*.

Trinity Richardson is a non-binary poet. They have a degree in communication and creative writing from the University of South Florida, are an editor for *West Trade Review*, and are a social media manager for *The Adroit Journal*. Their poems can be found in *Thread*, *Vagabond City Lit*, and other journals.

Emily Rinkema lives in Vermont. She recently has had stories in *Milk Candy Review*, *Flash Frog*, *Ghost Parachute*, and *Wigleaf*, and she won the 2024 Cambridge Prize and the 2024 Lascaux Prize for Flash Fiction.

Michelle Ross is the author of three story collections: *There's So Much They Haven't Told You*, winner of the 2016 Moon City Short Fiction Award; *Shapeshifting*, winner of the 2020 Stillhouse Press Short Fiction Award; and *They Kept Running*, winner of the 2021 Katherine Anne Porter Prize in Short Fiction. *Don't Take This the Wrong Way*, a collection cowritten with Kim Magowan, was released by EastOver Press in 2025. She is an editor at *100 Word Story*.

Josh Russell's work has most recently appeared in *Epoch*, *Northwest Review*, and *DIAGRAM*, and the most recent of his four books is *King of the Animals: Stories* (LSU Press, 2021). His novella, *Counting the Days*, is forthcoming in 2027.

Adrianna Sanchez-Lopez is a Southern Colorado inhabitant, community college professor, and writer. Her work has most recently appeared or is forthcoming in *Best Small Fictions 2025*, *Blood Tree Literature*, *The Citron Review*, and *Portland Review*. She holds an MFA in fiction from Antioch University, Los Angeles, and is currently working on her first short story collection.

Naphisa Senanarong is a fiction writer from Bangkok, Thailand, currently residing in Boston. Her work has appeared in *Gulf Coast*, *Bennington Review*, *Hawaii Pacific Review*, and is forthcoming in *Post Road*. She is a recipient of a Tin House scholarship. She received her MFA in fiction from Brooklyn College.

George Singleton has published ten collections of stories, two novels, and two collections of nonfiction. He lives in South Carolina.

James Keith Smith's work has appeared or is forthcoming in *Split Lip Magazine*, *Sierra Nevada Review*, *Pithead Chapel*, and elsewhere. He grew up in Michigan and lives in Tacoma, Washington, with his wife and two children.

Sarp Sozdinler, a Turkish writer, has been published in *Electric Literature*, *The Kenyon Review*, *The Masters Review*, *Fractured Lit*, and *Maudlin House*, among other journals. His stories have been selected or nominated for anthologies, including the Pushcart Prize, *Best Small Fictions,* and *The Wigleaf* Top 50.

Lana Spendl is the author of the fiction chapbook *We Cradled Each Other in the Air* (Blue Lyra Press, 2017). Her work has appeared in *World Literature Today*, *The Rumpus, Witness*, *The Greensboro Review*, *New Ohio Review*, *Zone 3*, and other journals. She is a queer writer and a Bosnian War refugee, her childhood divided between Bosnia and Spain.

Jenny Stalter is a writer and former private chef. Her work was selected for *Best Small Fictions 2024*, and she was a recipient of the 2023 *SsmokeLong Quarterly* Emerging Writer Fellowship. Her fiction appears in *Moon City Review*; *Longleaf Review*; *X-R-A-Y Literary Magazine*; *The Citron Review*; *Cease, Cows*; *Ghost Parachute*; *New Flash Fiction Review*; and other publications.

Alyssa McIntire Start is a writer and English instructor living in Grand Rapids, Michigan. She is currently a creative writing MFA candidate at Western Michigan University, where she serves as poetry editor for *Third Coast*. Her work has appeared in *Oyster River Pages* and is forthcoming in *I-70 Review*.

Mae Juniper Stokes (she/they) is a writer, painter, and librarian living in Vermont. Her work has appeared or is forthcoming in *The Rumpus*, *The Forge Literary Magazine*, *Foglifter*, *Strange Horizons*, and elsewhere. They are a 2023 graduate of Clarion West.

Justine Sweeney is an Irish writer. Her work can be found in journals such as *The Dublin Review*, *Banshee Press*, *Fictive Dream*, *Flash Fiction Magazine*, and *Inkfish Magazine*, as well as the *Bath Flash Fiction* and Fish Publishing anthologies. She has an MA in creative writing and is working on her first novel.

Justin Taroli is a writer based in New York City. His work is forthcoming in *Maudlin House*, *West Trade Review*, *BULL*, and *Eunoia Review*.

Alexandra van de Kamp is the executive director for Gemini Ink, San Antonio's Writing Arts Center. Her most recent book of poems is *Ricochet Script* (Next Page Press, 2022). Previous collections of poems include: *Kiss/Hierarchy* (Rain Mountain Press, 2016) and *The Park of Upside-Down Chairs* (CW Books, 2010). She has also published several chapbooks, including *A Liquid Bird Inside the Night* (Red Glass Books, 2015) and *Dear Jean Seberg* (2011), which won the 2010 Burnside Review Chapbook Contest.

C. Zhang read English at University College, Oxford. She desires, above all, to keep loving what she loves.

Ruiyan Zhu is a high school senior from Saratoga, California, who currently serves as the editor-in-chief of her school newspaper and literary magazine. Her work has been recognized by *JUST POETRY!!! the National Point Quarterly* and the Scholastic Art & Writing Awards.